Wilfred Thesiger

was born in 1910 at the British Legation in Addis Ababa, and spent his early years in Abyssinia. Educated at Eton and Oxford, where for four consecutive years he won his Blue for boxing, he joined the Sudan Political Service in 1935. During the next five years Thesiger visited little-known areas of the Sudan, Libya and the French Sahara. In the War, serving with the patriots under Orde Wingate in Abyssina, he was awarded a DSO. He later served with the SOE (in Syria) and the SAS in the Western Desert.

From 1930, always using traditional means of transport, Thesiger travelled through remote areas of Africa, the Middle East and Asia. For over twenty years, until 1994, he lived mostly among the pastoral Samburu at Maralal in northern Kenya. He now lives permanently in London.

Thesiger's journeys have won him the Founder's Medal of the Royal Geographical Society, the Lawrence of Arabia Medal of the Royal Central Asian Society, the Livingstone Medal of the Royal Scottish Geographical Society and the Burton Memorial Medal of the Royal Asiatic Society.

His writing has won him the Heinemann Award; Fellowship of the Royal Society of Literature; an Honorary D.Litt. from Leicester University and an Honorary D.Litt. from the University of Bath.

In 1968 he was made a CBE. He is Honorary Fellow of the British Academy and Honorary Fellow of Magdalen College, Oxford. He was honoured with a KBE in 1995.

Wilfred Thesiger's previous books include *Arabian Sands, The Marsh Arabs, Desert, Marsh and Mountain, Visions of a Nomad, The Life of My Choice* and *My Kenya Days*.

WILFRED THESIGER

The Danakil Diary

Journeys through Abyssinia
1930-34

Flamingo
An Imprint of HarperCollinsPublishers

Flamingo
An Imprint of HarperCollins*Publishers*
77–85 Fulham Palace Road,
Hammersmith, London W6 8JB

Published by Flamingo 1998
9 8 7 6 5 4 3 2

First published in Great Britain by
HarperCollins*Publishers* 1996

Author photograph © Paul Harris

ISBN 0 00 638775 6

Set in Linotron Minion by
Rowland Phototypesetting Ltd,
Bury St Edmunds, Suffolk

Printed and bound in Great Britain by
Caledonian International Book Manufacturing Ltd, Glasgow

*For Frank Steele,
my cherished friend for forty-five years*

CONTENTS

ILLUSTRATIONS

Waidellas in Aussa.
Das with upright stones.
Wooden *das* on the Kareyu plain.

The entrance into Aussa.
Soldiers of the Sultan of Aussa arriving in camp.
The Awash river in Aussa.
Fording the Awash in Aussa.
Goumarri precipes and Lake Adobada.
The swamps of southern Aussa.
Caravan on the way to Lake Abhebad.
Sinter formations in the south-east corner of Lake Abhebad.
Lake Abhebad where the Awash ended.
Camp on the way to Lake Assal.
Mimosa bushes near Lake Assal cut down for our starving camels.
Camels carrying salt.
Adoimara encountered near the coast.
Camp in the Marha riverbed.
Photograph of me by Umar.
A dhow.

PREFACE

THIS BOOK IS BASED on a diary I wrote in 1930 when I attended Haile Selassie's coronation as Emperor of Ethiopia – and afterwards spent a month hunting in the Danakil country of Abyssinia, as Ethiopia was known in those days – and on my diaries for 1933–34 when I spent a further six months among the Danakil tribesmen. In 1933, as soon as I had finished at Oxford, I returned to Abyssinia to explore the Awash river to its end. Shortly after my return to England in 1934 I wrote four turn-over articles for *The Times* describing my journey, and gave a lecture to the Royal Geographical Society which was published in the Society's *Journal*. In 1987 I wrote *The Life of My Choice*. In the present book I have included several, often lengthy passages from *The Life of My Choice* describing these journeys. I have also included letters which I wrote to my mother at the time.

Until recently the Afar had always been known as the Danakil, the name I have used for them in this book. I made a time and compass survey of my route through the Danakil country recording in my diaries the number of hours we marched and the bearings, maps of the country and sketches of the various Danakil monuments and graves, some of which are included here.

While I was with the Danakil I was anxious to record all I could learn about their customs and way of life. I was certain that no one else had previously done so. Some details of these customs are interspersed through the Diary. I believe I gave my original notes to Louis Clarke, at that time curator of the Fitzwilliam Museum in Cambridge. I am presenting the diaries of my Danakil journeys, together with the manuscript of this book, to Eton College Library.

The photographs reproduced are some of the first I ever took, using a Kodak camera which had belonged to my father. Unfortunately, the view-finder was slightly damaged and consequently the bottom of a number of photographs is missing.

Alexander Maitland, my official biographer and close friend, had read these diaries and insisted that they should be published. We therefore approached HarperCollins who were immediately enthusiastic. Without Alex's insistence it would never have occurred to me to publish these diaries. My sight has been giving me trouble and consequently I have relied on Alex, Lucinda McNeile and Anne O'Brien to edit my diaries for me. I am grateful to them for doing so.

WILFRED THESIGER
Chelsea 1996

INTRODUCTION

DURING THE SUMMER VACATION of 1930, my first year at Oxford University, I worked my passage as a fireman on a cargo boat to Constantinople. On my return home to The Milebrook I found two letters waiting for me. One was a personal invitation from Ras Tafari to attend his coronation as the Emperor Haile Selassie of Ethiopia, in November 1930. My father had been British Minister in charge of the Legation – today's Embassy – at Addis Ababa from 1909–19. He had died in 1920 and Ras Tafari had sent me, his eldest son, this invitation to his coronation – the only personal invitation he sent to anyone. The other was a notification from the Foreign Office that I had been appointed Honorary Attaché to HRH the Duke of Gloucester, who would represent his father, King George V, at the coronation.

I was born in the Legation in 1910 and spent my childhood, until I was nearly nine, in Abyssinia, as Ethiopia was called in those days. It was an extraordinary childhood and I am convinced that the events in which I was involved and the sights which I saw during those years had a permanent effect on the rest of my life.

My father, accompanied by my mother, travelling with animal transport, arrived in Addis Ababa in December 1909. With its people inheriting a civilization as old as that of Egypt, and a Christian faith dating back to the 4th century AD, Abyssinia resembled no other country in Africa or anywhere else.

When my parents arrived, the new Legation was still being built. At first they lived in circular, grass-roofed *tukuls* or mud huts, in one of which I was born; these *tukuls* still stand there today, a hundred years after they were built. I was the eldest of four brothers and, during the years we were in Abyssinia, there were no other European children to keep me company. Over the years I relied increasingly on my brother Brian, who was one year my junior, for companionship. We had learned to ride almost as soon as we could walk. There were no cars in Addis Ababa. My father had a horse-drawn carriage which he sometimes used, otherwise everyone rode everywhere, and we did the same. As I grew older, my father taught me to shoot and, enthralled, I listened to his stories about hunting big game, determined that one day I would do the same.

Menelik, the King of Kings of Ethiopia, and one of the greatest in the history of that country, was still alive when my father arrived, but he had recently suffered a stroke and was utterly incapacitated. He lived until 1913, but my father never saw him. Menelik was succeeded while still alive by Lij Yasu, his thirteen-year-old grandson, whose father was Negus Mikael, the despotic ruler of the northern province of Wollo. Lij Yasu was never crowned; cruelty and arrogance predominated in his character. He had always hated Addis Ababa and spent most of his time at Harar and elsewhere with the Somalis and the Danakil. He became increasingly attracted to Islam, and finally at a mass meeting of Somalis he swore on the Koran that he was a Muslim. As a result he was deposed in 1916 and Menelik's daughter, Zauditu, was proclaimed Empress with Ras Tafari as Regent. Fourteen years later Ras Tafari was to become the Emperor Haile Selassie.

Negus Mikael assembled his forces in Gojjam and prepared to march on Addis Ababa and restore his son to power. Ras Tafari took charge of the government and collected his forces to oppose him. My father was aware that Lij Yasu had been supplying the 'Mad Mullah' with ammunition and arms to assist him in his long-drawn-out war against the government of British Somaliland. It seemed probable that if Lij Yasu was restored this would bring Abyssinia into the war on the side of our enemies. We were already fighting the Germans in East Africa, the Turks in Syria, Mesopotamia and Aden, and the Dervishes in Somaliland. My father had a great respect for Ras Tafari and was therefore doing all he could to assist him. During those critical days, he even gave Ras Tafari's infant son safekeeping in the Legation.

Those were exciting days. Brian and I watched fascinated as Ras Tafari's Shoan army passed below the Legation on its way north to give battle to Negus Mikael. Armed with swords and spears, some of them carrying rifles, but all of them with shields, they hurried past on foot, closely packed about their mounted leaders. They were followed at intervals by bands of Galla on horses, wild tribesmen from areas in the south which Menelik had conquered and added to his empire. But this was nothing compared with their triumphant return after their decisive victory at Sagale, only sixty miles from the Legation. All day they had fought hand-to-hand in that desperate battle. Forty-two years later I visited the site of the battle and saw the hillside where Negus Mikael had made his last stand; crevices in the rock were still filled with skulls and bones. Now I sat beside my father near the Empress in an open-fronted pavilion, filled with notables, in all the splendour of their full dress. All day the victorious army passed before us, to the thunder of drums and the blare of trumpets, beneath fluttering pennons and glittering spear points. Negus Mikael was led forward to bow before the Empress, a proud figure even in defeat.

That day made a profound impression on me, implanting a craving for barbaric splendour, for savagery and colour, from which derived a lasting respect for tradition and a readiness to accept a variety of long-established cultures and customs. I grew to feel an increasing resentment towards Western innovations in other lands and a distaste for the dull monotony of our modern world.

In 1917, owing to the war and the difficulty of going back to England, my father took his leave in India, where his brother, Lord Chelmsford, was Viceroy. As a guest of the Viceroy I was conscious, even as a seven-year-old boy, of the majesty of the British Raj. We stayed with the Maharajah of Jaipur, there surrounded by all the opulence and splendour of his court; I rode about on elephants and was taken on a tiger shoot. While we were in Jaipur I had experienced a gratifying sense of shared adventure with my father. Always gentle, patient and understanding, he gave me a happy sense of comradeship.

Back in Addis Ababa, at the Legation, I lived once more the life I had always known, riding about everywhere with Brian, but this time on a new and bigger pony. We went again to our camp, an enchanted spot tucked away in the Entoto Hills, where a stream tumbled down the cliff opposite our tent and then flowed through a jumble of rocks among a grove of trees. Here were all sorts of birds: top-heavy hornbills, touracos with crimson wings, brilliant bee-eaters, paradise sun-birds, flycatchers, hoopoes, golden weaver-birds and many others. My father knew them all and taught me their names. I would watch the vultures through his field-glasses as they circled in slow spirals above the cliffs where they nested; and the baboons as they processed along the cliff tops, the babies clinging to their mothers' backs. Sometimes at night we heard their frenzied barking when a leopard disturbed them. Several times my father took me with him when he went up the valley in the evening, and I sat with him behind a rock, hoping he would get a shot at a leopard. At the Legation I always looked forward to the evenings when he read to me as we sat on the porch, looking out over the surrounding hills before the sun went down in a blaze of colour behind Mangasha.

Then one day in 1919 we all went to the station, got on the train and left Abyssinia. I could not believe we were never coming back. We were going to England. I had no more idea of what England was like than I had of India before we arrived there. I asked my father if there were any hyenas in England. No, there were no hyenas, no leopard, none of the animals I knew, not even vultures.

My father's house at the mouth of the Severn had been requisitioned by the Navy during the war, so soon after arriving in England we went to my mother's family home, Burgage, in County Carlow. Our visit to Ireland was great fun. Brian and I drove about in a donkey-cart, fished for eels and shot rabbits with a .410 shotgun. I spent a lot of my time with my father while he fished for salmon in the Slaney. Then we returned to England and Brian and I were taken to St Aubyn's, a preparatory school at Rottingdean, on the Sussex coast near Brighton.

Before I went to St Aubyn's I had never met any English boys. Here there were more than seventy of them, nearly all older than me. I found I was never away from them; in classrooms, on the playing fields or in the dormitory, I was always among them. I think that when I went there I was a friendly, forthcoming boy, only too ready to talk, and perhaps to boast, about the journeys I had made and what I had seen and done. Naturally my stories were greeted with disbelief and derision. I had arrived there without knowing any of the conventions that govern schoolboy life. I had not even heard of a game called cricket or seen a football. As a result I withdrew into myself and treated overtures of friendship with mistrust. But I accepted this as the life I was leading and was certainly not miserable, just lonely. In bed at night I was back in Abyssinia – I could recall it all so vividly.

My parents had taken rooms in Brighton, to be near the school. During my second term, my father collapsed while he was shaving and died in my mother's arms. Few marriages can have been as happy as theirs, and this was a devastating shock to my mother. Undaunted, she dedicated herself to looking after her four sons, found The Mile-brook, a house in Radnorshire on the Welsh borders, and there she gave us a lively, happy, self-sufficient home.

From St Aubyn's I went on to Eton. I had no idea what to expect; certainly I did not expect on the day I arrived there to find I had a room of my own. Eton was to mean a great deal to me; it gave me self-confidence. I gradually learnt to get on with my contemporaries, so that by the time I went on to Oxford I had found that others were prepared to accept me as a friend if I gave them a chance.

When in the summer of 1924, during my first year at Eton, Ras Tafari, as Regent of Ethiopia, arrived in London on a State Visit he invited my mother and me to call on him. As we left the room, I turned to him and said: 'More than anything in the world, sir, I want one day to return to your country.' These heartfelt words of mine were to decide the course of my life. He gave me his gentle smile and replied: 'One day you will come as my guest.'

Six years later I was granted a private audience with the Emperor two days after his coronation, a remarkable consideration during these eventful days to his youngest and least important guest.

He received me with grave courtesy and enquired after my family. When I expressed my appreciation of the honour he had done me by inviting me to his coronation, he replied that as the eldest son of his trusted friend, to whose assistance he had owed so much, it was proper that I should be present.

I told him how happy I was to be back in his country.

'It is your country. You were born here. You have lived here for half of your life. I hope you will spend many more years with us,' was his answer.

ETHIOPIA, SHOWING THE DANAKIL COUNTRY.

The Danakil Diary

Empire d'Ethiopie
Ministère des Affaires Etrangères

✦ ሰ ፴

ይድረስ · በወዳጃችን · በመስተር · ተሴገር ··
ሰላም · ለእርስዎ · ይሁን ··
አባትዎ · የግርማዊ · ንጉሠ · ነገሥት · ቀዳማዊ ·
ኃይለ · ሥላሴ · በተለየ · ወዳጃቸው · ስለ · ነበሩ ፤ እር
ስዎን · እኔስከግዜም · ኧንዋይ · ስለሚያል·ቀዋ ፤ ግንጉ
ው · ነገሥ·ቱ ·ዘውዱ · በሚጫ·ኑበት · በፕቅ·ም·ት · ፳፫·
ቀን · ፲፱፻፳፫ · ዓ·ም·ት · ወደ · አዲስ · አበባ · መፕ · ተው ·
 የደስታ·ቸው · ተካፋይ · እንደ·ሆኑ· · የግርማዊ · ንጉሠ ·
ነገሥት · ፈ ቃዳቸው · መሆኑን· እንደ·ስታ·ወ·ቅ·ም· ·ታዘ
ዣለሁ ·· ነሐሴ · ፮ · ቀን · ፲፱፻፳፬ · ዓ·ም·ት · አዲስ · አበባ ←

ᴸᴰᴰᴿ

(signature)

TRANSLATION:

Ethiopian Government
Ministry for Foreign Affairs

Let this letter come to our friend Mr Thesiger.
Greetings.

Your father was a cherished friend of His Majesty the Emperor Haile Selassie I and His Majesty knows you personally. I am charged to inform you that it is the pleasure of His Majesty that you should be present at the celebrations of the ceremony of Coronation to take place on 23rd Tekemt 1922 (2nd November 1930).

6 Nahassie 1922 (12th August 1930)

Signed: Blatengueta Herouy W.S.
Director General of the Ministry for Foreign Affairs

Seal of the Ministry

Coronation

I JOINED THE DUKE OF GLOUCESTER and his staff at Victoria Station on 16 October 1930, and from there we travelled by train to Marseilles. The Duke of Gloucester's mission comprised the Earl of Airlie, Major Stanyforth, Captain Brooke, Major 'Titch' Miles from Kenya, Mr Noble from the Foreign Office, and myself as an Honorary Attaché. The Duke was also accompanied by a delegation from the Sudan, led by Sir John Maffey, the Governor-General, who had previously served under my uncle when he was Viceroy of India. Earlier that year, I had stayed with him in Scotland, shooting grouse. He was six foot three, impressive in appearance, with natural charm and a spontaneous interest in others. Knowing him was a help in this unfamiliar setting. Lord Airlie, another impressive figure, also went out of his way to help me. Later, at the State Banquet in Addis Ababa, he wore the full dress of a Highland chief and looked magnificent. But it was the natural kindness of the Duke of Gloucester himself which helped me most.

It had been my ambition ever since I was a boy one day to join the Sudan Political Service and I listened with great interest one night when we were dining as Maffey told us about a recent killing by the Nuer of their District Commissioner. He said that two years earlier he had approved the Sudan Government's takeover of the Western Nuer. This naked, warlike tribe lived out of touch in the swamps of the White Nile. Hitherto they had been left alone, but their repeated raids on the administered Dinka eventually necessitated intervention. The Nuer had resisted fiercely and severe fighting had resulted before they submitted. Now they had killed Fergusson, the District Commissioner, and again taken up arms. While I listened I never anticipated that seven years later I would be helping their District Commissioner to administer these proud tribesmen in a virtually unknown area of the Southern Sudan teeming with wildlife.

We joined the SS *Rampura* at Marseilles and sailed for Aden. We had an entire deck to ourselves and all of us, with the Sudan delegation fed together at the same table. One of the first questions the Duke asked me was if I played bridge. When I admitted that I had, but was a very bad player, he said: 'That doesn't matter. Now I've got a four.' I was roped in to play on most evenings.

We arrived at Aden on 26th October.

October 26th

HMS *Effingham* saluted us with twenty-one guns. The *Dalia* and the shore battery also fired salutes. HRH went on board the *Effingham* at 9.30. Sailed at 10.30 a.m., arrived Jibuti 4.30. Averaged 28 knots. The French yacht fired a salute of twenty-one guns. Sir Sidney Barton came on board. Dined on board and joined the train at 10.30. Admiral Fullerton, his private secretary, Cooper, and Flag-Lieutenant Drage, are also coming up to Addis Ababa for the coronation, and the Marine band of the *Effingham*.

October 27th

Felt thrilled to be back in Abyssinia. As we travelled up to Addis Ababa in the train, stared at the arid landscape of the Danakil desert. Saw several dik-dik, baboons and a lesser bustard. Arrived Dire Dawa at 8 a.m. Gabra Mariam, the Governor of Harar, received HRH on the platform. The road to the palace was lined with troops, the station by regulars in khaki. The rest of the way by ordinary armed natives, and the steps of the palace by the Rases etc. in lion's mane crowns and velvet cloaks. An impressive scene. Here he gave us breakfast and we then returned to the train.

Troops turned out at all the stations as we passed through. Breakfast was not a bad meal, but the room was heavily scented, as was some of the food. Champagne afterwards. The Governor of Chercher gave us lunch at Afdam. The station being lined by his troops all in *shammas*. We arrived at the Awash at 9 p.m. and had dinner in the rest house. The train was quite comfortable. HRH had an apartment to himself.

October 28th

Had breakfast at Tafari's new house 'Mon Repos' two stations before the Akaki, at 5 a.m. A filthy meal. The coffee was scented. Two cars were provided to take us there. One ran out of petrol, the other out of water. HRH finished the journey on foot. An attractive spot overlooking a lake covered with wildfowl.

Arrived at Addis Ababa about 10 o'clock. HRH was met on the train by Ras Kassa and Belatingata Heroui. HIM Haile Selassie was on the platform and received HRH as he descended from the train. The Abyssinian band played the Ethiopian and English National Anthems (three verses of the latter). HRH was introduced by the Emperor to the leading Rases, and he then introduced the members of the mission to HIM. The station was lined inside and out by the regular troops in khaki, and two squadrons of cavalry, also in khaki, escorted HRH to the *Gibbi*.

The crowds lining the streets were not large and seemed rather listless. The baggage all went wrong and took the afternoon to sort out.

When eventually we arrived at the Legation we were put in tents in the compound.

October 30th

I do not think the Emperor is popular in the country. The Abyssinian mind is unable to appreciate him. Strange rumours are afloat that Lij Yasu is coming back in the role of a saviour of the country. He was in their eyes a real man and a true king and has gradually gained a halo. In reality he is, I believe, so dissipated as to be barely alive, and has disappeared from sight of late. Many, at least among the Europeans, say he is dead. He was invaluable to Kassa, giving him a great hold over the Emperor, but now that Tafari is to be crowned, Lij Yasu is no longer a real menace and must have lost his value to Kassa.

Gugsa's revolt seems to have been really serious for quite a time. Had it shown signs of being successful, I am sure several of the Rases would have joined him. Hailu was openly sitting on the fence, and Ras Seyum and Gugsa, although outwardly loyal, would have been on the winning side.

October 31st

As soon as you leave Addis Ababa, even for a short ride, you are back in the old Abyssinia. All the Emperor's reforms must be purely local until communications are improved.

Sandford thinks the Emperor forced the quarrel on Gugsa, having picked him as a representative of the old regime. He forced him into a position from which he could not withdraw and then smashed him, thereby greatly strengthening his position, and appearing as the champion of law and order against a mutinous subject.

The Emperor has a certain moral advantage in being the owner of a trained army, and has practically all the artillery and machine-guns in the country. The air force too gives him considerable superiority over any of the Rases (he has about six planes in flying order). But I think his position is far from safe.

November 1st

All the Legation and HRH's staff were photographed in the morning and then went to the unveiling of Menelik's memorial. The Emperor made a speech, which was translated into bad French, and then unveiled it. A bronze statue of Menelik on horseback. The square was lined by his regular troops.

The Emperor shook hands with each of us as we arrived, and we then formed up on his right. There were a few chiefs in lion's mane crowns and a certain number of priests present. There was a large crowd in the streets. The whole proceedings took about an hour and a half.

November 2nd

Coronation ceremony began at 7 o'clock. Left Legation at 6 o'clock. Estimated a hundred thousand people in the town, nearly all men and all armed. Streets seething.

Ceremony held in a canvas building added onto St George's Cathedral. Emperor and Empress observed an all-night vigil. St George's filled with priests dancing, beating drums, and chanting. Went in several times and watched them.

The church was surrounded by the captains and chieftains in their lion's mane head-dresses and silk and velvet cloaks. A wonderful sight.

The Emperor entered the outer church at 7.30 accompanied by a few attendants, and the Abuna, the Patriarch of Alexandria and the Etchege.

The Empress, accompanied by the ladies-in-waiting, entered about ten minutes later. The steps into the inner church were crowded by priests waving censers and holding very fine crosses. A special Coptic choir was present.

The heads of the respective missions sat in the front row with the most prominent Abyssinians. Ras Kassa, Ras Hailu, Ras Seyum and Ras Gugsa wore crowns. The Abyssinian diplomatic corps wore uniforms – a pity. The Emperor was presented with the robe, sword, sceptre, orb, ring, and two spears. The Abuna blessed each of these in turn and the Etchege actually handed them to the Emperor. The Abuna anointed the Emperor with oil and crowned him. A salute of guns was then fired.

The Crown Prince was then crowned, and the chief Abyssinians did homage before the Emperor. The Emperor signed his name. The Empress was then crowned and a salute of guns fired, after which the Abyssinian notables did homage before her. The Emperor and Empress then retired into the inner church to take communion. The Coptic choir remained chanting on the steps. The Emperor had been seated on a large red throne, the Empress on a blue one. More chiefs in lion's mane crowns were inside the church.

After a long wait, the Emperor and Empress, and the Abuna, Patriarch, and Etchege, came out of the inner church, walked in procession round to the other entrance of St George's Cathedral and then mounted two thrones set up opposite facing the priests and with the heads of missions on both sides.

The Abyssinian air force flew overhead and distributed pamphlets. The Emperor and the Empress and heir apparent then drove off in the state coach. (The state coach was the one the Kaiser used at his coronation.)

The streets were lined with the old army, and the effect was indescribably wonderful. Each chief surrounded by his brilliantly clad captains and officers. The missions drove back behind the state coach.

In the afternoon about forty Somalis came to the Legation and danced. In the evening the Emperor gave a dinner at the *Gibbi*. Attended the reception afterwards, but unfortunately all the fireworks went up at once. One child was badly burnt. HRH was given the Seal of Solomon.

November 4th
State procession in the morning. All the missions in a grandstand overlooking the street. The NCOs and chiefs passed first, wonderful in their lions' manes and many-coloured cloaks. Some on foot and some mounted.

The Regular infantry in khaki, followed by the cavalry, then marched past. The Emperor and Empress drove past, large red umbrellas with golden fringes held above them. Both were extremely dignified and very impressive. The old army then surged past with a traditional Abyssinian band in the middle.

Had a private audience with HIM at 6 o'clock in the *Gibbi*. Presented him with the books. He was extremely gracious. Saw Belatingata Heroui on leaving.

Attended the Crown Prince's dinner at the little *Gibbi* in the evening. The Emperor and Empress were present and the Crown Prince was rather crowded out. Kassa, Hailu, Seyum, Gugsa, Heroui and the Minister of Home Affairs and Minister for War were present. Had an excellent dinner off gold plates, with gold spoons and forks. We were to have seen the coronation of George V on the cinema afterwards, but after one or two flickering efforts it broke down. We then retired.

The Emperor is dissatisfied with the sceptre designed by Budge [presented to him by HRH], as it has Menelik's seal at the top, and his name only on the shaft. The idea was that Haile Selassie should gain power from wielding the sceptre once held by Menelik. Stupidly subtle. Zaphiro swears there are several spelling mistakes. It is a pity, as it was much the most dignified present, treating him like an Emperor, not a native chief. The French have given the Emperor an aeroplane and a field-gun. The Italians gave an aeroplane and an invaluable [sic] lace cloak for the Empress.

This is a letter I wrote to my mother at the time:

Wednesday 5th November

Dear Mother

The coronation was almost too wonderful to attempt to describe. It began at six in the morning and lasted till one.

The actual coronation was held in a canvas building added onto St George's Cathedral, which was well arranged so that it did not jar.

We were all able to get in and were not at all crowded. The Emperor and Empress (who is to have a child in a month's time and consequently has the European midwife as lady-in-waiting) had had an all-night vigil in St George's. The church was surrounded by all the chiefs and Rases in lion's mane crowns and velvet cloaks, outside them were the regular troops in khaki, and surging in apparently hopeless confusion beyond them again were the ordinary troops. The crowds were terrific, all men and all armed.

The Emperor and Empress entered the outer building accompanied by the Abuna, Patriarch of Alexandria and the Etchege and chief priests, all clothed in the most wonderful robes and with glittering crowns.

The Emperor was extremely dignified and the whole ceremony was intensely interesting. The Empress and Prince were also crowned, with rather awful European crowns.

The Cathedral of St George was filled with the rest of the priests. I went in and watched them dancing. All through the ceremony their chanting and the throbbing of their drums came faintly to our ears. In the outer church we had a special Coptic choir.

Kassa, Hailu, Seyum and Gugsa were present and wore crowns too, in their capacity of lesser kings I suppose. The church was filled with chiefs in lion's mane head-dresses, and all the European missions. The Abyssinian diplomatic corps wore European clothes and cocked hats, which was a pity.

Tafari was to have left in his state carriage, but the horses were unmanageable.

The streets were lined with troops in their native dress and every side street was packed with dense crowds. There must have been a hundred thousand people present. A wonderful spectacle.

After the ceremony the Abyssinian air force flew over the building (they have crashed two planes in the last fortnight).

In the evening Tafari gave a dinner party for the heads of missions. I went to the reception afterwards. There was a tremendous selection of fireworks, but unfortunately an accident occurred and they all went off at once.

Yesterday there was a state procession. An odd mixture of East and West. But I must say his regular troops are well disciplined and good at their drills. All the Rases and chiefs went past with their soldiers and looked very wonderful.

I had a private audience with him at six and gave him the books. He says he can never repay what you did for him. Zaff [Zaphiro, who interpreted] said I had the most cordial reception of anyone. Tafari is fixing up for me to shoot a bushbuck at Mangasha, and go down the Awash for kudu and oryx. Sandford is lending me boys and I am going to stay on the line to avoid a caravan. I am having an audience with the Empress later.

I dined with the Prince in the evening, a large party. The Emperor and Empress were present. We fed off gold plates with gold spoons and forks.

Afterwards we were to have seen King George's coronation on the cinema, but after a few flickering efforts it went out altogether.

The review is on Friday and should be quite wonderful.

The coronation and other ceremonies have had the strangest contrasts. Scenes which take you back a thousand years, and make the dead past live again. Robes and crosses, lion's mane crowns and incense, and the wail and throb of the bands; and then a dirty Greek in European clothes directing operations in the foreground, khaki-clad troops, cinema, motors and aeroplanes. In some ways it is rather pathetic, and in others it is incomparably magnificent.

I think he is staking his all on one great effort. If he fails Heaven knows what will happen. Kassa supports him, otherwise he could not hold his position. Hailu is just waiting for a chance to bid for the crown. He was only allowed to bring three hundred men in and I think the country is apathetic and would go either way. Gugsa and Seyum would probably side with the winner.

This coronation must have cost him hundreds of thousands and some one has got to pay. There are the oddest rumours afloat and Lij Yasu figures prominently in them. The country seems to be awaiting his return. They don't understand Tafari. Lij Yasu was a man and they say no man could look him in the eyes. In point of fact, he is I believe so debauched as to be barely alive – if still alive, which seems doubtful. But it shows the country is waiting for the coming of a prophet, so to speak. The Emperor looks very small and frail surrounded by great burly warriors such as Hailu and Gugsa, but he is almost inhumanly dignified. You can't help feeling he was born to be a king when you look at him.

His changes are very superficial. A thousand men in khaki, a few aeroplanes and ministers in European clothes. The crowds which line the streets are the crowds of twelve years ago.

I met Kassa, Hailu and the Minister for War at a garden party here the other day, also Doctor Martin. I met Heroui yesterday. He is Minister for the Interior and a thorn in the side of the Legation, I think.

I am loving my time here, and each day brings back the old days more vividly, and so many things which I have forgotten are coming back again. I have had several lovely rides.

Dear Mother, I think of you such a lot. There has never been anyone like you and Daddy here since you left and they know it.

I am longing for a letter.

Very very much love,

Wilfred

November 6th

The Royal Picnic at Addis Ababa. HRH and Brooke attended.

Busy all day preparing for the official dinner in the Legation.

Lit all the grounds with Chinese lanterns, and had three large bonfires on the hill. About a hundred Somalis danced on the lawn lit by flares. The Emperor and Empress attended.

Belatingata Heroui has very considerable influence over the Emperor. The Legation seem to have got badly on the wrong side of him.

November 7th

The Review held out by the station. The Emperor sat on a throne under an awning surrounded by the Abyssinian notables and the heads of missions. This was on the top of a small rise overlooking the plain. Troops were massed all round.

A large band of chiefs on foot then rushed up to within a few yards of the Emperor, so close that they had to be beaten back with staves. They shouted out their services on his behalf, and their prowess at the Battle of Adua and other battles, and worked themselves up into a frenzy. When these retired, more chiefs, mounted this time, rushed the royal tent, sweeping aside all opposition. It seemed for a moment that everything would be ridden flat. A very wonderful spectacle, and the Emperor never stirred. An exhibition of spear throwing then took place in the plain below. Well worth watching. Next the regular army marched past. The Emperor then retired to lunch with the [French] Marshal. Finally the irregular army streamed past, covering the plain with their numbers, and moving in every direction at once.

It is said that the Marshal had no answer to his invitation from the Emperor till the very last moment, and had a special train waiting with steam up to take him to Jibuti if the Emperor did not attend. He is a pompous little man, and greets everyone with his baton like a conjuror about to perform a trick. Cavalry and foot all mixed together, each man following his chief irrespective of all else. A whirlpool of colour.

Went back slowly through streets choked with troops to lunch with

Lady Ravensdale at the Hotel de France. Saw de la Rivière after lunch and talked with Ferra Ali. Fixed up quite a lot about a shoot. Dined with HRH at the small *Gibbi*.

Hunting

As a small boy in Abyssinia, at the age of seven, Powell-Cotton's *A Sporting Trip through Abyssinia* was the book I most enjoyed being read to me. While I was at Eton, I had already collected books by Selous, Baldwin, Gordon Cumming, Chapman, Millais and others on African exploration and hunting. Whenever I was in London, I visited the Natural History museum as often as I could to acquaint myself with the African game animals about which I had been reading. I was familiar with Rowland Ward's *Records of Big Game* and I had a well-thumbed copy of the book with me.

Now that I found myself back in Abyssinia for the coronation I was determined as soon as the festivities were over to spend a month hunting big game before I returned to Oxford. I had brought with me a .318 Westley Richards' rifle, which I had borrowed from a friend. My aim was to secure a good head of each species and, in consequence, except when I shot for meat, I shot selectively and seldom.

My original plan had been to accompany Sir John Maffey back to the Sudan and hunt there. However, when I discussed this with him, he said it would be expensive and it might be difficult for me at my age to secure the necessary permits to hunt. I asked Colonel Sandford for his advice. He had served under my father in the Legation in 1913 and had lived in Abyssinia for many years. He and his wife and family were now farming at Mullu, some fifteen miles from Addis Ababa. He suggested that I should spend a month hunting in the Danakil country.

I could get down by train to the Awash station where I should be on the edge of the Danakil desert. He said that the Abyssinians had wiped out the wild animals over most of the country, but they never ventured into the Danakil country where a man's status among his fellow tribesmen depended on the number of men he had killed. The Danakil themselves did not hunt, so there were plenty of game animals down there. He said at once that he would help me get a caravan together and he would lend me the necessary camping equipment. He advised me to take a Somali called Ali Yaya as my headman. Ali had worked for him for years and was utterly reliable.

The Danakil were camel-owning pastoralists, a Hamitic people resembling the Somalis, and like the Somalis they were Muslims. They inhabited the desert area north of the railway line that lay between the Rift Valley escarpment of the Abyssinian Highlands and the Red Sea coast. The Awash river which rose near Addis Ababa flowed northwards into the desert but never reached the sea. No one knew where it ended, for much of the Danakil country was still unexplored. Sandford suggested I should follow the river from the railway station as far as Bilen; here there were extensive reedbeds where I should find buffalo. He said he would lend me his double-barrel .400 Jeffery so that I should have a heavy rifle if I hunted them.

Sir Sidney Barton was worried at the thought of my going at my age by myself among the Danakil. After all, as he said, I had no previous experience of trekking in Africa, nor of big-game hunting, and above all the Danakil were dangerous – I already knew they castrated anyone they killed. He suggested I should join him and Lord Airlie on a short hunting trip which they proposed to make. I thanked him, but insisted that I must do this journey on my own to acquire the experience for the life I intended to lead.

After some further hesitation he agreed, but said: 'Don't go further down the Awash than Bilen. It would rather spoil the effect of the coronation if you get yourself cut up by the Danakil.'

November 12th
HRH, Stanyforth, Brooke and Miles left Addis Ababa on a special train at 11 a.m. Received a pair of elephant tusks, a golden cigarette case and the Star of Ethiopia (Third Class) from the Emperor.

Saw Moussa Hamma, the *shikari*, and Muhammad Sirage, the *aban*.

November 15th

Finished packing in the morning. Took luggage, tents, etc. to the railway in the afternoon. The railway station was a scene of utter disorder, twenty clamouring Gurages trying to get hold of every package, however small. Sandford authorized to lend me a Government tent and equipment. Pass not yet arrived and rumour that only allowed to shoot three heads. Same to apply to Airlie and the Minister.

November 16th

Said goodbye to the old servants. Left on 9 o'clock train. Nothing got left behind, more by good luck than good management, as there was an appalling scramble. Belatingata Heroui at the station. No pass arrived.

November 17th

Airlie and Sir Sidney Barton arrived at 7 a.m. at the Awash station and left with their caravan at 9.30.

Pitched the tent outside the hotel and bought flour and kerosene.

Went up the line with the .318 rifle in the afternoon. Moussa Hamma acted as *shikari*. Saw a hyena, and hit a jackal. Found a small lot of Soemering's just before sunset. Had a stalk of about 150 yards and shot a buck with quite a good head at 100 yards. Got back long after dark. Hyenas all round the station. Heard one laugh.

Six *zabanias* arrived from the Governor of Harar, to accompany me.

Grand Hotel Continental

Dear Mother

I came down here from Addis Ababa yesterday.

This place has not changed much. I have put up my tent near the rest house and am going to sleep in it tonight and go off tomorrow morning. My camels are here and an escort of six men from the Governor of Harar.

I saw Rhigas on the train. He recognized me from Daddy and

was full of enquiries about you all, and seemed delighted to see me. I must look him up again at Jibuti.

Everything seems to be going all right in spite of the usual last-minute difficulties, and I hope some riding mules may arrive any minute.

I have got a really first-class headman and interpreter called Ali; he is with the Sandfords.

I saw a lot of game yesterday, including oryx.

I am rather busy at the minute finding out about possible landing grounds, food, etc. for the air force. I have got to be rather discreet as the Abyssinians are not to know it is contemplated so don't say too much.

It is fairly warm here but not as hot as I expected. I have got an excellent tent off the Abyssinian Government.

The old servants all assembled to see me off and kept impressing on me to remember them to you. A faithful lot.

I was very sorry to leave Addis Ababa and hope to return there again some day.

I went out last night for an hour and shot a Soemering's gazelle as the sun set. We had to skin and bring it back in the dark. There were any number of hyenas laughing round the station during the night.

I am just off and will send back letters when I get a chance.

God bless you dear, and I am always thinking of you.

Love to every one,

Wilfred

November 18th

Bought a mule for one hundred dollars, and hired four camels at two dollars a day.

Got off about 2 o'clock and arrived at Moussa Alidas on the Awash an hour after sunset. Quite a good camp on a stony plateau, but naturally everything rather in confusion.

Just before getting into camp fired off a shot as a signal and heard a snake hiss in the dark at my feet. Threw a stone in its direction and went in the opposite direction. Very unpleasant.

Forded the Awash. The ford looked very crocodilish in the moonlight and seemed a long way across. Very white legs! Told the *zabanias* I would send them home unless they did well.

Shot a Soemering with a bad head and saw a sow wart hog on the way to the camp. Shot badly.

November 19th
Left camp soon after sunrise. Saw a herd of oryx on the hill opposite. Moussa Hamma ill with fever, so took Muhammad, who was very little use. Followed them for three hours, but Muhammad twice showed himself, so undertook a stalk by myself of about four hundred yards. Got a shot at about two hundred yards after a long crawl in the open.

Killed a bull with a nice head. Shot through the heart. He rushed about a hundred yards before falling dead.

Vultures soon began to appear and when we left the carcase was quite concealed by a scuffling mass of them. Reached Hindessa after a six hour march. Saw two female lesser kudu on the way. A great many camels and cattle being watered. Given three jars of camels' milk.

A herd of oryx stood on the hill overlooking the camp all the afternoon, and came down to drink as soon as the sun set. They then thundered back up the hill. Several other lots came down to drink during the night.

Had some target practice with both rifles, and bathed when the sun was setting. They say there are no crocodiles here.

Moussa, who had been left behind, arrived. Not at all well.

CARAVAN

self	
Ali Yaya	headman
Muhammad Sirage	*aban*
Moussa Hamma	*shikari*
Tukluh	cook
Lemma	boy
Alamou	mule boy and extra
Ababa	*zabanias*
Gabra Selassie	
Haile Miriam	
Tassabe	
Muhammad	
Hailu	
Farah	

3 camel men, 1 mule and 4 camels

November 20th

Left camp at sunrise. Arrived at Sade Malka at 1 o'clock. Took a circle round to look for game. Saw a great number of oryx and an ostrich in the distance. Went out shooting after lunch. Thick jungle all round the camp, a relief after the stony desert and scrub. Followed a waterbuck.

Good tracking on the part of three natives out with me, and after getting two glimpses of it, got a shot at it as it was standing by the edge of the river. A lovely picture. Hit it, and knocked it over with a second shot. The .318 rifle. The natives then rushed in and the water-buck scrambled up and disappeared. Followed it for two hours till sunset by the blood smears, which were plentiful.

The natives insisted on getting clear of the thick jungle before sunset. They are afraid of their neighbours over the river. So had to give up. The Danakil hunted like a pack of dogs, spreading out and casting whenever they lost the spoor. A very carrying call when they picked it up.

Saw two crocodiles, small ones, on the way home and hit one with a very long shot. Saw a lesser kudu bull in the twilight. Should have got a shot at it as I saw the does first, but stepped out into the clearing stupidly.

Sade Malka

Dear Mother

Everything is going very well. I have got an excellent headman. The caravan varies between fourteen and twenty people and we have four camels and one mule.

We have done three days' trekking and are now resting here. A lovely spot on the Awash river. We shall probably stay here two days.

There is thick jungle along the river and every sort of bird. So far I have shot one Soemering's gazelle and one oryx with a good head, also a bush pig. We went out yesterday evening and had a thrilling time following up a waterbuck. We tracked it for about an hour and then I got a shot and hit it twice. We followed it by the blood splashes for another hour until the sun set. I looked for it this a.m., but it is very thick bush. I have got four men out looking for it now. It was very badly hit and they should find it. The Danakil are quite wonderful at tracking and it is thrilling work.

I saw a lesser kudu yesterday. This seems a paradise for game. I shall go out again this evening. There are any number of oryx about and I am looking out for an extra good head. There are also plenty of crocodiles. I hit one yesterday but it got into the river. I also saw an ostrich yesterday.

It is a wonderful experience. Every evening we watch the game come down to drink and the hyenas patrol all round the camp and give the mule hysterics.

I am very careful about boiling all water and sleep under a net and take quinine.

I bit everyone's head off once or twice to keep them in order and now they are all very willing.

I am presented with camel's milk and sheep at every camp and sent a man off today to try and raise some vegetables.

I have just finished my air force report which took rather a long time.

Very very much love and a happy Christmas to you all. I should be home soon after it. I shall not be able to get a letter back again, but will wire when I get to Dire Dawa in about a month's time.

Very much love again,
Wilfred

November 21st

Went out with Moussa and another native to look for the waterbuck. Could find no trace of it. Saw one lot of about three others and several pig. Natives out looking all day but unsuccessful. It was hit high up and rather far back judging from the blood marks.

Went across the river in the evening with Muhammad and three local natives. Thick jungle, mud swamps, and bamboos.

Saw several waterbuck, but all females except for one. Got a shot at him as he was standing with three does on the edge of a clearing. Broke his neck with .400. Quite a nice head. Gave the natives the skin. Took plenty of meat for the camp.

November 22nd

Went out just before sunrise. Saw several waterbuck, one [a male], the far side of the river. Did not get a shot. Always hope there are no crocodiles about when fording the river.

Sand-grouse began to fly back from the river soon after I got back. Shot six. Quite amusing shooting. Not very good to eat.

Impossible to get eggs or any vegetables from the natives, and cow's milk only very occasionally. Get presents of sheep and goats nearly every day.

Sent a native to a plantation not far away. He came back with a great number of squashed bananas, twenty oranges, and plenty of lemons, a great treat.

Went out in the evening and shot a waterbuck. A slightly smaller head than the other, but thicker and prettier. A long shot across a clearing and then a bit of a chase. Walked right into a family of pig. Hyenas all round the camp.

November 23rd
Bitterly cold as we left before sunrise.

Arrived at Dopane about midday before the caravan. Thick bush and groves of aloe all the way. Saw two lesser kudu bucks and several does, but could not get a shot. Usually just a moving branch or a little dust as they disappeared. They were always in the centre of the thickest bush, where it was very difficult to move noiselessly.

Moussa rather better, but still not right. Saw a bateleur eagle.

November 24th
Left just before sunrise. Arrived at Werrer at midday to find camp pitched. Saw several lesser kudu does in the morning and the natives saw a buck.

Had a talk with the headman. The Danakil of this part have had a fight with the Danakil from beyond Bilen. Their king was killed and they say 80 of their men and 150 of the other side. He wished me to induce the Abyssinian Government to send troops to punish the other Danakils. Muhammad Sirage is in charge of the case.

Went out after lunch. Saw a lot of gerenuk. Had eight shots at the buck at an average of two hundred yards and missed every time – awful. Got three chances at a lesser kudu and missed. Shot vilely. Sickening. Legs very tired. Saw three lesser kudu does. Ali shot a dik-dik with the shotgun. He saw a hippo.

November 25th
Left for Badahamo just before sunrise and arrived at 11 o'clock.

Saw two hyenas and had an unsuccessful shot at one. Saw a family of lesser kudu; six in all including one buck with a good head. Could not get a shot. Saw a few more females.

Shot and hit a very large crocodile at Badahamo, but he got into

the water. Killed another small one of six feet with one shot from the
.400. The natives said it was a female. Shot it on the far bank and the
natives swam over and brought it back. They were very pleased. Broke
its back behind the shoulder.

Went out in the evening. Saw another lesser kudu buck and several
females. Could not get a shot.

There is a large village here, and consequently not much game.
Passed the village at sunset as all the camels and cattle were coming
home. A sight well worth seeing.

November 26th

Left for Bilen before sunrise and arrived at 2 o'clock, about half an
hour before the caravan. Great numbers of camels and cattle were
being watered at the hot springs.

The natives are burning the reeds. They lit them yesterday. Unfortu-
nate, as it will probably shift the game and disturb the buffalo. Whole
acres on fire.

An Itu Galla killed a Danakil here yesterday. The Itu Galla sent a
force to molest the inhabitants of Bilen. They took up their quarters
in the reeds and attacked and killed one person. The reeds were then
lit to burn them out successfully.

Went out with Moussa for a reconnaissance in the afternoon. Found
plenty of buffalo tracks about two days old, and the tracks of a lion
about four days old.

Great numbers of pigeons came down to drink in the late afternoon.
Shot nine. Moussa came back from the reed bed about an hour after
I had shot the pigeons saying he thought from all the shooting we
must have been attacked. Took him a long time to think this out.

Went out with Moussa and two natives to wait for buffalo at sunset.
Sat under a bush where there were most tracks. An eerie feeling. Plenty
of mosquitoes. Stayed about an hour and saw no signs of the buffalo.
Plenty of pig and three porcupines which came within a few feet of
us. The Danakil chased them. They went surprisingly fast.

November 27th

Went out at the first sign of dawn to look for buffalo, but without success. Saw a few lesser kudu does on the way back to camp.

As soon as I had got back, some natives reported having just seen a lesser kudu. Went out again. About an hour before sunrise. Found some oryx, who spotted us crossing open ground. Left the natives standing in plain sight, and stalked round behind them by myself. Shot a cow with a very nice head. Then went on to look for the kudu. Unsuccessful.

The camelmen have run out of flour so went out about 11 o'clock to try and get something. Missed an oryx and saw a few gerenuk. Went out again in the afternoon with Moussa to the hot springs. Saw great numbers of oryx, and a few gerenuk and lesser kudu does. Missed another oryx after a successful stalk by myself. Had some target practice. Shooting high with the .318.

Came to the reed bed just after sunset and heard the buffalo moving about just inside them. Sat down behind a bush and waited. Not at all a pleasant feeling as the light was shocking. There was thick bush all round and I only had the .318 rifle and none of the special expanding nickel-covered ammunition for dangerous game. The three natives also loaded their rifles. When it was too dark to see twenty yards a pig walked right in among us and gave us a severe fright as it bolted away. Gave up and came back to camp after about an hour.

November 28th

Went out just before sunset to try for the buffalo. Saw them moving in two herds about a mile away through the burnt rushes. They made a large cloud of dust. Found a broken tree about four feet high which gave us a fair view of the game path we thought they would use. Climbed onto it with the tracker. The other natives, the *zabanias*, and Muhammad stayed on the ground. Difficult to see much as there was thick bush about four feet high all round and the reed bed twenty yards in front. It grew very dark under the trees. The moon nearly half full, gave a little light outside. Numbers of fireflies in the reeds looking like myriad single eyes. Innumerable frogs croaking in the reed bed, and teal whistling in the darkness.

Could hear the buffalo coming closer and plenty of pig moving about. After an hour the buffalo splashed out of the reeds in two lots just out of sight. Waited another half hour, during which we heard them bellowing in the bush behind us, and then followed them. An extremely nervous job, and four loaded rifles pointing in every direction, often at me. Came to a small clearing, surrounded by bamboos, evidently well used from the tracks, and sat down and waited. The tracker, armed with a spear, went off to reconnoitre several times and said they were quite close. Mosquitoes very bad. Waited an hour and then as they did not come we followed them again but gave it up when they entered some very thick bush.

Tukluh had an excellent supper waiting. A hyena laughed round the camp during the night.

November 29th

Left camp about an hour and a half before sunrise. Pitch dark. Moon set. Had to wait about three-quarters of an hour for enough light to see our way through the bush, and by then the buffalo had gone back into the reeds. Had an unsuccessful snap shot at a lesser kudu on the way home.

Ali went out in the afternoon and made a seat in a tree overlooking the game path. Serviceable if uncomfortable. The tree a mimosa.

Went out in the evening after buffalo. All sat in the tree which Ali had prepared. Mosquitoes better off the ground. Neither saw nor heard the buffalo, but a large black cat called *ourie* by the natives passed right under the hide. As far as I could see, it was as large as a jackal, but shorter in the leg and with a short tail. It is said to be light-coloured underneath and occasionally to attack people. A hyena laughed within a few yards of us on the way back to camp. A horrid noise which makes the back of your scalp tingle.

Large herds of cattle and camels came to water all day. Muhammad always tries to make me eat my supper and go to bed in the dark. They have all been scared of a night attack since we left the Awash.

The *zabanias* chatter all night to keep awake. Have put a stop to this, and told them to walk about to keep awake. They will probably sleep if not too frightened. The Danakil would not, I think, attack the camp, though they might try to cut one of the men's throats while they were asleep. This seems to be the most likely camp for trouble. A Danakil until he has killed someone is called a woman and not allowed to marry.

A most pernicious custom. Moussa has ten men to his credit and is entitled to one ear ring. He has several appalling-looking scars on his body. One arm must have been nearly severed. A Frenchman was murdered not far from here three years ago. The remains of his corpse, one leg, was taken to Addis Ababa and formally decorated by the Emperor. Posthumous glory!

November 30th

Stayed in bed till two hours after sunrise, and then went out for a short stroll. Tried an unsuccessful stalk after gerenuk. Did not get a shot. One more gerenuk than one has first spotted always turns up to spoil the most careful stalk.

Shot a gerenuk in the afternoon. Hit him too low with the first shot but killed him with the second. Stalked him by myself. Not a very good head. None of the Muhammadans will eat gerenuk. They say it has the blood of a woman. They would not even carry any part of it back.

Saw a very large tawny owl with two large ears. There are any number of interesting birds about. Saw six marabout [storks] round the camp and any number of vultures who pounce on anything thrown away. Watching the kites is always an amusing way of passing the time.

Moussa, who has been seedy ever since we left Addis Ababa, went home in the afternoon. He has been spitting blood of late and complains of a pain in his side. Sorry to lose him.

Went out after buffalo again in the evening to the same hide, but with no more luck than the night before. Had one thrilling moment when a family of pig came through the reeds. At first we thought it was the buffalo. Hunted round afterwards to see if they could have slipped out of the reeds lower down, but they had not. The moon half-full but the sky very cloudy.

December 1st

Went out at sunrise. Saw a lesser kudu with a nice head watching us from some long grass. Left the natives and made a successful stalk. Killed him with one shot. A better head than the last. Left Bilen in the afternoon at 3 o'clock for the valley of the Mullu. Engaged an extra camel at a dollar a day to carry water. Trekked across to valley of the Mullu by the Plain of Alidak. Saw a great number of oryx and Soemering's and one ostrich. Walked right into a flock of sand-grouse. One, on rising, got caught up in a thorn tree and although scratched flew away when released. A lovely sunset.

December 2nd

Left before sunrise and reached Tardi on the Mullu at 3 o'clock. A long march with the Mullu always behind the next range of hills. One of the camel loads kept slipping, causing a good deal of delay. Kept two tanks of water in reserve in spite of protests from the Danakil, who are not nearly so good at bearing thirst as the Abyssinians. Walked all the way from Bilen to set a good example. Mountains all round.

Saw a number of harriers out in the desert. A seagull-grey colour. Found several greenish pools of water in the bed of the Mullu, but got some quite good water by digging a well.

As lunch was being got ready a large force of Galla, armed to the teeth and evidently quite ready to attack, appeared on the cliffs behind the camp. After a certain amount of talk they descended into the camp and sat about in sullen groups. They said they had mistaken us for a Danakil raiding party.

A large brown eagle spent all his time robbing the kites of their titbits. One stoop just overhead sounded like an express passing through a station. I think they are Tawny Eagles. Went out to look for guinea-fowl in the evening, but took the rifle as well. Walked practically straight into five greater kudu bulls one after the other. Got a shot at the last as he was disappearing over a ridge and broke his back leg half-way up. Followed him up – he seemed greatly handicapped – and killed him with a shot through the heart. A very nice head.

Sent a man back to camp to get men for the meat. A distance of about one mile. At the end one haunch would have had to be left behind, so carried it myself.

Rain in the hills had brought the river down meanwhile. A muddy torrent two foot deep. Feeling very pleased with myself.

December 3rd
The night passed off quietly though we posted the *zabanias* more carefully than usual.

Haile, who had overeaten with raw meat at Bilen, wanted a dose. Gave him five packets of Epsom salts, a cupful.

Went out at sunrise. The mountains all hidden in clouds. Very beautiful. The country round here is cut up by deep watercourses with red clay cliffs. Mainly mimosa with patches of aloe and bush. Saw one greater kudu, an easy shot at fifty yards, but spared him in the hopes of getting a better head.

Rained later and the river came down in flood. The Galla headman and a large band of armed followers came to camp and had a conference with Muhammad. They say they have seen lion tracks not very far away.

Went out again in the afternoon. Saw two lesser kudu bucks; easy shots, but did not shoot though one had a very nice head.

The cliffs round the camp are alive with baboons who make a great noise. The smell is very bad. Got up within a few yards of them from behind and gave them an awful scare.

December 4th

Rained at sunrise just as we were preparing to start, so waited an hour till it stopped. The hills all hidden in clouds and a fine Scotch mist. Shot my way to the next camp at Garissa further up the Mullu. Saw two lesser kudu and one greater kudu but could not get a shot. Camp was like a small village, all the natives having built themselves grass shelters.

Went out about 3 o'clock. Saw a hyena, two female lesser kudu and one greater kudu cow.

About 4 o'clock there was a heavy thunderstorm. Soaked in a minute. Got to the river in ten minutes, which, though swollen, was crossable. Suddenly there was a roar and down it came. It rose six feet in two minutes and bore down large trees and branches. Luckily none of us had yet attempted to cross. Reached the river opposite camp at sunset and fired shots to attract attention. Lemma succeeded in throwing us over some matches and at last got a fire going and got fairly dry. The river fell rapidly, but we were afraid of more rain sending it down again before we could cross. A hyena patrolled quite close round the fire. Ali did great work wading about trying to find a way across. Half an hour later there was another downpour. About an hour before we got across. Ali threw us over a tin of sardines and some meat for the men, Ali Muhammad Haile and Muhammad. Eventually at midnight we succeeded in getting across. Tukluh had hot soup and food waiting.

December 5th

Out at sunrise. Very misty and damp. All the *zabanias* said they were ill, but soon persuaded two to come.

Went further up the Mullu and got back at lunch time. Very heavy going except on the mountains. Saw one kudu cow on the shoulder of a hill early on and another in a similar position at the end of the morning. River quite low again and it cleared up about 11 o'clock.

Heard the Galla uttering their rallying cry. Apparently a large force has gone off to raid the Danakil. Have had an unpleasant feeling lately of being in a hostile country. No Galla ever come into camp or bring

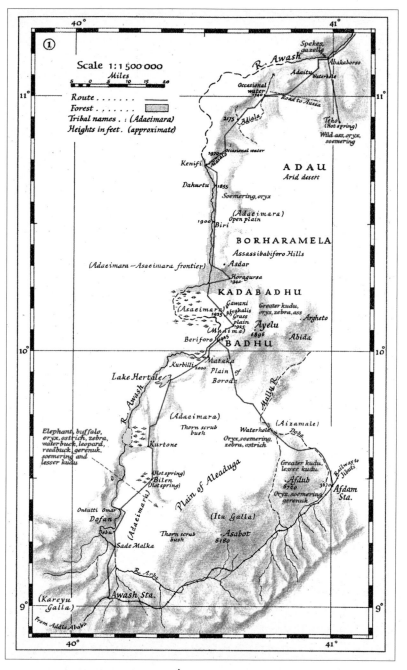

WILFRED THESIGER'S DANAKIL MAP 1, 1933–34.

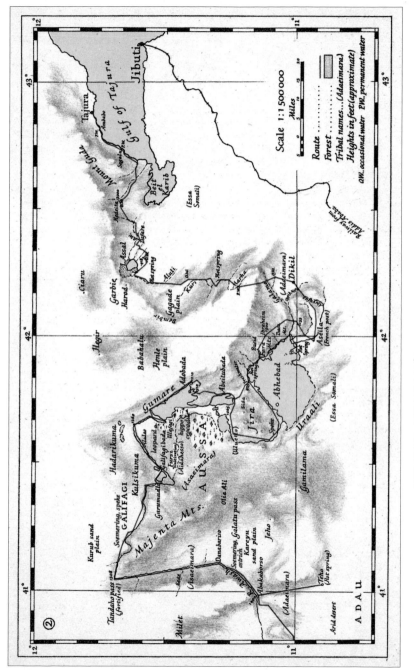

WILFRED THESIGER'S DANAKIL MAP 2, 1933–34.

us presents. We are constantly being watched from the hilltops, but they always vanish as we approach. In the Danakil country, crowds of natives sat round the camp all day.

Muhammad has not been fit and is very weak. A long day tires him out. I don't think he is getting proper food. He has eaten and given away all his flour, and does not like meat. Gave him some tinned milk and more flour.

Tukluh has had a bad eye. Gave him some boracic powder. This has a great reputation and a pinch of it is more valued than several dollars. At every camp a crowd sits round and begs for some of it. Give it out occasionally to headmen and favoured trackers as a very special gift. At Bilen the Danakil would do anything for a pinch of it.

December 6th
Left camp at sunrise and reached Lobi at midday. Saw five hyenas on leaving camp. Got within twenty yards of them. I think they had been having a drink. Saw a female kudu and young soon afterwards.

None of the people I had with me seemed to be very sure where Lobi was. Luckily when I thought we were lost Ali heard a shot we fired.

The drought of last year has given the countryside a very burnt up appearance. There is no grass and all the game has gone. Passed a few deserted Galla villages. There being no pasture for their flocks, they have had to move into Danakil territory and this has been the cause of the troubles.

Passed through some very mountainous country. Rode the last two hours. The water was a few very muddy puddles. Went out in the afternoon at 3 o'clock. Saw one large tortoise, and a few gerenuk and pig, and found no tracks of anything else. Ali shot two partridges.

December 8th
A cold night and heavy dew. Left before sunrise and got to Afdam soon after midday. Saw no game, but the caravan walked into a female greater kudu.

The Chief of the Railway Police was travelling up to Addis Ababa on the 12 o'clock train, and very kindly came and saw I had all I wanted. Did not go out shooting in the afternoon, but got a jackal round the camp with the shotgun.

December 9th

Went out an hour before sunrise into the foothills across the line. Good kudu country, but at the moment everything is disturbed by herds of cattle and goats.

Had an unsuccessful shot at a gerenuk. Muhammad, the *zabania* who was out with me, got lost and only turned up at camp at 3 o'clock. Boiled all the heads I had shot in salt water. Some of the horns have loosened sufficiently to come off.

Went out at 3 o'clock and went half-way back to the last camp. Got back to camp two hours after sunset. No moon and a difficult walk through scrub country largely composed of wait-a-bit thorn. Saw a family of gerenuk and a kudu bull just before sunset. Followed him up and saw what I took to be him standing in some thick bush. Fired and hit a male lesser kudu. A stupid mistake, but I was in a hurry because of the failing light. The lesser kudu made off and I missed with two other shots. Followed him up and came on him lying dead within a hundred yards. Hit rather too far back. He had a much better head than the other two I have got, but this does not make up for losing the greater kudu.

December 10th

Had a long lie-in in the morning and then settled the wages. Took a photo of the caravan and paid off the camels and muleman. Gave letters of recommendation to Ali, Muhammad, Tukluh, and Lemma, and a letter to the *zabanias*.

I am extremely pleased with everyone except the three younger *zabanias*, who were idle, never doing anything unless they were told to and watched all the time. Only gave them half the *bakhshish* I gave the other three. Ali and Muhammad were quite splendid. Tukluh an excellent camp cook and Lemma very willing, if not overburdened with common sense. The extra man Alamou, who looked after the mule, was always quietly efficient and was very useful.

December 11th
Paid off the remaining people and struck camp. Sold the few remaining stores, and the buckets, tanks, lamps, etc.

STORES

Drank tea without milk, and coffee sometimes after lunch. Always had porridge for breakfast.

Did not take enough dried fruit and could have done with some more macaroni. Forgot to order curry powder, a serious mistake. Found sardines and packets of dried pears very useful. Did not use the tinned kippers, lime juice, and very little jam and flour. Tinned milk useful for cooking, but not used otherwise, and did not use any tinned butter. Custard useful as a change from rice puddings.

Zaphiro came up on the train from Dire Dawa. Had lunch with him and then went down on the train from Addis Ababa. Rather a rush at the last moment, but finally everyone and all the tents etc. were got on the up train.

Arrived at Dire Dawa soon after 4 o'clock. Plowman [the Consul] met me at the station and we both spent the night at the hotel.

Hear the coronation is estimated to have cost over a million pounds. This will take a bit of raising.

There is considerable excitement because Dunkley, the manager of the Ethiopian Produce Company, is said to have gone off with £400. He was going home for leave with his wife when the man he had left in charge wired to have him arrested at Jibuti. The French said they had not got the right to do this, so Dunkley has gone on home.

December 12th

Left Dire Dawa at 7.30, got to Haramaya at 12 o'clock and had lunch there, and got to Harar at 4.30. Rode slowly and did not hurry. It is a lovely ride up the Harar mountains. Everything was very green after the recent rains. Saw a bateleur eagle soon after leaving Dire Dawa.

There is a very fine view back from the top. Ranges of hills in the foreground and the plains stretching away endlessly beyond. The smell of junipers was very reminiscent of the old days in camp at Addis Ababa.

A new motor road is being built from Dire Dawa to Harar. It has just reached the top of the mountains. It was badly damaged in places by the recent rains as the drainage is very inadequate. There were any number of duck and geese on the lake at Haramaya.

December 13th

Rode round Harar in the evening. The houses are square with flat roofs made of stones set in mud. The whole town is surrounded by a wall with five gates. The streets are very narrow and rough. There are only a few modern houses, mostly with zinc roofs and, except for these and the *Gibbi* and two or three mosques and churches, the town has a chocolate appearance. It is situated on a small hill but looks down in the valley from the Consulate, which has a lovely view of the town and the mountains beyond.

The Harari people are quite distinct from the surrounding Galla and are much lighter in colour. They are of mixed extraction and have a lot of Arab blood in their veins, being the descendants of the old traders who lived there. They are Muhammadans. The women look very bright in their Harari clothes. Red, yellow and orange are the favourite colours. They also favour large red and yellow beads. They are, on the whole, very light-coloured and good looking. It is incredible, however, the number that are blind in one eye.

A family of genet cats live under the roof of the Consulate and come down every evening.

The gardener killed a mongoose in the garden two days ago. In the evenings hyenas prowl all round the house and come quite close to the tent in which I am sleeping.

December 15th
Went down to Harar in the afternoon. Bought two silver bracelets. The hyenas came very close to the tent in the night. The Plowmans have a tame young baboon called Granville. He is quite fascinating and devoted to the children.

December 20th
Left at 2.30 with Plowman for Haramaya. Got there in two hours, had a cup of tea, and went out after duck. Shot twelve, mainly shovellers but also one widgeon and several duck I did not know.

Collected several boys and got them to drive two small pools near the hotel. There were a lot of duck on these pools, but they came over rather too much together.

Have never seen so many kites. There were literally hundreds flying round over us while we were shooting. A most disconcerting background. They roost in the eucalyptus trees by the hotel, the only trees round about. Saw also several harriers.

December 22nd
Shot the two pools again at sunrise. Got five duck. They came even faster and higher than usual, and after so much rifle shooting I did not expect to hit much, but have been shooting rather well these last two days. A few geese went past out of shot, disturbed while feeding on the Indian corn.

Got to Dire Dawa soon after 11 o'clock.

The lake looked very beautiful as I left, half hidden in the morning mist, and the view from the top of the mountain seemed even more magnificent than before.

Packed the heads in a case during the afternoon. Alamou, an old

Legation *syce* and now Plowman's head *syce*, came to Dire Dawa with me.

December 23rd
Left Dire Dawa at 7.00. Arrived Jibuti at 5.30. The Italian minister was travelling on the train. A special coach.

Saw a great many mirages, some like the sea, others like lakes, quite close at hand. Lowe met me at the station. Went to Rhigas Hotel, a fly-infested spot.

December 24th
Saw about my luggage which had been sent from Addis Ababa. Wandered round a bit in the evening. A godforsaken spot.

December 25th – Christmas.
Caught the MM *Azay-le-Rideau* at 6 p.m. Second class. Turkey truffles for dinner at 6.30.

Somali boys came on board and dived for pennies. Ship coaling. Left at midnight.

A detachment of the Foreign Legion is on board. A tough-looking crowd.

December 26th
Fairly hot. Saw the coast of Eritrea in the morning. Volcanic mountains.

December 27th
Still hot. A dull crowd on board. Everyone comes to breakfast unshaven and in pyjamas. A family of children spend their time being a nuisance.

December 28th

Hot, especially at nights. A few cockroaches two to three inches long about. Loathsome animals.

December 30th

Arrived at Suez at 7.00. Very beautiful in the hazy light. Entered the Canal at 10.30. The Foreign Legion were all put under the hatches and guarded to prevent their deserting. Arrived at Port Said at 8 o'clock. Went ashore and wandered round for a couple of hours. Very cold in the evening.

On January 5th, six days later, I arrived in Marseilles.

Arussi

I N OCTOBER 1931 I went back to Oxford for a further three
years, and while I was there I thought incessantly about that
month I had spent among the Danakil. I had gone down there
to hunt, but this journey had meant far more to me than just the
excitement of hunting. The whole course of my life was to be permanently affected by that month. There had been the constant and exciting possibility of danger, as occurred when we encountered the Itu
Galla, with no possibility of our getting help if we needed it. The
responsibility had been mine and, even though I was only twenty years
old at the time, men's lives had depended on my judgement. I had
been among tribesmen who had never had any contact with a world
other than their own, and only accepted to some extent the authority
of their tribal leaders.

At Bilen I had watched the Awash flowing on northwards through
the desert to its unknown destination. Ali, my headman, had constantly
made enquiries on my behalf, and had told me that the local Danakil
said that the Awash ended against a great mountain in Aussa, where
there were many lakes and forests; this however was hearsay. I had
felt then the lure of the unknown, the urge to go where no white man
had been, and I was determined, as soon as I had taken my degree,
to return to Abyssinia to follow the Awash to its end and to explore
the Aussa Sultanate. With this end in mind, I joined the Oxford
Exploration Club. The President of the Club was John Buchan, who
lived at Elsfield Manor in Oxford. I had always enjoyed reading his
books, and his novel *Prester John*, with its Zulu hero fighting against
the whites, had made a profound and lasting impression on me. On
hearing of my ambition to explore the Danakil country, Buchan helped
me with encouragement and advice.

During my last year at Oxford I wrote to Sir Sidney Barton, who was still the British Minister in Addis Ababa, requesting him to obtain the Emperor's permission for me to undertake this expedition to follow the Awash river to its terminus. When the Foreign Office informed me that the Emperor had given his consent for me to do that journey, I set about raising the money. The Royal Geographical Society gave me a grant, as did the Percy Sladen Trust of the Linnean Society. The Natural History Museum undertook to purchase any collections I made of birds and mammals; my collection of birds, in the end, totalled 872 specimens, comprising 192 species including 3 new sub-species. Most firms I approached agreed to provide rations, films, ammunition, medicine and other requirements for the expedition, either free or at a considerable discount.

My uncle, Lord Chelmsford, had taken a great interest in my plans. He was Warden of All Souls at Oxford and I saw him frequently. He died, suddenly and unexpectedly, in the spring of 1933, but his widow insisted on my receiving from his estate the sum he had intended to give me.

On my last day at Oxford I met the President and dons to say farewell. The President wished me well on my expedition and then, quite unexpectedly, announced that the College had decided to contribute towards its expense. I was very moved by the gesture.

My mother was all too well aware of the risks which this journey would involve, but she never tried to dissuade me from undertaking it. She realized its importance to me and gave me encouragement and helpful advice while I was making my preparations. She did however insist that I must have a companion with me. I had expected to find someone from the Oxford Exploration Club, but I failed to do so. Fortunately, David Haig-Thomas, a fellow Etonian, heard about this and volunteered to come with me. His father, who had hunted mountain nyala in the Arussi Mountains of Abyssinia, invited me to stay and agreed that his son should accompany me.

David Haig-Thomas and I left London on August 24th, 1933 for Marseilles. From there we travelled third class on the MM *Chermonceaux* to Jibuti. The food was reasonable and we had a cabin for the two of us. Most of the third-class passengers were Asian and we shared a deck with the steerage passengers. Meals tended to be chaotic, for most of the other third-class passengers had children with them who were noisy and ill-disciplined.

We arrived at Jibuti on September 14th. Salmon, the Vice-Consul, met us when we landed and helped us with the customs, permits for the rifles, and, the following day, getting our cases out of the warehouse and onto the train where they were loaded in a sealed van.

I heard from Salmon that the French had recently had trouble on the Danakil frontier involving fierce fighting with the Danakil from Aussa.

On September 8th, Dan Sandford and Frank de Halpert met us at the station in Addis Ababa. Sandford was accompanied by a tall, powerfully-built, middle-aged Somali called Umar. Sandford instructed Umar to secure the release of our luggage and get it down to the large empty house which he had hired for us in the town. Umar's quiet authority in dealing with the Abyssinian officials impressed me and I was glad when Sandford told me that he had engaged him to be our headman. He said that Umar had been with him since he was a boy, spoke good English and was utterly reliable.

During the following nine months, Umar more than justified Sandford's strong recommendation. Thanks to him there was never any trouble among my followers, though they comprised Amhara, Galla, Gurage, Somali and Danakil; all of them, whether Christian or Muslim, accepted his authority without question. Umar was a devout Muslim, and like the best Somalis, was proud and fearless.

Helped by Umar, we spent the next few days selecting the men who were to go with us. The Sandfords provided us with an elderly Amhara called Habta Mariam as our cook. I liked him as soon as I saw him and came to do so even more over the ensuing months. At first I was doubtful about taking him because he looked frail, but the Sandfords assured me that he had stood up to several long treks with them, invariably producing good meals even under the most unfavourable conditions.

Umar produced two Somalis to be our gunbearers. Abdullahi was small and slender, with vigilant, intelligent eyes and an engagingly ugly face. Said Munge was short, stocky and impassive, though like all Somalis he could occasionally get worked up. As our head *syce*, we chose Kassimi, a middle-aged Amhara. Bearded, dignified and quietly authoritative, he was to become our second headman. Goutama, whom I had known as a young *syce* at the Legation when I was a boy, was of slave origin and very black. Like Kassimi he was a devout Christian and good with animals.

As a personal servant, I chose Birru, a young Christian Galla, and Haig-Thomas chose Said Boy, a Muslim Gurage. They got on well together. Umar had a young Somali called Demise as his personal servant. There was another fifteen-year-old lad called Yusuf Nico, who attached himself to us and proved to be useful.

Since we needed someone to skin and look after the bird specimens, we eventually employed Yusuf German, who had worked for a Greek taxidermist in the town. He spoke a little French and sounded plausible, but he looked unreliable and indeed proved to be so.

Sandford told me that before we arrived he had sent Umar down to the Awash station, on the edge of the Danakil country, to buy eighteen camels and employ six Somalis to look after them. He said I would be better not to start my Danakil journey for another two months, to lessen the chance of getting malaria which was always bad along the Awash after the rains. He suggested that instead we should visit the Arussi Mountains, south of Addis Ababa, where we could try and shoot mountain nyala. These large antelope, resembling the greater kudu, were to be found nowhere else in the world other than in the highlands of Arussi and Bale, where Ivor Buxton had discovered them in 1910. My father had shot one, as had the Duke of Gloucester during a hunting trip which he made to the Arussi Mountains after Haile Selassie's coronation. Otherwise few Europeans had ever seen a mountain nyala, so Haig-Thomas and I were naturally eager to secure one. We also hoped to obtain a specimen of the cuberow, the so-called Abyssinian wolf, for the Natural History Museum. This animal was confined to the highlands of Abyssinia. I looked forward very much to seeing this little-known mountainous region and I had every intention of penetrating at least as far as the Webi Shebeli river.

This journey would also give us a chance to assess the men who were with us and, if necessary, make changes before going down to the Danakil country. Umar assured us that the Somalis he had engaged would wait contentedly with the camels until we turned up.

Haig-Thomas and I each bought a horse and a mule for ourselves, and four additional mules – one each for Umar, Kassimi and the cook, and a spare one. We intended to hire eighteen baggage mules from a *negadi*. In those days, there were no roads or any form of motor transport in Abyssinia. Consequently almost everything was carried on mules.

On September 22nd, Haig-Thomas and I were granted an audience by the Emperor and the next day we rode out to stay with Dan Sandford and his wife on their farm at Mullu. The house overlooked the sheer, two thousand-foot gorge of the Muger river and had a magnificent view down the valley towards the distant canyon of the Blue Nile.

I had been specially asked by the Natural History Museum to try and get a specimen of the blue-winged goose. They only had one specimen in the museum, brought back after Napier's Magdala expedition in 1868. There were many of these geese here, as elsewhere, and we obtained several specimens for the museum.

The Sandfords' house had an earthen floor, mud walls and a thatched roof, and the furniture was home-made; but it was imbued by these two remarkable people with a warmth that few houses can ever have equalled. It was a rewarding experience to stay with them, for their knowledge of the country and its people was outstanding.

October 1st

Train left at 9 a.m. Told Umar to be at the house at 6 a.m. so as to have plenty of time to get our last things through the customs and on the train. At 7.30 he had not turned up, and I then heard he was in prison. Rushed up to see and found Abdullahi had been arrested for debt of forty dollars and Umar as his guarantor. Paid the debt and got them both out by 8.15. By a miracle caught the train. Last man and last parcel on with three minutes to spare. Thought the customs would prove impossible but they gave way just in time.

Three hours later we arrived at Mojjo. We eventually got away from the station and camped two hours later near a marsh, where we shot some duck for dinner, and two lily-trotters for our collection. As Haig-Thomas and I returned to camp, the summits of the Arussi mountains far in the distance glowed in the last of the setting sun. The tents were up; the fires were lit; everyone sounded cheerful, happy to be off at last. The stars came out and several hyenas howled round the camp. Eventually Birru brought us the ducks that Habta Mariam had cooked. They tasted delicious, a happy augury for future meals. I went to bed utterly content; ahead of me were weeks of hunting and travel in remote mountains, and later the excitement of exploring the Danakil desert.

October 2nd

Left camp at 8 o'clock. Mules slow getting off. Arrived Koray camp about 1 o'clock. Mimosa scrub country rather broken. No game – shot a few guinea-fowl.

Excitement with a *shifta* on the way. Suddenly a great uproar broke out at the back of the caravan. Told that a *shifta* had stolen one of our rifles. Saw him on a broken hillside covered with scrub. Gave chase – only Abdullahi would follow me. Had a shot at the *shifta* and hit rock about a foot over his head. Instantly he dived into cover. Followed him, very ticklish work as thick scrub and I thought he would fight. Lost him, but Umar, Makonnen and Kassimi surrounded him later in a patch of bush and forced him to surrender after putting two shots close to him. Tied up, he looked a very spectacular brigand, with his face and clothes soaked in blood from a cut on his head. Luckily it turned out he had no ammunition for the rifle he had stolen, otherwise we might have had some casualties. We handed him over to the village headman.

Had target practice. If this is an example of their shooting, they are very much maligned as shots, and would be extremely formidable at bush fighting.

October 4th

Arrived Bovu about 2 o'clock. Open cultivated plains at foot of Chelalo, after leaving mimosa bush. Climbed steadily all day. Passed a hanged *shifta*, fairly ancient and the hyenas had got his legs, also a monument to a famous Arussi brave made of wood. From the horizontal piece some dozen pieces of cloth were hanging down, representing the men he had killed. Hung on the top of the uprights were three round loops of fibre and wood, representing the shields he had taken. Passed numerous Arussi graves – fairly elaborate and one or two had crude figures carved on the upright stones.

October 5th

Left camp at 7.30. Mules arrived Chelalo at 1 p.m., several of them very exhausted after a steepish climb; it was here that we expected to find nyala. We entered a forest of wild olives and massive juniper trees resembling cedars, many of them festooned with lichen. I had never been in such a forest and found it fascinating. We camped on the edge of the moorland among magnificent red-tasselled hagenia trees and clumps of yellow-flowering St John's wort; above us the mountain was covered with giant heath ten feet and more in height. Only the high tops, at thirteen thousand feet, were bare; there, tussocky grass, patches of everlastings and a scattering of giant lobelia were interspersed among crags of weathered rock.

We had previously passed through open cultivated country. The Arussi Galla are a cattle-owning people, but the rich plains at the foot of Chelalo have recently been extensively colonized with people from other parts.

The Arussi Galla womenfolk dress in skins – mostly pagans with some Muhammadans.

Camped in a belt of *kauso* trees. Very attractive and masses of wood for fires, had huge ones for which we were very grateful. Above the belt of forest is the heath country, this grows in places to twelve feet high and covers practically the whole mountain. The country is extraordinarily like Scotland, and there are large numbers of hares and a bird very like a grouse, now always in pairs.

October 6th
Out after nyala at 5 o'clock. Extremely cold. Hunted on different sides of the mountain.

October 7th
About 12 o'clock came to the top end of a large valley with very steep sides. Saw two nyala bulls and three cows in one place, and at the top of one of the sides about a dozen cows and a good bull near them. Had lunch and tried to think things out. All but one bull of the first lot moved gradually away. The big bull had also seen us and moved slowly over the sky line with the cows. Persuaded to have a closer look at the first bull, whose head I could see was small. Got up to within a hundred yards, when he saw us. Had to decide instantly and no time for another look at his head. Standing facing us. Shot him straight through the chest and smashed his heart to pieces.

Nyala head twenty-four inches along curve. Disappointingly small – smaller even than I had thought. A lesson never to go against one's first impression of a head, and also a punishment for going for the bird in the hand.

When we first saw them all the nyalas were grazing. Usually they lie up soon after sunrise till about 4 o'clock, I gather.

Heard two cuberow calling – a most weird noise, faintly resembling a baboon's bark. They answered each other across the valley.

My Galla tracker says that the Arussi Galla used to collect together from seventy to two hundred nyala, and armed with spears surround and kill them, getting as many as thirty in the day! This driving seems only to have stopped since the Emperor's order protecting nyala. The local headman is held responsible, and it is impossible to kill them surreptitiously in this manner. He says nyala have got considerably scarcer of late. I gather, however, that Fitaurari Birru still allows the Galla to spear nyala on his ground.

October 8th
David shot two nyala. A complete mistake. He jumped one in thick bush, and then saw it hide soon after in another patch of thick heather.

Stalked it and shot at it, when it apparently bolted. Fired four more shots and killed it. Found the head very much smaller than he had thought. When Umar arrived with the mule, he found another one – the original one – lying dead where first shot at. A great nuisance as David only paid for one on his licence.

October 11th

Climbed up to a big open plateau south of the main range and connecting it with another. Here it was bitterly cold. After a time you climb above the heather level to open rocky slopes and flats with some grass and a short, very whitish plant. The lobelias grow here, and occasionally in the top valleys along the streams. Much of the heath lower down is burnt in large patches by the Arussi for their cattle.

Ground white with frost in the mornings on the tops. Practically always a very blue sky when the sun rises and every promise of a fine day. About 11 o'clock it clouds over and the mists come down on the tops – then nearly always there is an hour of very heavy rain and sometimes hail between 2 and 3 o'clock. After this it often clears up a bit, though on the tops the mists hang about.

About 10 o'clock Makonnen suddenly spotted a cow nyala grazing. Through the glasses made out an extremely fine bull lying down, two other bulls, one very small, and another cow. Luckily they had not seen us though they were only four hundred yards off and the ground was very flat and open. Lay and watched them anxiously for an hour, after which the big bull got up and started to graze. Cautiously made a big circuit on hands and knees, and then got to some rocks and heather. Worked nervously through this and saw them about one hundred yards off.

At last spotted the big bull end on. Left Makonnen behind for the stalk. Terrified the whole time that he would raise his head and be seen by the nyala. Waited till the bull turned side on and then shot. He staggered and then recovered. Gave him two more shots for safety. A very fine head of forty-nine inches [an unofficial record]. A real triumph, and I am so glad I did not take another indifferent head.

In the evening great excitement as the leopard trap was heard to close. The camp turned out with lamps and armed to the teeth to find a rat caught by the hind legs. A small mammal for the museum. During the night Abdullahi killed a large water rat. Ergay sets traps every evening but so far has not been successful.

One of the *negadi*'s ponies died while I was away from a mysterious Arussi sickness. Several others are ill.

October 12th

A terrible trek with all the mules looking sick and failing at every difficult place. Muhammad Denkali, Yusuf, Said and two or three others chose to go fast on ahead with all the rifles, to get to the next village. They knew the mules were sick and that this piece of country has an extremely bad name for *shifta* ambushing caravans. Sent Kassimi to fetch them back; in future anyone leaving the caravan loses two dollars. The Abyssinian servant of a Greek was recently murdered here by *shifta*. It was the *shifta*'s hanged corpse we passed on the 4th. His three comrades were hanged in other places.

October 13th

Passed the remnants of a big Muhammad Ali caravan. This passed our camp at Chelalo two days ago. Out of fifty mules they have lost forty and are now completely stranded.

October 14th

My pony Emir died during the night, and also one of the *negadi*'s mules. My pony has been listless for several days. Two other *negadi* mules sick, and Gama, my grey.

The local Galla persuaded the *negadi* to try their cure. They bought a sheep, drove all the mules round it three times and then killed it. They ate the flesh, but made collars of the skin which they hung round the mules' necks. There is nothing known among the local Galla or the *negadis* about this sickness. Some say it is picked up on the Awash or at Jilli and is a form of fever.

46

Some say it is bad grass at Chelalo. This is the only route where it is got, except possibly in Walega. Mules and ponies practically never recover. Stricken animals first get listless, and then in two or three days they begin to breathe with difficulty, making much noise, and are usually dead in about twelve hours. Sometimes, however, it is very much more sudden, the animal dying two or three hours after the first symptoms. Just before dying they lie down, often getting up once or twice, and being very restless. They continue to take mouthfuls of grass up to the end.

With one of my mules a white frothy fluid came away from the nose in a continuous stream for two hours until we shot him. In breathing he bubbled through this. In this case the mule collapsed very suddenly. This appears to be what also happened to the cook's mule, though he was ill two days. The *negadi* said there is never any hope when they run from the nose.

Except for the listlessness and restlessness the animals show no other sign of illness apart from a slightly swollen stomach. They do not appear to become thirsty, but it seemed to me that a drink usually hastened the end.

October and November appear to be the only months when this sickness is about. At other times of the year the Arussi country is as healthy for mules as any other. These months are directly after the rains. But there is no evidence of which I have heard that it recurs again after the little rains.

As long as kept on the move they keep alive, but die as soon as they are allowed to lie down.

Engaged a local Galla with three ponies but his friends said all our mules were dying and he would never get paid. He then went off, and my boys beat the man who had dissuaded him. Nearly a fight with the village.

While we were waiting, a man passed on his way to be married. He was accompanied by about fifty friends, all on horses and armed. A very wild and impressive crowd. They very readily allowed us to photograph them. Several of them indulged in spear-throwing on horses.

The Galla here swear that there are lion in the forests on the mountainside, and this was confirmed by the village headman. He also said that there were plenty of nyala there.

October 15th

The mules now seem to be free from fever, but they are all in a bad state and have the most awful backs. One of the *negadi*'s boys ran away during the day.

October 16th

During the night, nine of the *negadi*'s mules ran away and were only recovered at 8 o'clock this morning. The *negadis* then refused to march and demanded a day's rest. Endless discussions till 12.30 when we started.

Bought two ponies off the headman of the Arussi village, an ancient who claims to be one hundred and twenty years old and to have killed one hundred and forty men. Umar was masterly in his handling of him. In the middle of the discussion the Arussi would suddenly break into ancient battle cries and songs. Humoured him with handfuls of salt and sugar, and an old fruit tin.

October 17th

Sent Ergay and Goutama to Gaba to try and engage camels to take us to Sheikh Husain, where I shall arrange for my camels to meet us. If they cannot get camels, and I do not know if camels can get from here to Sheikh Husain, they are to get a new *negadi* and mules. I then sacked Bayenna, but as he owed me twelve dollars I made him take me across the Webi to the foothills of the Gouba Mountains, and gave him eight dollars for this.

Left camp at 1 o'clock and arrived at camp at 4 o'clock. A most attractive spot, close to an Arussi village, in juniper trees and over-looking the Webi plain – well sheltered from the wind. Passed a small patch of cultivation. The Arussi are in a few cases doing a little cultivating as a result of the example set them by the Abyssinians. This Arussi has often been to Addis Ababa.

The Arussi have a bad reputation, and still kill and mutilate on the sly when an opportunity offers. The Abyssinians are gradually stamping out this practice, however. In many ways the Arussi resemble the Danakil.

Only just got the mules across the Webi – the water reached to the bottom of the loads.

The country here is too populated for there to be any game, and the Arussi have vast herds. But there are said to be leopard, bushbuck and bohor reedbuck further up in the mountains.

October 20th

Small naked Arussi boys herding the cattle, armed with large spears. The Arussi women and girls dress in skins and wear a great quantity of small red, blue and white beads, often also woven into their hair in patterns. Many of them wear brass ornaments in their ears. These ornaments are three inches long. Fairer coloured than the men, and some very light.

Many of the men wear Abyssinian clothes. Headmen wear a brass circlet round their throats. This is also a sign of having killed many men. Another proof of having killed is a bracelet round the arm, or a ring. Some wear a ring on their toe.

About half Muhammadan, the rest pagan. No Christian converts.

October 21st

Ergay and Goutama returned about 4 o'clock with mules from Gouba. Nineteen mules, several spare ones, and men to look after them. But he misunderstood my order and engaged them to go back to Gouba. At first they pretended they could not go to Sheikh Husain as it was bad country for the mules, but eventually agreed. Agreed also to march six hours a day.

October 22nd

Left camp at 8 o'clock. A certain amount of delay with slipping loads, but by 9 o'clock had got to Haro. Here we had serious trouble with the customs. Told they were in church. Went to look for them, and sent the mules on. Found, however, that they had stopped the mules. Refused to let us pass and said that our permits said 'to Webi' and we could not go into country on far side as no mention of Bale. Explained that we wished to go down the Webi to Sheikh Husain, and that the only caravan route went this side. No good. A large crowd collected, and they all shouted at once. Feeling very much against us, and the customs officer nervous of stopping us but afraid of going against public opinion. Consequently he blustered.

They then refused to let us go back, and tried to shut us up inside a wooden compound filled with nettles etc. Finally insisted on our camping on some open ground in the centre of the village.

October 23rd

Left camp at 5.30. Saw no game, though bohor are said to be very numerous and to feed within two hundred yards of the village.

Got back to camp about 9.30. Heard that the customs officer had been to see us. Very frightened over what he has done and Umar gave him an unpleasant half hour. It appears that they were all drunk yesterday.

October 24th

Feeling seedy, a chill on the stomach.

Market day. Market opened at midday. Before this the Arussi collected and sang, beating a drum. Market quite interesting, but very difficult to get photos. Bought some Arussi pots.

The Arussi appear to possess practically no rifles and never to wear swords. They have a barbed hunting spear unlike any I have seen elsewhere, and keep them very sharp. Have since this seen one or two straight swords.

An Abyssinian from the village brought me a young bull, two

chickens and nine eggs. Accepted them after making very sure that he had nothing to do with our detention here. Tossed whether Christians or Muhammadans got the meat, and the Christians won.

October 25th

A woman brought a very small bushbuck into camp, but wanted three dollars for it. It was blind in one eye. Umar bought a small *medaqua* (duiker) for four piastres in the afternoon. It is remarkably unafraid; a weak bleat is the only noise it seems to make. This it makes constantly. It seems very petulant when being fed. Feeding it on milk out of an HP bottle fitted with a teat made of leather. Feeds readily. It is a female about ten days old.

Shot on the hill opposite camp. Thick forest at the bottom of the hill, above the cultivation in the valley. This consists of juniper, a fir-like tree, and a tree resembling an olive, also a few shola trees. It is particularly thick on the edges of streams, and this seems to be the favourite resort of bushbuck. The trees grow to a considerable size. Towards the top of the hill the forest becomes very open and consists mostly of junipers. The very top is crowned by a battlement of precipitous cliff.

Kassimi returned from Dedjazmatch Nasibu with apologies for our treatment, and vegetables and two sheep as a present. Nasibu sent an old man with Kassimi who arrived very tired after his long ride. He is telephoning Addis Ababa for permission for us to go to Sheikh Husain, and Ergay has remained behind to bring us the answer.

October 26th

Insisted on, and received, a public apology in front of all my men from the customs officer for his treatment of us.

October 27th

Felt very seedy on waking up. Sick several times. David also says he feels sick, and so did not go out early. Habta Mariam also unwell with similar symptoms. David went out in the evening. He climbed to the top of the cliff where he could look down into the scrub. Saw some six bushbuck, does and small bucks, but nothing worth shooting. Felt better in the evening after taking castor oil.

October 28th

Went out at 2 o'clock. A native, whose brother's foot I doctored, insisted on coming with us. Dressed in a newly washed *shamma* he was visible several miles off. Took me for the usual peregrination after reedbuck. Finally went for my usual walk after bushbuck, but the pleasure spoilt by this man. He would talk and try and get in front.

Ergay has not yet turned up, so decided to re-cross the Webi tomorrow and go down the far bank to opposite Sheikh Husain, and there collect our camels. Previously they all said it was impossible to go down the Webi and that we must cross the mountains here. Now Yusuf says he has actually been down the Webi. He is, however, most unreliable.

October 29th

Delayed for nearly an hour starting, first by the escape of Shaitan and then of two of the *negadi* mules. Most exciting, galloping and rounding up.

The Abyssinian Sunday and also the feast of Gabriel. Heard the chanting of the priests and the throbbing of drums from the time I woke. Most attractive in the distance.

Marched along well, and crossed the Webi lower down where it was much shallower. Drenching rain from nine till 10 o'clock, and after we had crossed the Webi it blew a half gale till about 12 o'clock. Very heavy rain all round in the hills. Level plains with an occasional *kopje*, extremely stony and burnt up. No trees or shrubs. Where the ground is very dry and stony there are a great number of the spotted cactus with white flowers.

The Webi runs at the bottom of a very deep valley with precipitous sides probably fifteen hundred feet deep. The view across this gorge to the mountains opposite is very fine.

Found a place for camp where a stream came down. Impossible to get water up from the Webi. No firewood about, but my man took a considerable amount of wood, including the rafters, from what looked like a deserted *tukul*. Soon after the owner galloped up and demanded it back, but we bought it for four piastres.

Ergay arrived, accompanied by a man from Nasibu. Permission cannot be obtained from Addis Ababa for us to enter Bale. Belatingata Heroui issued the pass, and the second-in-command now in charge dare not alter it.

October 30th

Another chase after escaped mules. Country at first very burnt up and rocky, then came to long but dry grass, and finally to extremely fertile upland downs. A very fine crop of grass. Some streams and occasional single trees. Fairly thickly populated. The dry plain country is inhabited only by Arussi encampments, but up here settled villages. Short of wood but an attractive camp. Very rugged country and deep canyons beyond the Webi, all thickly wooded. All shrouded in rain clouds all day, as was Ankole, but we had no rain.

November 1st

Went out at 5 o'clock to look for bohor reedbuck. Soon saw two does by a stream. When alarmed, one of them whistled but this was more wheezy than I expected. Allowed me within fifty yards. Then got hold of some Arussi and walked some country in line. Put up two does in a small valley and shot a duiker. Saw him lie down under a tree. Walked up to him and he jumped when I was twenty yards off. A very satisfactory shot as he bobbed away in the tall grass.

Then had two very long shots at a reedbuck ram. He was in the same valley as the two does. Following him we jumped another doe lying in tall grass. The reedbuck again showed up most distinctly while feeding, more so than any other antelope I know.

One mule fell into a crevasse and was being abandoned by the *negadi* when Umar arrived and got it out with ropes.

Sent Kassimi to [some] Belgian planters to try and buy sugar as we are right out. Just as the sun set one of the Belgians rode up, and asked us to come over and dine. An amusing moonlight ride.

There used to be waterbuck here before the ground was cleared. Leopard were common till a few years ago, when their skins fetched a large price at Addis Ababa. In eight years they have only heard lion twice.

One of the *negadis* has had toothache. Asked us to take it out. David tried with some wire cutters, but unfortunately only broke the tooth.

November 3rd

A good day's trek. Left camp at 6.30 and camped by water in the middle of the Plain of Deda at noon. Mules getting tired when we got in, but no complaints.

Always takes two hours to strike camp, tie up the loads, and then load the mules.

Passed through Robe after one and a half hours. A small town, but the biggest market in the Arussi country. Flat open plain, burnt-up but tall grass. Little cultivation as water scarce, but thickly populated in patches by Arussi and some Abyssinians. The Arussi houses are good permanent structures and they are now settled, only taking their cattle down into the low country for the salt earth for two months a year.

November 6th

Went out shooting at 4.30. Followed the stream up, but the furthest I went was twenty minutes' walk from camp.

I must have seen about eighty reedbuck, feeding on the slopes like cattle. Difficult to be certain of the numbers in each party, as they were strung out in a practically continuous line as far as one could see, whenever there was suitable ground. They were usually in parties of six or seven, though I saw fourteen young rams together. The big rams were usually either by themselves, or with two or three does close by. They were feeding on the open slopes of the stream, tall grass sprinkled with bushes. Along the stream there is a considerable reedbed. It is very tussocky and difficult walking, but never very wet. There were reedbeds in every direction, both in dry places and also on small raised islands where it was wet. There are well-worn paths through the reeds.

The reedbuck here are incredibly tame. They are easily approached to within fifty yards and never run far. Sometimes they will even walk towards you if you stand still, stopping and gazing every few yards. But they go off at once if they get your wind, and then seem very alarmed.

A wonderful view from the edge of the plateau out towards Abu el Kassim. A bad descent, but the mules managed it well. The mountainside is clothed with dense forest. A small village at its foot. Little naked boys armed with slings keep the birds off the crops of Indian corn. When throwing they pass the sling across the back.

Passed incessant bands of pilgrims to Sheikh Husain. They carry peeled forked sticks as tokens of their pilgrimage.

November 7th

There are three vultures nesting in a tall mimosa near camp. The nests are in the tops of the trees, and not bigger than a buzzard. Kingfishers, like the one at home, are common, and there is a lovely red and green bird with a long white tail about the size of a small dove.

November 8th

Went out to get honey from some Galla hives upstream. Placed in the most impossible places in very tall trees. Demise got to one and dropped it down. The fire not ready and he was covered in bees before he got down, badly stung. The comb ready, but only a small amount of honey – delicious. Took it back to camp, about three-quarters of a mile. Half an hour later the bees arrived and made life impossible.

In the evening discovered that they had sucked the honey out of all the combs, so our labour was in vain.

November 9th

Did not go out early, but found on getting up that Kassimi, Demise and the *negadis* have cut down one of the trees with the hives in and broken the hives. They got no honey and this is almost certain to cause trouble.

November 10th

Expecting the camels all day, who should have arrived last night, so did not leave camp in the morning except to go a quarter of a mile to look at some wild bees' hives. These were in the rock and defied our every effort. One is said to be forty years old.

Heard that the camels have made another detour. Adam says that now they may not be here tomorrow.

David successfully extracted another of the *negadi's* teeth, not the one he broke last time. The poor man has not got a sound tooth in his head.

November 11th

The Galla owner of the cut-down hives arrived in the early morning and made trouble, justifiably. Demanded forty dollars, but finally settled for six dollars.

A party of Arussi on their way to Sheikh Husain had a dance. Two oldish women danced with the men. One man beat a drum. Resembled the one I saw the Somalis doing at the Legation during the coronation. Mimicked animals.

The camels arrived at 9 o'clock. Have had a hard march getting here. Brought me only 160 dollars out of the 250 dollars, having spent the rest, so 40 dollars short to pay the *negadis*. They took it very well, and finally took the white pony for 20 dollars and an IOU for the other 20 dollars. Most satisfactory as it might have been very unpleasant. Umar extraordinarily good settling it. I hear that one of my camels has died, they think from eating a poisoned tree.

Gave the *negadis* knives, soap and celluloid tumblers. They were delighted with them. Parted the very best of friends, and I am most sorry to say good-bye to them.

Muhammad brought me a fossil from Sheikh Husain shaped like a bird's head. There are, I gather, numerous rocks there like life-sized men and women and animals. The country round here is full of fossils. The rocks round the camp look like the molars of prehistoric giants.

November 12th
David heard a lion roaring about half an hour after dawn, in the direction of our next camp.

Marched almost to Abu el Kassim, and then left it on our right and camped lower down on the Daro River at 9 o'clock. A very fine valley, big cliffs and dense bush. Two difficult places for the camels, leaving our camp and then re-descending to the Daro. Managed them all right, but necessary to do some road building.

Half an hour before getting into camp found fresh lion tracks up the path. Told the men to camp by the river, and followed them with Umar, Abdullahi and Adam. Probably the lion David heard roaring. Difficult ground to track on, dry gravel. Adam's heart was not in it, and he lost the tracks after half a mile, just after where the lion had lain down by a game trail.

Raining in the mountains around and from 5.00 till 8.30 we had some very heavy rain in camp. Had intended to sleep out, and our tents not up. Covered the beds etc. with the ground sheets. When the rain was over found the ground sheets had let the rain through and our beds sopping wet, also my camera, rifles and a number of exposed films. The rain had no appreciable effect on the river.

November 13th
Left camp at 5.30 and arrived in new camp on another river at 1.30. Marched through mimosa scrub and forests of euphorbia. The rain

made the ground slippery for the camels, but it was fairly level and they went along well.

Came on a patch of cactus with fruit, and all had a good feed, though most people got the bristles in their tongues.

November 14th

The guide has made a considerable detour to avoid some bad road, though he assured me he knew every inch of it, and it was quite practicable. Expected to get to Mini tomorrow, but shall not do so now. Accurate information about the road is quite impossible to get in this country.

David wants to go to Addis Ababa to have some boils on his leg looked at.

A Galla who had just married passed with his wife and a large attendance of friends. Muhammadans. He was taking her home to his village. His mouth covered with his *shamma*.

November 15th

David and Kassimi left camp at 5 o'clock [so that David could go ahead to the Awash station and catch a train to Addis Ababa]. The camels left at 6 o'clock. At 7.30 David caught us up, having lost the road and been a considerable detour through the bush.

In very dry bush the far side of the Elala river there is a shrine to Sheikh Husain, built to commemorate where he lived alone fasting and praying for years. A white-washed dome with four turrets. It is called Audou Sakina. The Muhammadans entered and prayed. A well-like structure inside. All gave presents to the local mullah. Abdullahi his orange turban. Goutama also gave a present. Umar says that Abyssinian Christians also venerate Sheikh Husain, and go there on pilgrimage. Then shortly after the road climbed two thousand feet over a pass in the mountain chain. As Umar said it was a road up which you would hesitate to take loaded mules, I shudder to think what we turned aside to avoid. Then descended again towards the Magna river. An awful road, quite impracticable as it was. Worked frantically to make it fit for the camels. Luckily the rock is sandstone here and easily broken up.

At 3.30 we camped by an Arussi village near some water in a deep natural well in the riverbed. Joined soon after by one of the Somali camelmen and four camels, and four more men. No tent, no food for the men, and none of my bedding. But had the stores with us, and gave out six pounds of my flour to the men. Made quite good pancakes.

Stupidly let our camels wander off and could not find them. Nervous lest a lion should get any of them. Got a good fire going and made a very reasonable bed out of groundsheets.

One of the camels, I hear, gave out at the top of the mountain. More nerves than exhaustion, I think. Muhammad Denkali, Yusuf, Ergay, Indieray, Ahmed and the other Somali camelmen with it. Have got a rifle. Leopard heard in the night, but no lions.

November 16th
A considerable amount more road making, and tree cutting. Heard another honey bird but again too busy to investigate. The natives say he will sometimes lead you to a lion instead of to honey [as in Fitzpatrick's book *Jock of the Bushveld*]. Umar says this bird will lead you sometimes to a lion, leopard or python.

Worried about David, who will get two nights in the bush. He has no food but some bread, but he has a rifle and Kassimi with him. I hear there are villages not far from the river so they shall get cover.

Went out to look for game at 2 o'clock. Said to be lion, pig, bushbuck and waterbuck here. The jungle is in many places impenetrably thick except for pig runs, and there are dense beds of reedlike grass ten feet high. There are also magnificent trees. A few open places along the river bank. Saw and heard a large number of *guerazas* [colobus monkeys] feeding, I suspect, on the oranges and lemons. Have seen several small spiders with shells on their backs. Biting flies unpleasantly common. There are also large numbers of spiders in the jungle, some of them large. I have an instinctive loathing of them. Cockroaches common as they were on the Daro. Saw no game and no tracks by the river. The local Arussi returned to camp breathless with excitement saying he had walked into a lion. Declined to take us back to the place, and no one believed him.

November 17th

Took most of the men and prepared the road towards Mini, very overgrown in places, and took us three hours to clear what we walked back in an hour. Met three Arussi who were decidedly unpleasant and wished to know why we were spying out the land, and if we hoped to take it from them. Dread, I suppose, that we have a concession from the Government. Found David's tracks. Had already found them as far as the Magna, but wondered if he would strike the right road from there on. This valley is wonderfully fertile. Besides oranges and lemons we passed quantities of *berberi* [red pepper] growing wild. Sixty dollars a sack in Addis Ababa. Collected a lot to take with us. There is also a salt lick. Coffee would grow well here.

November 18th

Woke up sitting among my tent ropes dreaming that we were trying to get the camels through the forest in the dark and had just run into an army of ants.

Muhammad Denkali, Ahmed and Said Munge returned with the tail of the camel. Found it dead yesterday evening quite close to their camp. Say it was ill when they lost it. This may or may not be true. They arrived at 11 o'clock, and so I decided to march at 1 o'clock. Bedi and Muhammad had not returned when we left, though we blew the trumpet. Afraid to try the other road without news. They joined us as we made camp. The other road far better than the one we used.

Mountains all in cloud. A nice camp, good water and plenty of wood. Several villages and crops of durra when you get to the foot of the mountains. Umar traded an empty tin for a considerable quantity of durra. The camels excited much curiosity among the Arussi. Certainly I cannot believe that any other camels have ever been here.

We are, I hear, regarded as *deus ex machina* since the Arussi wished to go on a pilgrimage to Sheikh Husain, but regarded the road as impracticable. They have no tools for breaking rocks.

November 20th

Sent Muhammad Denkali and Goutama to the Belgian coffee farmers at Gulucha to try and get news of David. Heard that he had been there and gone on to Mini. They lent him a mule. I hope there is nothing wrong with Fitaurari – I am afraid David spent two nights in the bush.

Makonnen is again making trouble and trying to dissuade the men from going into the Danakil country. Demise told Umar. Shall turn him out of the camp if he does it again.

Saw bateleur eagles, Abyssinian buzzards, numerous hornbills, two very large, and several black-and-white pied kingfishers. These rise to a height of fourteen or fifteen feet when hovering before diving.

November 22nd

Left camp at 6.15 and marched till 10.30 when I decided to rest and feed the camels at Dumuga. A Greek gone native beginning to cultivate coffee here. Muhammad Denkali, whom I sent yesterday to Mini, joined us as we started. Brought a letter from David. He spent one night out on the Magna and got to Gulucha next day. Thinks the road quite impracticable for camels.

Marched again at three thirty and camped after three hours at Lagaoada on a small stream. A three-day-old moon. The men don't like this midday halt, but I shall continue it as it is better for the camels and you can march longer. Had dinner with the Ticklers, the Belgian planters at Bakaksa, who were most kind. A doctor staying with them had lanced an abscess in David's throat and sent him on quite recovered.

The Arussi mule and horse sickness appears to be called 'morre' and to be extremely contagious. They say it occurs all round here and in this area is not, it appears, restricted to October and November. At Chelalo this may be due to the cold killing the bacillus.

November 23rd

A *shifta* has here written on the bark of a tree the names of three other *shifta* who recently killed some men here. Underneath, the *choum*'s answer – 'You have done well, but are a *shifta*.'

November 24th

Drenching rain at 3 a.m. Got my bed under cover, but not till it was drenched. Delayed starting till 6.45 and everyone a bit under the weather. Arrived at Balbalata at 9.30. Anticipated trouble with the customs as this is Chercher and is not mentioned in our pass, and we now have camels and not mules. Rode on ahead, and when the camels arrived unloaded just beyond the town. The head of the customs accepted thirty cartridges and allowed us to go on at 2.30.

A largish town in close touch with Addis Ababa and evidently considerable trade here. Coffee plantations all round. Two men have recently been flogged for picking durra as they marched along the road, ten and forty lashes. A great sensation. Before reaching here everyone does this as a matter of course. Umar says forty lashes sometimes kills and always cripples for life. Fifty lashes is sometimes given.

Extremely heavy rain at 1 o'clock and drizzle afterwards. The road very slippery for the camels. The moon did not give much light. Camped at 7 o'clock near Galmuso. Country much less wooded. Have at last reached the end of this eternal tableland and come to hills which we can cross. Put up tents and placed everything carefully under cover.

Said Munge ate a great quantity of *qat* leaves and then ran round like a hungry camel looking for work. All the men eat these leaves, which are slightly intoxicating. The Hararis are very partial to it.

November 25th

Left camp at 6.30 and almost at once climbed the chain of hills separating us from the Awash. Rested at Hardina. A very large cemetery here. One grave covered by a thatched roof.

Remained behind with Umar trying to pick up some camels as I want five more, and we were now in camel country. But nearly all females kept for milk. The Somalis deliriously happy at getting camel milk again. Shot a female duiker for food for the men. An extraordinarily low altitude for duiker. Thorn scrub – she was in milk but we did not see the young one. A long march by the moon. The unmistakable warm wind of the desert after sundown.

November 26th
Left camp at 5.45, everyone being very quick. Descended gradually through thorn scrub till 10.00 when we rested at Katchinwaha. The men saw aoul, and I saw some fresh oryx tracks and quantities of dik-dik. Haile Moidaje lost. Probably gone to Boroda. Am anxious as the Itu here are as bad as the Danakil and would certainly mutilate a single unarmed man.

Marched again at 2 o'clock and arrived at the Awash at 6 o'clock. Open country with grass two feet high and scattered bushes. Ground dry. Hills all round.

A steep descent and ascent to and from the Awash. David waiting for us and much better, also Jama Guleid the *shikari* from Somaliland. David has had him out and says he is good. He shot a male and female aoul and missed a big oryx. Saw masses of game.

Camped close to the station. The *syces* lost all three mules, which wandered off in search of grass. Everyone out all night, but unsuccessfully. Afraid the Danakil will steal them or hyenas kill them.

November 27th
Mules found in the morning. David has developed another attack of tonsillitis, now in both tonsils, and cannot feed or speak properly.

Telephoned to the acting Governor of Chercher and ten soldiers and three camels are being sent off at once.

Have got 'chiffy' in my right foot. Swollen and itchy. I don't know what causes it, but think pricks from grass seeds which enter your socks. These seeds have been terrible since we left Chelalo. A very common disease. Muhammad Denkali has it too. Trying mercurial lotion. David had the same thing, but just under his knee. It was to have these looked at that he went up to Addis Ababa.

November 28th

David caught the train back up to Addis Ababa in the morning, and I very much doubt if he will be able to come with me.

The following day brought a wire from David: 'Cannot come.'

I was content to be on my own, glad that I should have no need to accommodate myself to a fellow-countryman, that any decisions in the days ahead would be entirely mine. Haig-Thomas had been cheerful and good-natured, and never once had we quarrelled. No one, indeed, could have been more easy-going; but we never got on close terms or found much in common during the four months we had been together since leaving England. I did not feel I should miss his company, and the fact that I should have no fellow-countryman with me to take charge if I fell sick or was wounded did not worry me, since I had every confidence in Umar.

The journey I had just completed in the Arussi had been the first I had undertaken in the highlands of Abyssinia. I had travelled through remote and spectacular country among exciting, barely administered tribes, and had secured the record head of a much prized quarry. I had enjoyed the last two months greatly but the journey, though arduous, had involved no real danger. I knew conditions would be different once we crossed the railway and entered Danakil country.

Danakil I

IN ADDIS ABABA I had heard from Sandford that somewhere on the Awash was the virtually independent Danakil Sultanate of Aussa which was ruled by an autocratic Sultan who acknowledged no allegiance to the Abyssinian government. No European had as yet succeeded in setting foot in Aussa, though a number had tried. I learned that in 1875 an Egyptian army commanded by Werner Munzinger, a Swiss mercenary who had served under Gordon in the Sudan, had set out to invade Abyssinia, only to be defeated by the Danakil. Not one of his men survived; all carried on their persons trophies which the Danakil were anxious to acquire. Then, in 1881 an expedition led by Giulietti and Bigliore, accompanied by thirteen other Italians, had been wiped out somewhere to the north of Aussa. Three years later an expedition led by Bianchi with two other Italians had met a similar fate in the same area.

Ludovico Nesbitt and his two Italian companions had enjoyed greater success in 1928, travelling through the Danakil country from the Awash station to Asmara in Eritrea. I do not think that when I was there in 1930 anyone in Addis Ababa was aware that Nesbitt had made this journey – I had heard no mention of it.

Nesbitt published an account of his journey in the October 1930 issue of the Royal Geographical Society's *Journal*. Three of his servants were killed by the Danakil during the course of the journey, and when Nesbitt was in Bahdu there was every chance they would all be attacked and killed. Nesbitt then crossed to the northern side of the Awash, and kept away from the river. He rejoined the Awash at Tendaho and followed it eastwards to the border of Aussa. Here he met the Sultan and was given permission to continue northwards towards Eritrea.

When, one evening in my digs at Oxford, I read Nesbitt's description of his journey in the *Journal*, it brought home vividly to me the risks I should be taking when I made my own journey. The Danakil were armed with spears and every man, after being circumcised at around the age of fourteen, wore a large, broad-bladed, curved dagger across the front of his stomach. I never saw any shields, but many of them were armed with *fusil gras* rifles. These single-shot weapons fired heavy lead bullets which inflicted appalling wounds. Formerly the standard weapon of the French army, these rifles were now being disposed of into Abyssinia by traders in Jibuti.

At first in 1930 I had disapproved of the incessant killing by the Danakil, but fairly soon I accepted this as the way they lived, and I never felt any desire to see them brought under alien control and civilized. Instead, I set about recording as much as I could discover about their tribal customs, including the practice of rating a man's prowess by the number of his kills:

A man can marry before he has killed, but no other woman will sleep with him. 'I am a woman and you are a woman. Why do you come to me?'

A man child of any age, even at the breast, counts as a kill. They invariably castrate their victim, even if still alive, if it is possible to do so. There are numerous instances known of wounded Danakil and Galla who have been castrated recovering. De Monfreid [a Frenchman who lived with the Danakil] was told that it is necessary to plug the wound at once with a bundle of grass or leaves.

Where it is however impossible to castrate their victim, as when they fire into a camp at night, certain knowledge or the production of witnesses suffice for it to count as a kill.

In his book *Desert and Forest*, published in 1934, Nesbitt wrote: 'It is the custom among these bloodthirsty slayers to dry, and display in their huts or on their person, those organs taken from the body of their victim.' I myself never saw such a trophy – indeed, the Danakil I encountered denied emphatically that they would ever wear the testicles of the men they have mutilated:

The trophy is exhibited round the village and then thrown away. They deny that they ever preserve it, or that their tombs are ever decorated with these trophies as Nesbitt says in his account.

They do, however, wear the testicles of animals they have killed in the belief that this trophy brings them good luck when hunting.

The Danakil were divided into two hostile sections, the Asaimara and the Adoimara. The Danakil at Bilen were Adoimara, whereas in Aussa and Bahdu, an area downstream of Bilen, they were Asaimara. During the course of my travels I learned to tell at a glance, from the decorations he wore, which tribe a man belonged to and how often he had killed:

Amongst the Bahdu Asaimara it is almost universal for the young men to wear a thin band of leather, sheepskin or tape round the neck, waist and ankle. Even small boys of ten years old will wear it. It is a special medicine to bring them success in killing a man and is obtained from a sorcerer who can be distinguished because he wears an amulet round the waist as well as the neck. When they have killed a man they replace this band by a bead necklace. Before raiding, or generally to bring them luck, they will tie a special creeper round their necks and waists. This creeper grows in the forest by the river.

A man who has killed ties one thong, decorated with brass, to his knife or rifle for each man killed. Coloured loin cloth. Ring (also worn by old men and magicians.) No man may put an ostrich feather or even grass in his hair until he has killed at least once. To do so is great shame.

A man who has killed two men will cut a hole in his ear and expand it with a wooden cork. The cork is removed when the hole is healed. This custom is far from general.

I could not find out for certain how many men it is necessary to kill before you can wear an ivory bracelet above the elbow. Most people said ten, but Ali declared it was only one. I myself think ten is probably correct.

More than ten men: signified by a narrow iron bracelet with a small hump. This is the highest decoration which an Asaimara can obtain.

ADOIMARA KILLING DECORATIONS: After having killed one man, they will wear a comb decorated with brass, a bead necklace, a coloured loin cloth, or an iron bracelet, known as maldaya, *on their left wrist. Having killed two men they may cut a hole in each ear, though this is far from universal.*

Having killed ten men they may wear an ivory bracelet above the right elbow. They also change the iron maldaya *to their right wrist.*

At a feast those men who have not killed have to clean the animals and carry away the heads and insides. The other men will throw the insides of the animals at them or hit them over the head with it. They will also rub cow dung on their clothes and hair.

At the feast they get only the worst meat, and the others will wipe the grease and food off their hands or their clothes.

There is a most intricate system of tribal marks. The Asaimara scarify the forehead and cheeks, and the Adoimara the nose and cheeks. The men also scar their chests and stomachs in crude patterns. The women scar their breasts and stomachs.

My immediate concern as I waited at Awash station in December 1933 for the ten-man military escort to arrive was not the murderous reputation of the Danakil, but the prospect that the Abyssinian authorities might forbid me from progressing any further.

December 1st

The Emperor's Secretary rang up to say that there was fighting where we are going. He did not, however, ban the trip, though he strongly advised us to go elsewhere. The acting Governor of Chercher [Lij Seifon] then rang up in an agitated way. Said we should require one hundred soldiers. Forbade the ten to move till they heard again. Said I should go anyway and he removed the ban. In a fever to get off before it was definitely banned.

Lij Seifon definitely refuses to take any responsibility for us – very insistent on this. But has got the wind up and thus cannot judge the risks.

Have twenty-one men to feed, since Habta, Birru and Said wanted the money and undertake to bring their own food. Have bought seven sacks of flour, six of rice and three of *teff*. Also three sacks of corn for the mules – six of them.

Excluding my rifles we have ten and the *zabanias* have another thirteen as three more soldiers came with the camels.

After getting Chercher to remove the ban gave the telephone man ten dollars to keep away from the telephone for the rest of the day.

Got away at 6.30 after many delays. A full moon – marched to Kolba. Camped just short of the hot springs, as these had a way of continuously withdrawing before us. Numerous hyenas ringed the camp round.

The camels are too heavily loaded. The soldiers have no idea how to load, though they seem to have nothing but two tents to put on their three camels. They look a good lot of men, and the commander speaks English, but they are none of them anxious to go on this trek.

December 2nd

Left camp at 7.30 and arrived Sade Malka at 11.30. Shot a waterbuck almost at once. Open park country, near the hot springs. Large numbers of doum palms by the hot spring. One or two bucks very tame and allowed all the caravan within 150 yards. Then passed along the edge of a marsh covering a large area, and running north to the forest. Only saw two oryx, but fresh tracks everywhere, also tracks of lesser kudu. Saw seven aoul, but all very small heads.

Camped by the river. Dense jungle along the edge of the river, covering a large area. Also patches of tall grass. Rumours of buffalo here and also elephant.

Went out with Jama, Abdullahi, and a Danakil at 2.30. Saw a waterbuck with average head with twelve cows and three calves. Stood on edge of river watching us from fifty yards. Put up two others, and later saw five cows, but probably more, feeding with warthog. Approached to within twenty yards while they stood and watched. There seem to be more waterbuck here than four years ago. Fresh tracks and droppings everywhere. Had a shot at a swimming crocodile. Hyenas very common. Guinea-fowl abundant. Built a *zariba* [thorn fence] round the back of the camp. One camel climbed down to the river and then could not get back. Umar and the men carried it up.

December 3rd

The Danakil say that a bull elephant, the last one, is on the river close by at the moment. Wanders between here and Bilen.

Wished to march again in the evening as camp in thick bush. All the village headmen opposed this, and asked us if we wished to be killed. Some raiding and killing here very recently. Moved camp about one mile into open country and built an effective defence with chop boxes and sacks of flour. The men rather jumpy.

December 4th

There is evidently bad trouble beyond Bilen. The Danakil have there renounced their allegiance to the Government and defied them to do their worst. Over tribute.

Balabat here called Bilo. Entuti Umar also came to camp with his son. Entuti Umar is the chief here, the same as when I was here before.

Met a young boy, at most fourteen, who had recently 'cut' [castrated] a man. His hair plastered with ghee. This is the dream of every boy.

December 5th

Left camp at six-thirty and arrived at Bilen at 11.30. Continuous opposition from Entuti Umar and two other chiefs at our going on. Wished us to camp after two hours. Said impossible to get there in the day, which I knew was untrue. Could not fathom their motive. They threatened repeatedly to turn back and said it was unsafe to go on without them. Paid no attention.

Bilen is on the frontier of the Itu country, and the Danakil and Itu are hereditary foes. The Itu seem slowly to be encroaching. Entuti Umar's son has killed one, and hopes to find another by himself.

Camped on a rise above the hot spring. The level of the hot spring has dropped considerably since I was last here – some four feet.

At 3 o'clock went out towards the north end of the marsh after buffalo. Heard innumerable pig in the reeds, but almost certainly two buffalo as well, very close to us. Bamboo-grass and thorn thickets on the edge of the reeds.

Trouble with the Danakil over food in the evening. The men pander to them in a disgusting way. The Danakil refused a sheep and insisted on having bread. They are most grasping and insistent, and collect like hungry vultures. Gabrisgael told me in the evening his men had come out with only fifteen days' rations and now had only eight. Wishes me to stay here twelve days while they send to Asba Tafari for more. Refused and told him to put them on half rations till we get to Aussa, and I would shoot them meat. Suspect they wish to inform Addis Ababa of the Asaimara trouble, and get our further advance forbidden. Told him I could not risk this.

December 6th

Left camp and went to the same place as yesterday to look for buffalo. Saw none, though we found fresh tracks. At most there are a dozen using this feeding ground. There must be a large herd in this reedbed since they are never shot and do not move away from here.

The Danakil with me found the fresh tracks of Itu sandals by the marsh and got very excited.

Went out at 2 o'clock to get some meat. Shot a bull oryx but with a bad head, and the point stubbed. A considerable number here in lots of five to ten. Vultures collected with incredible rapidity.

Entuti Umar and the other Danakil returned home. Angry with him, as he has not even given me any milk.

Someone has stolen fifteen of my pieces of tobacco.

December 7th

A Danakil chief I met last time came to the camp. More talk about the dangers from the Asaimara, whom these Danakil declare to be extremely savage. We shall be in Asaimara country two to three days immediately after passing Mount Ayelu. Collected birds 2–3.

December 8th

Went into the reed bed. In the centre a dry island thickly covered with dead rushes where the buffalo lie up in the day. This is surrounded by water between one and two feet deep and dense rushes fourteen feet high. Through these rushes there are well-beaten paths, leading to open spaces in the middle of the reed bed. Here the grass and small rushes are grazed short. There were numerous open spaces like this, but none more than thirty-five yards across. Saw some snipe and two quail on the edge of the reeds. Quail common in the open country round about. Numerous warblers. Disturbed two buffalo in the centre island. They got our wind when we were about fifteen yards off. Had been following them up by the mud splashes on the reeds. They made a considerable noise as they galloped off. Jama useless, and the Danakil only tracked after we had disturbed them. Put up two lesser kudu bucks in the thick bush not far from camp. Shot one of them running at a hundred yards. Fetched him into camp on a camel.

Extremely strong wind about 11 p.m. This happens every night.

December 9th

Camels nearly loaded when I got back. Abdullahi has lost six Legation cartridges. Fined him a dollar for each one.

Left camp 7.45 and arrived at Kurtuni at 12.45. North for three and a half hours along edge of escarpment. Then at 305 degrees for half an hour to edge of swamp. Native villages on terraces half-way up escarpment which is volcanic. Grass plains very cracked between escarpment and swamp, but to north mimosa bush and lava rock. Hills to the north of us.

Camp defended with *zariba*, and sandbagged inside this. The *zabanias* say the Danakil here are worse than the Asaimara, and made the fortifications without any encouragement. A bad place for defence in thick bush. A very steep ridge of lava rock all along the edge of the swamp here. Extremely cracked on top, some of these crevices fifty feet deep. Numerous baboons. Camp at south-east corner of swamp.

This swamp is very large, stretching as far as I could see to the Awash. Mostly mud and bushes here, but a large patch of vivid green in the distance. Found spoor of zebra and oryx, and one old set of hippo tracks. Yusuf declares he disturbed two hippo when fetching water. Several Egyptian geese and herons.

Mosquitoes unbearable. The Danakil guide shouted out a warning to any Danakil lurking round not to attack the camp.

Rode Fitaurari to press the poison out of his back.

Almost innumerable flights of sand-grouse to lesser Bilen spring at 8 o'clock. Stop only a second. Shot three, excellent eating. Came from every direction. A baboon's garden close to camp. They have grubbed up two or three acres for the roots of a rushlike grass. Exactly like a ploughed field, and more thoroughly done than most natives' ploughing.

About two hundred guinea-fowl feeding together here in the evening.

Collected birds 7–11.

December 10th
Left camp at 7.45 and arrived at Lake Hertale at 5.15 – a long and hot march, mostly over lava rock which threw up the heat. Numerous hills, mostly between us and the river. These either black rock or covered with burnt grass. East of us a mimosa-covered plain as far as you could see. A glorious view of Lake Hertale as we crossed the intervening mountain. Had a bathe. Camp on a lava terrace well above the lake. No mosquitoes. Great numbers of bats at sunset. The lake runs north-east by west-south-west. Narrows at the western end but broad at the east, fringed with marsh. A chain of mountains run down to the lake, and then along it at 30 degrees. Lake vivid blue.

Marched at 5 degrees for two hours along another escarpment parallel to yesterday's. During the march our guide ran away, but was luckily caught. Serious if he had escaped. Then set two *zabanias* to guard him.

Saw several bateleurs during the day. Saw a bittern, and several birds like cormorants.

Jama drank the water in my bottle which he was carrying – unforgivable. He is very unsatisfactory, interferes with the headmen and tries to incite the others.

December 11th

Left camp at 10.00 and arrived at Mahedilla near Kurbilli at 1.30, camped close to the Faradai river which flows out of Lake Hertale and parallel with the Awash.

Camp not far from a Danakil village. Here three from a party of four Greek merchants were murdered eight years ago. The Abyssinians decimated the Danakil – men, women and children. Loathe the Government in consequence. The headman begged us to be wide awake and to allow no one out of camp. Four Adoimara killed two hundred yards from our camp a few days ago by Bahdu Asaimara. Funeral feast and we were given much meat. The Danakil here all carry rifles or spears, never sticks – a sign we are in a disturbed area.

Saw numerous aoul going back from water at sunset. Shall give the camels a rest here tomorrow, though the feeding is very poor.

December 12th

Stayed in camp all day as there was very strong opposition to my going shooting – incessant talk of the Asaimara. Extremely difficult to judge how great the danger is. Completely filled all belts with my cartridges so as to appear well armed, rather like getting out cartridges for a big pheasant shoot.

December 13th

Left camp at 8 o'clock. Crowds of Adoimara came to see us leave. Marched for two hours north-east towards the escarpment, and camped not far from it near a hot spring and marsh. Awash river half a mile from camp. Camped at 10 o'clock, as it is important to get the *balabat* here to take us on to the next. Marched in very close formation. This *balabat* saved one of the Greeks when they were massacred here, and for this he was made *balabat*. Now thinks himself rather too clever, and wanted absurd sums to take us on. However, said tomorrow we should go without him and he would be responsible if we were killed. He then gave way and presented us with three sheep. Maddeningly insistent in his requests for presents, and produced first his children and then his wives, and finally all his relations asking for presents for each.

A pleasant camp under some big mimosas.

This is the frontier of Asaimara country. What makes it dangerous is that Dedjazmatch Abashum came here with a large force two and a half months ago to enforce the payment of tribute, but was afraid to enter their country and withdrew. They naturally think in consequence that they are too strong for the Government. The *balabat* will, however, take us as far as the next, though it is very doubtful if he will hand us on again. In that case there will be a big risk. They appear to be a rich and powerful tribe.

When Yusuf fired off a shot at birds near camp the Danakil talking to me made a grab for their rifles. Even after this they moved instinctively each time. Shows the state of tension in which they live.

December 14th

Left camp at 7.30 and arrived at Beriforo at 11.15 where we camped. Marched due north along edge of escarpment for one hour. Marsh then ended, escarpment changed direction.

The first part of the march through a bad country for ambushes, a narrow path between the escarpment and marsh. This place is well known for surprise attacks. Kept stopping and closing up. The Danakil with us very insistent on this. The marsh is fed by numerous small springs flowing out from the foot of the ridge, all hot. The marsh itself is long but narrow, and of tall rushes as at Bilen. Saw some old hippo tracks. Then came to a grass plain about one mile wide between the escarpment and the Awash river. Rich grass and in several places standing water. Thickly populated on both banks of the river and large herds of cattle and sheep, also a few ponies and donkeys. The richest country we have seen so far in Danakil.

Thought at first we were going to have trouble. The Asaimara remained squatting when we approached, and shuffled round till their backs were to us. They were very numerous and all armed. It took some time to find the *balabat*, Bilo, and then much talking before he became friendly. Camped not far from the village under a few trees. Crowds of Danakil round camp. This was within one hundred yards of the river.

Innumerable crocodiles, some very large, on the mud at the river's edge. Unlike previous crocodiles they paid no attention to us even when close. Two Danakil waded the river, which is waist deep, and had a bathe. They don't seem to fear the crocodiles. Kassimi caught two small catfish. Marabout common, and white ibis flying up and down the river.

The *balabat* gave us five jars of cow's milk. The men, on finding that they have not been killed as they expected, have now swung to the other extreme and declare that here is no danger. This is not true and I don't want them to think so or they will get careless and then be killed and mutilated. The men over the river don't come under this *balabat*, and I mistrust those on this side as much. They are preparing a big raid on the Issa, with whom they are always at war. Heard my men talking Somali, and at once said they were Issa. They say now that they are satisfied that they are not, but I am not sure. The young men might easily get out of hand. We pretend my gun case contains a machine-gun, and talk of it a great deal.

The *balabat* wears a coloured Abyssinian shirt given him by the Government. The *balabat* at Bilen also wore one and a cheap black cloak.

One man wearing an ivory bracelet above his elbow. This is the sign that he has killed at least ten men. He killed two Issa in a recent raid. They do not all seem to cut holes in their ears when they kill, though many do. Women also scar their breasts and stomachs, usually in rough rectangles. Many women have scarred their backs into crude patterns, and also tattooed in blue round their eyes. They are good-

ABOVE: A 1930 Legation group for Haile Selassie's coronation. (*Left to right*) *1st row* Sir Harold Kittermaster (Governor, Somaliland); Sir Sidney Barton (Minister, Addis Ababa); HRH The Duke of Gloucester; Sir John Maffey (Governor-General, Sudan); Admiral Fullerton (East Indies Station RN) *2nd row* 1-4 Sir Stewart Symes (Resident, Aden); Lord Airlie; H. A. (later Sir Harold) MacMichael (Civil Secretary, Sudan); J. M. (later Sir John) Troutbeck (1st Secretary) *3rd row* 2 & 3 Majors R. E. Cheeseman (Consul) & A. T. Miles (ADC) *4th row* 1 & 3 P. Zaphiro (Oriental Secretary); myself *5th row* 1 E. A. (later Sir Edwin) Chapman-Andrews (Vice-Consul).

RIGHT: Emperor Haile Selassie wearing his State Crown after his coronation, November 1930.

ABOVE & ABOVE RIGHT:
Adoimara Danakil at Bilen
watering camels.

LEFT: Moussa Hamma, my
shikari (left) and Muhammad
Sirage, my *aban*.

OPPOSITE: My camp on the
way to Bilen.

ABOVE LEFT:
David Haig-Thomas with an
African tawny eagle.

ABOVE RIGHT: Camping
in the Arussi mountains.

LEFT: A *shifta*, captured
and hanged in the area. His
legs had been eaten by a
hyena.

OPPOSITE: The *shifta*
(centre) captured on October
22nd, 1933. We handed him
over to the local headman.

Arussi Galla woman with children.

LEFT: A spectacular view in the Arussi mountains.

BELOW: Our caravan on the way down to the Webi Shebeli

Crossing the Webi Shebeli.

Arussi Galla tribesmen.

Arussi horsemen arriving at our camp.

looking. The men have not got such fine features here. One or two are six feet tall.

December 15th

Moved to a small village and camped on some dry ground in the centre of a bog. Wished to go on to the next *balabat,* who is close, and a relation of the Sultan. The *balabat* of this village, an old and rather doddering man, would not hear of it, and as he is a man of great authority, we were forced to comply. He threatened indeed to become unpleasant. Could not have a worse place for camp, and as it was so close to the village impossible to keep the Danakil out.

Passed two small boys and a young man driving some sheep. They all three carried crude toy bows, and arrows of sharpened stick. Saw some children playing with similar bows near Bilen. When here before I saw two children using them near the Awash station. They shot at one another from a few yards with the bow laid flat along the ground.

A messenger arrived from the last *balabat* carrying letters from the Government. These ordered me to return at once as the road was very dangerous. If I refused to do so I was to sign that I had received the message, and the Government would not be responsible for me. In any case, the thirteen soldiers were ordered to return since the Government did not wish them killed.

Ato Gabrisgael read the letter out on receiving it. Thus all the camp knew at once, and also the Danakil standing round. The soldiers cannot conceal their delight. Infuriating as all was going so well, and I am certain I could have got there. Went to bed undecided whether to risk it and push on, or turn back in the hopes of being able to start again. Umar says he will follow me, but that he thinks we should stand no chance.

December 16th

Made up my mind that I must go back. Started at 8.45 and marched back a mile beyond our last camp. In camp at 11.00 under some trees, dirty, dusty and alive with flies. Listless and depressed. If we go on I think we shall certainly be killed. Most of the servants would follow me, but some would certainly go back. We should be about fifteen people, and almost impossibly short-handed. The Danakil would be encouraged by the return of the thirteen soldiers with nearly half our rifles. They also know the Government does not hold itself responsible, and would think that they would not be punished if they murdered us.

The *balabats* would be only too glad not to protect us, and even before we were dependent for our safety on their controlling the tribes who would gladly attack us. Nor could we find the water-holes on the short road to Aussa without their guidance. If we could go this road we might be able to race them for it. There is no hope if we have to follow the river. News travels incredibly fast in any case. I cannot describe my bitterness at this idiotic interference. Four years' planning and some thousand pounds thrown away.

When it was known that a Government letter had arrived, about thirty armed young men gathered round the old chief. Practically certain that these already knew its contents. In any case, Ato Gabrisgael would insist on my signing it before the *balabat* so that he was not responsible if I went on.

In the evening the nephew of Miriam Muhammad, the big Danakil chief round here, arrived in camp. His name is Ali Wali. Said that his uncle had refused to hold himself responsible for my safety in the Asaimara country. Government became nervous and sent off the telegram in consequence. I understand from him, however, that they are collecting two hundred soldiers to accompany me down here again. This is a gleam of hope, and if it is true I may yet get there. I do hope this is true, but I think the Government will have made a mistake; with two hundred soldiers the Danakil will think us potentially aggressive and be inclined to attack on the principle of attacking first. With thirty rifles they could not think this, while we were too strong to be an irresistible temptation. Also, so far we have succeeded in always getting hostages from the *balabat*. Himself during the day and usually his sons at night. This made it almost certain that the whole tribe would not attack us, and we could deal with odd young men out for trophies. Every night the *balabat* has warned anyone lurking round camp that he is like a hyena and will be shot on sight. This removes all responsibility from us if we kill anyone round camp while it is dark. Honest men must stand far off and proclaim themselves.

December 17th

Camped at 2.45. Took one hour to arrive at foot of escarpment. Difficulties getting camels up it; wasted much time. Volcanic rock, then grassy plain dotted with mimosa.

Saw an ostrich on this plain which is called Boroda. Second escarpment low and flat grassy top, with a steep descent to the plain of Aledea. Some Adoimara here with camels and they gave us milk. The Adoimara country stretches to the escarpment bordering the Asaimara Awash plain. On Boroda plain saw numerous tracks of oryx, aoul and gerenuk. Collected two locusts here, the only ones seen. Saw a few oryx round camp. Kassimi tried unsuccessfully to shoot one. No water here, but we have carried enough for one night from the Awash.

From the Awash to Bilen we were in Debinet country. From there on to the hot spring at Mataka in Waima country. The defile there is the Waima-Asaimara frontier. The Adoimara stretch to the Mullu river, across which it is Itu country.

December 18th

Flat open country, mostly bare earth covered fairly thickly with the usual evergreen plant (round leaves and a small yellow flower). Saw a very large herd of oryx, these cannot have been far short of a hundred, and a few aoul, also gerenuk tracks.

Passed the scene of a recent Asaimara raid on the Adoimara. Sixtyone people, including women and children, are said to have been killed. The *zariba* torn down and huts destroyed. They penetrated as far as the Mullu. When in camp several Adoimara said it was a miracle that we had escaped alive from the Asaimara country, they certainly have the moral ascendancy in these parts.

Where first crossed, the Mullu river had no defined course in the ground though its line was marked by trees. Later there was quite a deep riverbed, quite dry, water being struck in the wells at a depth of nine to ten feet. Soil at this depth gravel. Numerous wells, many dry. A man stands at the bottom and throws up a jar filled with water to a small boy, who catches it cleverly, and empties it into a mud trough for the cattle. Though the jar is full, little is upset. Numerous cattle being watered.

A large Adoimara village near these water-holes. Passed the first lot of holes, and camped further on where there was luckily some mimosa for the camels – none further back. Got within thirty yards of and watched eight aoul in the evening. A small buck, four does and three kids, two half-grown and one rather older. Shot a dik-dik with the .22.

Heard jackal chorus an hour after sunrise and again an hour before sunset.

December 19th.
Left camp at 5.45, carried no water as I hoped to get to Afdam in one day.

Very broken country round the foot of Mount Afdub, mostly volcanic rock. The camels came along well and we got to the station at 2.30. An interesting account of the Harar massacre from Umar. Tried unsuccessfully to telephone Broadmead at the Legation. The Abyssinian headman came to see us. Gave him tea. He says we were called back because there is trouble on the Aussa frontier. I cannot believe this, as we should certainly have heard of it. Several Danakil offered to guide us to Aussa, and would not have done so if they had expected us to be massacred. I think we were probably through the most dangerous area, the entry to the Asaimara country. However, he held out hope of our being able to return. I think Martin regards this man as the authority on the Danakil country.

Got hold of a large shed, built for a recent conference between the Danakil and Itu, and pitched camp inside it. No other shade anywhere. A gallows outside where an Itu was hanged five days ago for murder. The people round here are said to take Danakil to the Awash station for a fixed payment, and there introduce them to the inhabitants, thus giving them every opportunity to 'cut' a man. Mostly Somalis, but very mixed. Collected birds 31–36.

December 20th

Caught the train to Addis Ababa at 12.30. Umar to keep everything together here till I return. Took Birru with me.

Heard that there is trouble in the Ogaden. Gerazmatch Muhammad has been chained up. The Somalis waylaid and captured some Government lorries – four, I believe. The 'Mad Mullah's' son is down there. Disturbances probably instigated by Italy.

December 21st

Arrived at Addis Ababa at 7.30. Went to de Halperts and then saw Sandford. Went and saw Broadmead at 11.00. He did not know I had been recalled. I think the telegram was sent to Awash on December 11th. But the Minister of Foreign Affairs asked Broadmead to communicate with me at this date. Barton returns tomorrow. Sleeping in the padre's house and feeding with de Halpert.

December 22nd

Sir Sidney and Lady Barton, and Wally [one of the Consuls] arrived at 4.30.

December 23rd

Lunched at the Legation. Barton has agreed to do all he can to help me. He sees the Minister of Foreign Affairs on the 27th.

December 23rd
Addis Ababa

Darling Mother

Everything has crashed at the moment, but I hope to be able to pull things round. When I was within a week's march of the end of the river and everything going splendidly, I received an order from the Abyssinian Governor to return. They had suddenly got jumpy over the Asaimara. We were through the place where any trouble might have been expected, and I have not the least doubt that I should have reached the end of the river from where I was without difficulty. You cannot imagine my bitterness. However, to have pushed on despite this order, and though my soldiers were ordered to return, would have been suicide. The men were prepared to follow me if I went on, but I came to the conclusion we should not stand a chance. We should have lost half our rifles.

We did four forced marches and struck the railway between Awash and Dire Dawa. I have left the caravan there ready to return the moment I get leave. I have seen Barton, who has returned, and I hope he will be able to obtain permission for me to go back. However, nothing can be done for a day or two and I shall go out to the Sandfords for Christmas. I had hoped to spend it at the end of the river.

Everything was going simply splendidly. We were being handed on quickly from one headman to the next, and secured hostages for good behaviour off each headman. It is infuriating that the Government should suddenly have developed an attack of nerves. Nor was there the least reason for it, beyond the usual risks inseparable from travel in such an area. These risks they knew before they gave me leave to go in England, and before they issued my pass here.

However, I still hope for the best. The Legation are out to do what they can for me.

Darling Mother I suppose it is good for our souls, but it is bitterly disappointing to be baulked like this. It makes it more bitter when it is not your fault that you have failed, and you believe that except for this you could have done it. I have staked such a lot on this venture; not only money, though there is £1500 of that, but everything. However, I shall fight desperately to get back there. I have not wired as it was impossible to put all this in a wire and a short and unintelligible wire would only have added to your anxiety.

I will write again very soon.

Love from your son,

Wilfred

December 24th

Rode out to the Sandfords. Left at 8.15 arrived 1.30. Gama very lazy.

December 25th, Christmas

Rode to the second waterfall and had lunch there. Very fine, and a good view down the Muger valley from the point.

January 1st

Tea at the Legation. Taffera Work arrived with Sedalo's answer just as I was leaving. Martin has wired that the state of the Danakil country is very dangerous, and he could not recommend my being allowed down there. The Emperor is away at the moment. Nothing further can be done till he returns.

January 3rd

Went to the station to see Broadmead off. Barton has enlisted Heroui in my support. He has a strong dislike of Martin. Lunch party at de Halpert's. Belgian Minister there.

The Emperor was away. It turned out later that he had been to Ankober and released Hailu's son. This looks as if he may be going to be sent back to Gojjam. Imru is definitely leaving.

The Emperor on his return ordered Martin up from Chercher to discuss my return with Barton and me.

January 12th
Martin and the Scriveners arrived.

January 13th
Rode to the Legation in the afternoon. To go and see Martin tomorrow – gather from Sandford that Martin says that there is fighting between the Asaimara and Issa on the Aussa frontier.

January 14th
Saw Martin at 10.30 at his house. He is rattled over the question of responsibility. Barton and he evidently had a strong interview yesterday and reached no agreement. Barton claims that as the Government have accepted the expedition they are responsible for its safety. They should otherwise have said that Danakil was a closed area. Martin denies that the Government are bound to give me an escort and says that they did so as a compliment. They are ready to help, but I go on my own responsibility and no action lies against the Government if I am killed. Cited expeditions in the Burmese hills.

Forced Martin to admit that the conditions down the Awash are not more unsettled than usual. The Issa fighting is not exceptionally severe, and raiding in this area is chronic. Told him that I was confident that, except for the Government's interference, I should have got through last time, and given an ordinary run of luck that I could do it now. I am against a large increase in my escort. Said that several Asaimara offered to accompany me to the Aussa as guides and to come back with me. As they would thus place themselves in the position of hostages, they would not do so if they expected us to run into trouble. Nor had I heard anything to lead me to believe that there was big trouble in front of us, though I knew the Asaimara were raiding the Issa. This is a return raid for last year.

Then went and saw Barton, and Martin joined us for lunch. A compromise reached after lunch. The Government is responsible for my safety, but can discharge that responsibility by taking every reasonable precaution, by providing me with an adequate escort. After this should I be killed it would be an act of God and no action could lie against the Government.

Martin will see the Emperor and let us know the answer as soon as possible. He is not anxious for me to come back through his province, and is going to do what he can to get me permission to go out by Tajura or Dessie.

Wally says that Holland shot a bongo in the forests close to Maji. He also believes that giant bushbuck and forest hog are to be found there. Captured a young pig which he believes to have been a young forest hog and which someone else also identified as such, but he says it was red in colour. I don't know if young forest hogs are red. It was very savage. Wally says that conditions down at Maji are as bad as ever. Slaves are still seized, and quite recently there was a raid sixty miles across the frontier. The local tribes are harried and oppressed.

January 15th
Muhammad Ergay came and saw me. He has heard from Umar, who is down with fever, and most of the caravan. Rang up, relayed on from Awash, and Umar says they are better. Wants medicine for the camels, which I sent down by the night train. Worried about my caravan. Told him to pay Jama off. Ever since he has been with me he has made mischief, inciting the others to demand larger food and pay. Should have sent him straight back from the Awash station. He also drank the water in my bottle on the long march to Hertale. Heard from Martin that six of my escort were badly ill with fever.

January 17th
Ramadan over. Several thousand Muhammadans marched down to Filwaha for a prayer meeting. Very spectacular.

January 18th
Went up to the polo ground in the evening and watched the priests and crowds arriving for tomorrow. The Emperor came down with them and then went back.

January 19th

Went to Timkat ceremony which began about 7 o'clock. A large crowd and the war drums accompanied the Emperor to the Cabana. Here were the tents of the priests. The Emperor and various Rases and chiefs, and also the Abuna with a small group of priests, then blessed the waters. They formed a very colourful group. After this the priests danced on the slope opposite. When this was over everyone moved up to the racecourse. A magnificent sight. All the priests with the arks in front under their coloured umbrellas, followed by the Emperor and chiefs with their retinues. Their chargers were led in front of them in full trappings. Got caught up in the throng, but got ahead of them by doing some steeplechasing. On the racecourse the Emperor and the chiefs sat in a pavilion, while the crowd formed up in a circle round it. The priests were formed up in front, and the dancers danced before the Emperor. This was very effective and the drums had a lovely note.

When it was over they streamed back to the town. Various horsemen played at *gougsa*. Had breakfast at the club, then went to the Legation. Martin there. He has had a row with Salah Sedalo, the Minister of Foreign Affairs. The Emperor has told him to reach an agreement with Barton and me. The Government will give me fifteen soldiers but have no Lewis gun to spare.

I gave Martin a letter stating that I agreed that this escort constituted a discharge of the Government's duty to take adequate measures to safeguard my expedition. He says that the escort will be ready in a week. It is an enormous relief to have got this settled. I have had a very weary month with my hopes see-sawing between optimism and the blackest depression.

Danakil II

I WAS IN ADDIS ABABA for a month. Shortly after my arrival Sir Sidney Barton returned from leave, which was fortunate for me: he had approved my plans and obtained the initial permission for me to undertake the journey and now his persistence eventually obtained the permission for me to resume it. He insisted that Dr Martin, Governor of Chercher Province, should be summoned to Addis Ababa from Asba Tafari to discuss the matter. Dr Martin was an Abyssinian who had led an extraordinary life. As a small boy he had attached himself to an officer on the Magdala Expedition as it returned to the coast in 1868. The officer took him to India, educated him and gave him a medical training. Martin served for a time as a doctor in northern Burma before eventually returning to his homeland, where his European background made him easier than most Abyssinian officials for foreigners to deal with. At a meeting with Dr Martin, Sir Sidney pressed for me to be allowed to resume my journey; he also suggested that my escort should be increased but I opposed this, still sure that too large a force would risk provoking hostility. Dr Martin eventually agreed to sanction my return, but insisted that I first gave him the following letter:

January 20th, 1934
Addis Ababa

Dear Doctor Martin,

With reference to the permission given to me by the Ethiopian [*sic*] Government to travel along the Awash river to the place where it disappears in the Aussa Sultanate, I agree that the provision of an escort of fifteen men, to accompany me and remain with me until I return to the Awash station or leave Ethiopian territory at the French frontier in the Aussa country, together with letters recommending me to the tribal chiefs *en route* will constitute a discharge of the Ethiopian Government's responsibility for the taking of reasonable measures to ensure the safety of my expedition.

Yours sincerely,
Wilfred Thesiger

His Excellency Dr Martin
Governor of Chercher Province,
at Addis Ababa

The following day, I returned by train to Afdam. Ali Wali had turned up at Afdam from Bahdu while I was in Addis Ababa, and Umar, realizing how useful he might be, had looked after him. Ali Wali now suggested that I should ask Dr Martin to release his uncle, Miriam Muhammad, who was still in detention at Asba Tafari; he maintained that his uncle's return with us to Bahdu would ensure us a friendly reception. I telephoned Martin, who agreed to this.

While I was with the Danakil I was anxious to record all I could learn about their customs and way of life. Fortunately I found that Ali Wali was very ready to help me. He was intelligent and grateful to me for having secured his uncle's release. Umar translated my questions to him, using Amharic, which they both spoke fluently. Umar was obviously interested and he often enlarged on the questions I had asked with others of his own. I wrote down the results of our discussions at the time. I regretted that I had not studied anthropology instead of history at Oxford.

January 22nd

Arrived at Afdam at 12 o'clock. Found an excellent atmosphere in camp. They really seem anxious to get off again. Umar has done splendidly to keep them together.

The camels are all right again and well rested, and Fitaurari's, Desita's, and Shaitan's backs recovered. Muhammad Denkali and Araby have been turned out of camp for making trouble.

There are said to be four lion not far from here – I must investigate this.

The men gave a dance for me in the evening.

January 23rd

Went to the wells at Maghou to investigate the rumour of lion. Denied that there were any about and said the nearest they knew of were on the Erer, a day's journey off. There evidently are lion there. Possibly so few in the Danakil country because, except for the river, there is almost no water which is not at the bottom of deep wells. The mosquitoes on the river are very bad and drive them away from there. On the Magna and other rivers in the Arussi there were no mosquitoes. I do not think lions were ever numerous in the Danakil country, and that the Danakil have wiped them out since they have had rifles. The Danakil are not hunters.

The wells were very deep and the water was good. Three persons at different depths are required to throw the jars up. They climb down a tree trunk. The men work naked. There are some six wells.

Shot a gerenuk on the way back. Saw one oryx and one aoul, also three single gerenuk males, and a pair of males. In November four years ago the males were with the females. A leopard has killed a sheep at the back of the station. Came back early as I was extremely thirsty.

January 24th

Ordered thirteen sacks of No. 6 flour and seven of *teff* from the Awash; also two sacks of barley.

Went up into the hills at the back of the station in the evening. Looked for the leopard on the way. Found this morning's tracks but no sign of him. Thick aloes and scrub in a dry water course. He hung the goat which he killed in a tree here.

Heard and saw a woodpecker drumming.

January 25th

Gave all the men a month's wages in the morning. Birru is over his fever but very weak. The others are getting stronger daily. Re-engaged Araby.

Paid off O'Ahmed who says his children are ill. Really nervous of going back down the Awash. All the other men, whom I asked in turn, say they will come with me. Told them it was their last chance to back out and get paid. After today I will pay no arrears of wages to anyone who does not come, unless, of course, they are very ill.

January 26th

Had a long talk with the Asaimara chief in the evening. The Abyssinians lured him in here and now refuse to allow him to go back. He is very bitter with them. Wants me to get permission for him to accompany us back to his country. Shall try to arrange this, but Martin still in Addis Ababa. Told him to send a message to his tribe that I was returning and must be well treated.

Heard from Barton that the Emperor has given permission for me to go from Aussa to Tajura. Now awaiting an answer from the French Governor.

January 27th

Telephoned Lij Seifon asking about the escort. Denies that he has received any orders. Wired the Legation.

January 29th

Yusuf pretended to be ill, all day. Says he is too ill to go into the Danakil country. The truth is that he is in a blind funk. He was terrified all the time he was down there. Gave him the alternative of coming or staying behind and losing two months' pay. He is the only man except Umar who is difficult to replace.

Found that Araby had bolted on today's train. He has left nearly a month's pay.

Went out in the afternoon towards the foothills to the east of Mount Afdub. Flat scrub-covered country with thickets of aloe, cut up by numerous dry riverbeds, but Mount Afdub and numerous hills close. Shot a greater kudu with forty-nine-inch horns. A bad shot, running at about fifty yards through the haunch and forward through the stomach. Missed with a long second shot. Cast forward and came on a kudu which allowed us fairly close three times; thought it was the wounded one. Lost it and casting back came on Abdi and the Issa skinning the kudu. They had tracked it up and come on it where it had fallen into a watercourse which it was trying to get out of. Satisfactory.

Martin has arrived at Asba Tafari. Heard that the Governor of French Somaliland has given me permission to travel through the colony from Aussa, but by Dikil, Alisabiet and not by Tajura as I had hoped.

January 30th
Yusuf is in an abject funk. Told Umar he would not come even if his pay was doubled. These desertions will rattle everybody unless we get away soon.

Arranged to buy four *fracillas* of coffee. Coffee has a very great value down in Aussa, and this should be most useful as presents.

Rang up Martin. He says that my escort will arrive on the train on the 1st. Their camels have started today. Asked if I could have a *balabat* to accompany me.

January 31st
Yusuf has left the camp. Rang up and sent a letter to Dire Dawa to try and get a man from there.

February 1st
No soldiers arrived on the train as promised. Hear that they were only given their money at the last minute and had no time to buy food.

They are to come on the 5th and Lij Farada is also coming here, I gather. A Somali, Ali Nur, arrived from Dire Dawa in answer to a letter to Hajj Fara Umar from Umar asking for a bird skinner. Asked for sixty dollars. Found that he knew nothing about skinning birds, and is in every way unsuitable.

February 2nd

Heard in the morning that there is trouble at Kurbilli. A Danakil arrived and informed the *dagnia* that a large number of Danakil were collected there with their horses, and making ready for a raid. What tribe they were he could not say. The *dagnia* suspects it is the Asaimara and imprisoned their *balabats* who are here. Lij Farada rang up and wants me to put off going again. This I refused to do and asked for the soldiers on the 5th. He consented.

Went out shooting at 2.30 towards the flat-topped hill east of Mount Afdub. Shot an aoul with a wide and pretty head, one of eight. Though just on sunset vultures arrived, making a great rushing with their wings as they planed down. A jackal also arrived hot haste and almost ran into us as we were leaving.

A sandstorm lasting for about half an hour just after sunset. Shut out everything thirty yards off. Looked like a heavy rain storm only yellower as it approached.

Collected birds in the morning. Shot a large woodpecker, black-and-white crest and no red, drumming on a mimosa. This is a female. The male has a red crest. Unfortunately badly knocked about. Have only seen one of these before. Bedi promises to be good at skinning.

February 3rd

Collected birds in the morning and again in the afternoon. Have collected all the birds here along the edge of the dry riverbeds, where there are tall mimosa trees and a certain amount of undergrowth.

It is not the Asaimara who are on the war path at Kurbilli, but as far as can as yet be gathered a tribe from across the Awash. No fighting yet. The Asaimara visit me daily. My return is interpreted to mean that I gave a good account of the Asaimara to the Government. I tell them it is up to them to give me cause to say good things of them when the trip is over. Their big chief Miriam Muhammad is to accompany me. Delighted as he did not expect, I think, ever to get away from here. They are also relieved I fancy to find it is not their tribe which is now raiding. They always pose as innocents whose every action is misinterpreted to the Government by their enemies the Adoimara. My recall was due to this chief refusing to make himself responsible for my safety – says he was afraid the Adoimara would kill me in his territory, when he would be responsible.

This policy of detention makes the chiefs hate the Government very bitterly.

February 4th
Collected birds in the morning. Got a male and female of the large woodpecker. These woodpeckers again drumming. This gave them away. Saw two, one, and three greater kudu cows, all in the thickets along the main riverbed. Barked repeatedly. Heard a leopard twice in a thick patch of jungle, more of a roar than a snarl and quite unlike the noise I heard one make at Hako. This was at 3.30. Could see no trace of him except for fresh tracks.

Abdullahi had a very badly poisoned right hand and arm while I was away. Have got it healed up, but don't know if he will ever get back the movement of his little finger. Treating a local Somali whose hips and loin are riddled with poison.

February 5th
Shot a little owl in the morning, sitting in the top branches of a thick mimosa. The soldiers and Lij Farada arrived by the train. Their camels have not arrived, though they should have come yesterday. A letter arrived from Martin prohibiting me from shooting more than two head of any animal. The question of food will probably make it impossible to observe this, and in any case I have bought the Government licence, cost forty dollars, permitting me to shoot any number of animals,

except for the prohibited six. Lij Farada says Martin said nothing to the Emperor, as he promised he would, about having the Sultan warned of my approach – Lij Farada seemed to expect me to avoid Aussa by going direct to Dikil. This I told him I would not do. My pass authorizes me to go anywhere I like on the river. I shall write to Barton asking him to get the Government to announce my arrival to the Sultan.

Beret has got dysentery – I hope this won't spread. The thought frightens me.

February 6th

Intended to march in the afternoon, but the soldiers' camels have not come. The Danakil won't start tomorrow, as it is an unlucky day. Paid off Beret. He was very reluctant to go and swears he would be all right, but I cannot risk it. Engaged another man who can speak Danakil, useful for overhearing conversations.

February 7th

Engaged another camelman, Roblie, in place of Beret. The soldiers' camels arrived in the evening. Shall leave tomorrow. Lij Farada tried to make me agree always to do as the *balabats* said. Said I should consider anything they said carefully, but did not promise to fall in with it. Also said I was determined to go to Aussa. One *balabat* then swore the road was unsafe. There is a section of Adoimara territory between. Have written to Barton.

February 8th

Got my camels off by 10 o'clock. Carried water on one of the spare camels on an improvised saddle. One of the soldier's camels died on the way here, so that they are short. Succeeded in hiring one, but left very late.

Lij Theodore's *warquah* arrived by the train with letters for the headman. Made Miriam Muhammad sign for my safety. Gave him another copy of the letter I gave Martin as he has lost it. The *dagnia* of Afdam died last night after only two days' illness. I gather he was an extremely nice man. Lij Farada saw me off. He is a rather striking-looking man, and has taken a considerable amount of trouble on my behalf.

Got into camp at 5.45. The camels had arrived half an hour before. Abdullahi lagged behind and was very late turning up. Umar and I began to be afraid he had been 'cut'. He was unarmed. Apparently he had twice hidden on seeing Danakil and thus wasted a lot of time. A jackal chorus just before sunset. Did not put up a tent. Had to share the water with the soldiers.

Provisions for the men: 2 sacks of rice, 13 flour, 7 *teff*, 1 tin of ghee. Adam, Said and Birru have received money. Umar $7, Bedi $9, Kassimi $9 [Maria Theresa dollars].

The two *balabats* who are coming with me are Miriam Muhammad and Ahamado. Ali Wali, nephew and adopted son of Miriam Muhammad, is also with us. Ahamado and Ali are coming with me to Aussa.

Gabrisgael was ordered to come with me again. He absolutely refused to do so, however, and told them they could flog him or put him in prison, but he would not go down into the Danakil country again.

Except for one of the camelmen, all these soldiers are a new lot. They seem thoroughly depressed.

February 9th

Left camp at sunrise. Marched for three hours to the Mullu waterholes. The Danakil anxious to get rid of us as they were afraid we should drink all the water.

The remaining soldiers caught me up just before we got into camp. They only have fifteen rounds each which is idiotic, and too little food. They say they only have provisions for one month. They also have no proper water carriers. I have lent them two of mine now but they must buy skins. I think their headman will prove useless.

Miriam Muhammad begged me to stay here tomorrow as one of the women with him is ill and his mule has not arrived. Agreed to as

I do not wish to have a disagreement at once, but said I would not do it again.

Country round camp earth plain with a little grass and dotted with evergreen bushes. A fringe of trees along the riverbed. The wells are very deep.

I understand that Miriam Muhammad is credited by his tribe with the powers of a rain doctor. His return is eagerly expected so that he shall make rain. He has promised to give me a great dance.

The head of the Bahdu Asaimara is the Hangadaala, *currently Miriam Muhammad. The* Hangadaala *is always from the Madima, and is the eldest of the ruling family of the Asboura or Badogalet sub-tribes. Miriam Muhammad is an Asboura. The previous Sheikh was Ahamado's father, chief of the Badogalet.*

The Hangadaala, *on being invested, changes his name. He obtains the power of bringing rain and not a single Asaimara doubts his powers to do so. Only the* Hangadaala *can control the rain.*

An interesting ceremony takes place when the Sheikh is invested. They bring him a red and also a white cloth, and clothe him in these. The right of clothing the future Sheikh is hereditary. He is next smeared with ghee, after which he may not put his feet on the ground. He is placed in a special chair, and four men take the four legs of the chair. The right of carrying the chair is also hereditary, and each man always takes the same leg. There would be a fight at once if anyone else tried to usurp these functions. They carry him about two hundred yards towards the rising sun, and then back to his home. The Danakil believe that it always rains on this day, even out of a clear sky. Having returned to his home, they place the chair on a bed outside the house. They then bring earth from the top of Mount Ayelu and rub it on his hands, clay from the bottom of the Awash river and rub it on his forehead, and earth from under a big shola tree which they rub on his feet.

They then pour quantities of ghee over him and his clothes. For a week after this he will not drink water or take a bath. The crowd now fight to touch him.

They next bring a red and white goat, and two bulls, one red and the other white. The Masara then lift up the red bull and hold it over him

while they cut its throat so that the blood runs down over him. The
Asada then seize the red goat and cut its throat so that its blood too
flows down over the Hangadaala.

His son or nearest relation next cuts the throat of the white bull and
of the white goat, and his tribe rub themselves with the blood. The men,
and then the women, and finally the children of all the Asaimara tribes
pour a further quantity of ghee over him.

After this ceremony they kill up to a hundred sheep and drink quantities
of milk. Only the Madima may eat the flesh of the red bull and the white
bull, and of the red and the white goat. The skins of these animals are
dried, and the Hangadaala *uses them for sleeping on. The chair carriers*
are given the skins of the legs.

February 10th

Shot a dik-dik in the morning and picked it up at once. Half an hour
later a large number of vultures were circling round the place. Makes
one wonder if they do hunt entirely by sight, though there was a good
deal of blood. But if you hide an animal you have just shot under a
bush and cover it over so that it is not easily seen, the vultures do
not find it. Shot a female aoul for food.

Miriam Muhammad has had one of his camels stolen. Told the
local *balabat* it must be found. Ali Wali swears he saw some cows here
which were recently stolen from his tribe.

In the evening some Danakil arrived at the wells with several donkeys, the sentry gave the alarm and we advanced on them with the
light of the searchlights. The poor people were terrified.

If one Adoimara steals from another Adoimara for one sheep he has to
pay for four, for a cow forty dollars, for a bull thirty dollars, and for a
she-camel one hundred and twenty sheep. If an Issa steals from an
Adoimara for one sheep he is fined two, for a cow or a bull six sheep,
and for a camel twelve sheep. This is in conformity with Issa custom,
which prevails. It is reciprocal.

Unless the man is killed when he is caught, the punishment is always
a fine. Any old men who are present when the thief is captured prevent

*his being killed. They bind him and take him before the old men of his
tribe. Then standing far off they demand the fine.*

*For constantly lying or stealing, or for constantly committing adultery,
the offender is tied up in a ball, with his arms and legs together, and
submerged in the river until practically drowned. When he is condemned
to this punishment his relations will come and beg for him to be forgiven.
The length of the ducking is sometimes shortened in consequence.
Occasionally he is drowned by mistake, in which case his family can take
no action.*

*A man from another tribe who is captured when stealing or raiding,
if he escapes being killed at once, is flogged with the branches of a thorn
tree. If he is in any way related to the tribe he is ducked instead, since
members of the tribe are never flogged.*

*A man who entrusts cows, camels, etc. to someone else to sell for him
or to take to a distant town has no redress if this man later refuses to
hand over the money or the animals. He should have known what he
was doing when he handed over his animals, and if he has been a fool
it is his own fault.*

*A man who breaks a water pot belonging to someone else is fined two
cows. A man who steals a spear is heavily fined, and the gravity of the
offence is very much increased if he changes the wooden shaft of the spear.*

February 11th
Started to load two hours before dawn with lamps. Carried six tanks
of water on the spare camels. Marched for one hour up the riverbed,
past the wells we used going to Afdam. Great numbers of camels at
them. Took a lot of photos.

Shot a fairly large-eared owl. It flew into the evergreen tree we
camped under just as we arrived. Country waterless and stony with a
good deal of thorn scrub, but very few green trees.

As we left the Mullu river a party of Danakil arrived. They told us
that there is fighting on the Awash, and that they were moving away
from it. Probably untrue. A most attractive camp without tents. Ayelu
dominating the landscape.

February 12th

Camped under two trees by the river where we camped on December 16th. The *balabat* here is Abdullah, sometimes called Abdo.

Large numbers of Danakil came into camp to welcome Miriam Muhammad, though his country is lower down the river. Gave him the luncheon tent in which to hold his court, which pleased him.

They killed and gave us two oxen in the evening and quantities of milk. We also caught about a dozen catfish of about five pounds. There was in consequence a sound of revelry by night. One old Danakil has been shot in the arm above the elbow and the bone shattered. It has, however, healed well. He has besides this two spear wounds. He was one of a deputation of eight old men recently sent to the Adoimara. They were feasted and then murdered. He alone got away badly wounded. The big raid, the scene of which we passed on December 18th, is claimed to have been a return for this.

The Asaimara seem genuinely friendly to us. I am said to be their friend at court. The only danger to the camp is, I think, that there may be an anti-Abyssinian party who wish to throw off their allegiance to the Government. By murdering us, the whole tribe would inevitably be involved in hostilities with the Government and the young party would triumph over the party of reconciliation. One young man when ordered 'by Haile Selassie' to move off said, 'I don't know Haile Selassie.' There must be a large number who feel like this, and would be willing to commit the tribe to war. The other risk is that one tribe should kill us in another's territory in order to involve them with the Government. The *balabat* says this is our only danger, and that the Adoimara would be very pleased to bring trouble on them.

Found when the camels came into camp that Bedi had left one behind in the last camp saddled but not loaded. I could not think why there seemed more than usual on the camels. Stupid, but easier to do than it sounds with twenty camels. Miriam Muhammad is sending men to look for it. Asked me not to send mine as he is afraid they would be 'cut'. Should find it, I think.

If the Asaimara fought the Government, the Government could count on the support of the Adoimara. The Waima, the Debinet, the Issa, the Itu and the Galla from the edge of the mountains. All these tribes would be delighted to help smash the Asaimara, of whom they all stand in fear. When Fitaurari Takla Warat avenged the Greeks at Kurbilli, tribesmen came from as far as Asba Tafari to share in the fighting and lost. (The Waima and Debinet both sub-tribes of the Adoimara.)

A small boy with a toy bow spent much time trying unsuccessfully to shoot small fish in the shallows. Can find no evidence that they have ever used bows and arrows for fighting.

February 13th

Very cloudy in the morning. The Danakil said it was going to rain because the *balabat* had arrived. Miriam Muhammad lays no claim to supernatural powers, such as the Danakil believe he has, and says the rain comes in answer to his prayers. Crowds of Danakil in camp all day. A strange feeling, being watched continuously, and it is very difficult to keep them away.

A *zabania* fired off his rifle while cleaning it after dark, and brought everyone tumbling forth. A hyena round camp.

The Muhammadans held a prayer meeting in Umar's tent. Lightning to the west but no thunder.

Caught numerous catfish. Said got one of eleven and a half pounds. Camp festooned with meat drying, and quantities more milk given us today.

The *zabanias* have had a row. The Shanqalla, a powerful man, bullies the others and threatens them when they resist. Their headman seems quite incapable of dealing with him. Umar settled the trouble and said I should flog him if he caused any more trouble.

Harla and Yusuf had a row the day before yesterday over water. Fined them both two dollars. These Somalis are too fond of threatening to shoot or knife one another.

February 14th

Cloudy in the early morning. Went out at 7 o'clock to look for hippo. Had two shots, but they were too far off. Counted thirty-four showing

at one moment. Saw one of them raise his whole chest out of the
water. Grunted a certain amount. Large numbers of Danakil gathering
grass in the marsh, in water three feet deep. They then take it home
on donkeys or camels. Collected birds round the marsh. Got several
chocolate and white rails. These show a very considerable difference
in size and colouring. Quite a lot of snipe. The blue and rose bee-eater
very common. A water lily with a white flower common. Numerous
ibis and egrets. Harriers plentiful.

Posted a *zabania* in front of my tent to keep the Danakil a few
yards off. Crowds came into camp. The flies are very bad here.

Heard a Danakil playing on a reed instrument in his hut.

Asked about zebra. Was told that these, and what evidently are wild
ass, came down to drink in the evening at the hot spring at Mataka.

I think it must also be true here that crocodiles live but little on
fish. There are such enormous numbers of crocodiles that I think they
would soon clear up the fish if they subsisted on them to any large
extent.

February 15th

Left camp at 8 o'clock and marched for two hours down the Awash.
Bedi and Moulatto arrived just as we left camp which relieved me.
They had a bad time with thirst. Bedi got separated and was nearly
shot when the others first saw him in some bushes.

We are now in Miriam Muhammad's district. The Danakil held a
janili dance. They form up in a circle, clapping their hands to a varying
rhythm, and chanting. The *janili* [a man renowned as a soothsayer],
stands in the centre covering his mouth and eyes with his *shamma*.
Suddenly he starts to speak and the clapping and chanting instantly
stop, to continue again whenever he ceases. He said God had sent me
to their country, and that I had averted great trouble with the Government who, except for my visit, would have come and fought them.
He predicted a raid from the Issa in the near future to avenge the
capture of some women and children by the Asaimara. The Danakil
have absolute faith in him and believe every word he says, so it was
just as well he pronounced a favourable verdict on us. The features

of the Danakil dancing were of every type – some as tall as six foot, but most about five foot nine.

Ali Wali told me that this dance was peculiar to the Asaimara and that the Adoimara have no janilis. I think this is, however, incorrect and the Debinet round Dikil claim to have several janilis. Probably the Adoimara bordering on Bahdu have none.

The men – I always saw about twenty taking part in the dance, though they say many more often compete – form a close circle shoulder to shoulder. They chant and clap their hands periodically ending in a long drone. They are summoning the janili, who is sitting close by, and are not singing anything in particular.

At last the janili joins them, entering the circle and standing on a sheepskin or pile of grass in the centre. He is covered to the eyes with a shamma and leans on a staff. He spits continuously. The clapping and chanting starts again but the janili remains silent wrapped in contemplation. Suddenly he speaks in a high singing voice and the clapping and chanting ceases abruptly, commencing again immediately the janili stops prophesying. The janili seldom says more than a single short sentence, which is immediately chanted back by the surrounding circle. The dancers bend more and more forward, swaying from the knees, while the chanting and clapping gets faster and faster. They straighten up as soon as the janili speaks. Throughout they never move their feet or stamp the time. The Danakil who are watching join and leave the circle continuously.

Sometimes one of the circle asks a question which the janili answers. I never heard a janili prophesy anything which he could not already have known, or which was not too vague to commit him. The Danakil, however, have absolute faith in them. Janilis are consulted before a raid, and the raid is postponed or abandoned if the janili gives an unfavourable verdict. They are also consulted in times of drought and after a circumcision ceremony.

After a successful raid they have another dance. Two or three warriors with feathers in their hair dance and jump about in the centre of the circle.

They also have an enormous feast lasting for several days. This feast is at the expense of those who have not killed on the raid, unless they already have two or more kills to their credit. They smear themselves with ghee and then wipe off the ghee and fat on the clothes of those who have never killed, also smearing cow dung on the bodies and hair of these unfortunates.

Went a short way down the river in the evening. Thickly populated below the camp. A great number of horses in this country and big herds of cattle, but no camels here. The cows have extremely large horns. The river bank, which was steep here, was fringed with bamboo rushes, with paths through them. Shot seven crocodiles with eight shots on the way back which very much impressed the Danakil. This is useful.

Ali Wali says he has heard that the Sultan of Aussa expects me.

Collected birds 131–140.

February 16th

Miriam Muhammad walked out of Umar's tent during the night, and straight over the bank into the river. The bank is about fifteen feet high and the water is deep. Luckily he can swim, and succeeded in attracting attention. Had he been drowned or been taken by a crocodile, we should have been accused of murdering him.

Climbed Mount Ayelu. It took five hours counting a half-hour's wait. Left camp at 5.45 and reached the top at 10.45. Started down at 11.45 and in camp at 3 p.m. Volcanic rock, but covered, except on a few small precipices, with long grass. Extremely difficult walking and steep in places. Some mimosa trees in hollows and good feeding. No sign of water, but there evidently is some in the rains. The Danakil take their cows, goats and horses very near the summit, probably in the rains when they are drawing away from the river. Numerous round stone circles, about three to five yards across. There are some trees on the summit and a rectangular area of stones ten yards by twenty yards. The wall is one to two feet high. This rectangle is on the very summit and approached by a well-marked overgrown path.

There is a pilgrimage every year at the end of the rains to the summit of Mount Ayelu. Women and children can, but rarely do, make the pilgrimage, though there are nearly always some old women who accompany the men. The date of the pilgrimage is known beforehand, and Danakil come from as far as Daoe and Aussa to take part in it. They start in the afternoon, spending the night half-way up the mountain and reaching the top early next morning. This is probably for convenience.

They kill some sheep inside the stone square, burn incense, eat the meat and drink milk and coffee. (There is a spring of water somewhere near the summit which I did not see.) The magician prays but does not sacrifice the sheep.

They pray for good health, prosperity and success in war. They undertake pilgrimages at other seasons to invoke assistance in the case of a drought or of defeat in war.

Saw several single oryx and a herd of eight. Some of these were very near the summit. Saw also three greater kudu cows, and what I am almost certain was a lesser kudu buck in the trees on the summit, though I only got a glimpse of it. Put up a light-coloured nightjar about half-way up the mountain. If a lesser kudu an odd place for it. Abdi collected several birds, including a cuckoo.

Nesbitt says the Danakil do not know how to swim. This is not true. I have several times seen them swim across the river, to cross it, or to fetch a shot crocodile. The *zabanias* can also swim.

From the summit of Mount Ayelu the Asaimara belt of good pasturage along the river showed up very clearly. The river here is sparsely dotted with large shola trees, starting from the pass at Mataka. The rest of the country looks completely waterless and arid. Thinly covered with scrub.

February 17th
Passed through a continuous succession of villages immediately after leaving camp. Big heads of cattle and sheep, and plenty of good horses. Bamboo-grass round camp. A large open plain with one or two big trees. Forest along the river visible in the distance. Grass fires in the

distance. Miriam Muhammad dressed in all his finery to arrive at his village. Larger crowds than ever in camp. Except that they push in everywhere they are well mannered, but Umar has a bad time with the *balabats* who beg unceasingly. I am thankful I cannot talk their language.

At Gawani, a local *balabat* gave us nine sheep and half a dozen skins of milk. A good-looking young chief called Hamdo Ouga visited our camp. He looked about eighteen; he had a ready, friendly smile and considerable charm. His father, a renowned warrior and influential chief, had died and some of the tribe had objected to Hamdo Ouga succeeding him since he had only killed one man.

Hamdo Ouga went down to the Issa territory with some friends. When we met him he had just returned with four trophies; no one any longer questioned his right to be chief. He now sported a wooden comb in his hair, which was dressed with ghee, and five leather thongs hung from the sheath of his dagger. He struck me as the Danakil equivalent of a nice, rather self-conscious Etonian who had just won his school colours for cricket.

The custom of splitting the ear is far from universal, though a large number of these people do it. Several men in camp with ghastly wounds. The *fusil gras* makes an unpleasant mess, but they seem to heal very quickly. One man with his knee shattered. Most of these men, who are older than boys, seem to have killed at least once. Their war chief, an elderly man in filthy clothes but with an amusing face, spent the night in camp as a hostage.

Ali Wali and Ahamado have evidently been quarrelling. Ali and Miriam Muhammad promised me a big dance, Ahamado says the Danakil here probably won't give a dance, and he never promised me one. He also tried to dissuade me from going to Aussa, saying the Adoimara were not to be trusted and would make trouble for me. He had previously said all this at Afdam.

Have taken on Abdi as bird skinner. Replaced him as camelman with an Abyssinian who was with Miriam Muhammad as servant. A good man who knows how to mend saddles. His name is Alamou. Flies bad and a midge which is almost unbearable.

February 18th

Went out in the morning down to the river and shot a solitary hippo with the .450 and a solid bullet. He sank at once to the shot. Heard that a hippo I shot on the 15th has been eaten by the Danakil. I had asked them to let me know when it rose, but they said there was no sign of it. Umar and the Somalis are disgusted with them because they eat dead hippo, and ask how they can call themselves Muhammadans. Shot this hippo at 10.30. Went down there at 4 p.m. Found that the Danakil had pulled it up on the opposite bank and cut it up. It must have taken them an hour to do this, so that it must have risen in about four and a half hours. Had a row with Ali Wali in the evening over this. Told him they could have the meat but I wanted first to see it and take the skin.

Hamdo Ouga gave me seven sheep and a large quantity of milk. He also tried to sell me an old and half-blind pony for fifteen dollars.

A large number of marabouts [storks] and vultures round camp, and saw eight jackals in the morning.

The Danakil have a peculiar method of shaking hands. They touch the palms of each other's hands with a stroking movement, sometimes only using one hand, but more often both. After shaking hands with their chief they raise his hand to their lips. After a Danakil has kissed his chief's hand, the chief in turn raises his man's hand to his lips. They kiss the knee of a great man and the foot of a king. The women stroke the hand to the tips of the fingers with a milking movement. They think that if a man eats meat and drinks milk the same day he will poison himself. They were astonished to see Abdullahi doing so and said he was like a hyena.

No Danakil will mix the milk of two cows, or two goats, or two camels if he can help it. Their favourite drink is curdled milk with some ghee and *berberi* in it. They prefer camel's milk to cow's milk. Occasionally they get a load of durra from Aussa or Afdam, but they live otherwise entirely on meat and milk.

February 19th

Saw a flock of about 150 flamingos. They let me approach quite close and looked very lovely as they rose. Vast flocks of some large sandpiper.

Numerous Egyptian geese, spur-winged plover, and egrets. Very few duck.

A large quantity of milk from Miriam Muhammad. They have asked me to stay here two more days so that Ahamado and Ali can settle everything before accompanying me down to Aussa. They have got a case on at the moment. One of Ahamado's village speared a woman in the dark, and says he thought she was a hyena. An old mad woman in camp laughing incessantly like a hyena. She made sleep difficult.

Deribet shot off the .410 I had given him, by mistake, and nearly killed Demise, who was sleeping next to him. Took it away from him.

February 20th

Violently sick all night – Heaven knows why. Spent the day in camp. Bought a pony for four dollars. Rather a crock, but he may be useful. The Danakil had another oracle dance. Later my Somalis gave a dance. Miriam Muhammad gave me four sheep. No Danakil will give a present of milk today, as it is Monday.

A Danakil was brought into camp for me to cure. His right thigh and leg were one huge suppurating sore. I don't know how he is still alive. Gave him some permanganate of potash. Various other complaints I am asked to cure are piles, retention of the urine, and legs shattered in old fights.

Said Boy has got some trouble in his chest. Birru and Minda [the interpreter] have got violent headaches. I hope it may be a touch of the sun and not fever.

The soldiers say that unless Miriam Muhammad comes to Aussa with us they are going back to Afdam. Lij Farada told me that Miriam Muhammad would come with us to his village, Ahamado and Ali to Aussa. The soldiers are frightened, but I think this is only bluff to try and force me to take the short road to Aussa instead of following the river. I shall order them not to go back 'by Haile Selassie', but don't really mind if they do. Why did they give me another Gabrisgael as their commander? It is strange that my Abyssinians are excellent here, and better than the Somalis, while both lots of soldiers have got jumpy and gone to pieces. Kassimi is an excellent headman.

My pony escaped back to its home in the evening; it is notorious for doing this, perhaps they hope to get my saddle by this means.

The Danakil have no special type of spear. Their spears vary from heads of five inches to broad heads of more than a foot long. Several of them carry round sticks with sharpened points, and I have seen one spear made of oryx horn.

No Danakil, after he has been initiated, is ever seen abroad without his knife.

February 21st
Bought two baby ostriches about nine inches high in the evening. They make a fairly loud trilling noise at frequent intervals.

February 22nd
Left camp at 7.45 and camped on the Awash at 10.45. Passed through open mimosa forest, all evidently under water during the rains to a considerable depth. A fringe of dense forest along the river bank. Impossible to get the camels through this, and so had to camp some way back from the river. Followed a cattle track to the river. It is narrow but deep here and thickly shut in. The river was almost liquid mud, and an endless stream of an aquatic vegetable-looking plant was borne down on it. I think it must have been raining in the hills. We have cut off a considerable bend of the river where it evidently passes through large swamps. Several crocodiles here who paid even less attention than usual to us. We were certain they were dead until they moved.

A very important *balabat* here called Ahamado, who is related by marriage to the Sultan of Aussa. A large fat man with bad features for a Danakil. He was wearing a very fine knife. He was very angry with Miriam Muhammad and Ali for not having warned him of my approach. He has no use for Ali, who, he says, never speaks the truth. Nearly all the Danakil dislike Ali.

Very large herds of cattle here. The usual throng of Danakil in camp. This camp is called Kadabadhu.

The ostriches, who travelled on top of a camel in a dog box, are flourishing. Gave them the run of the camp.

February 23rd

Left camp at 8 a.m. and marched till 10.15. Very hot today. Passed through open mimosa forest for the first hour and a half. Then came to a large open plain, bordered on three sides by forest, and on the fourth by a range of hills running on 180 degrees. Two shallow pools of water in the plain. As the huge herds of cattle and sheep which cover the plain all drink here the water was unspeakably filthy. Though very thirsty, I simply could not drink more than one cup of tea. Camped by some bushes near the hills. The name of the water here is Horagursa, but the general name is still Kadabadhu.

The Danakil in this camp were more than usually penetrating, and insistent in their demands for almost everything. They gave me an oracle dance in the evening by the light of the moon. The *janili* here was a woman. This dance was far the most impressive of those I have seen – probably because it took place at night.

February 24th

Left camp at 8 and camped again at 10 a.m. Marched along the edge of the Asdar chain of hills. These hills are a most extraordinary sight, being streaked with every colour: mauve, orange, brick-red, yellow and white. They are broken by numerous valleys. The western slope is covered with a succession of small villages. These and the numerous defiles are strongly fortified for this country. The villages were all surrounded by stone walls. This is the Asaimara–Adoimara frontier. Saw one large cave in the hillside. Camped by the river on the edge of a large open space surrounded by forest. Not a good camp for defensive purposes and the Danakil with me say this place has a bad reputation. Ali and Miriam Muhammad were overheard discussing the chance of their border villages following us into Adoimara country and then attacking us. Had a long discussion in the evening about the road to Aussa. As far as I can gather, the road follows the river for some eight days. You then have to leave the river and take the Daoe caravan road across the desert to Aussa. To follow the river for more than eight days they all declare to be impossible.

The Adoimara beyond here seem to have suffered badly from drought this year which has made them savage. I gather we shall have a hard time with food for the camels and especially the mules before we reach Aussa.

They say that beyond this point the country by the edge of the river is broken by numerous and impassable ravines. They also say the feeding for the camels is worse along the river than away from it, which sounds improbable. Shall see what it looks like when we get there.

February 25th

Overcast in the morning. Miriam Muhammad left us to go back to his village. He was a nice old man, and the Asaimara have a great respect for him. Ahamado and Ali are coming on with me. Left camp at 7.45 and camped again at 10, as I want to collect birds in the forest by the river. Marched in the open country on the edge of the forest, which is here a narrow belt. Very few places where it is possible to get water from the river for a camp, owing to the thickness of the undergrowth and the steepness of the banks. Marched well closed up. The *zabanias* in the rear blew the trumpet whenever a camel was stopped to be reloaded.

Camped in the open a little way from the river. Good feeding for both mules and camels. Probably the last good feed the mules will get till we arrive at Aussa.

About two hours after we camped, the camelman found a camel was missing. Ali and several Danakil said they would find it, but came back to camp after pottering round for a bit and said it was gone. Left a few rifles in camp and organized the rest into proper search parties. It seemed obvious that the thieves would keep along the forest and cross the river as soon as possible. Bedi and some other camelmen recaptured the camel about two miles upstream. Two Danakil, probably Adoimara, driving it off. They bolted when a long way off, so the camelmen unfortunately did not get a chance of shooting at them.

This is a lawless strip of country and there is no *balabat* here. As far as I can make out, this is where Nesbitt's *syce* Bayenna was murdered. The man who killed him has crossed to this side of the river two days ago, according to Ali. I also hear that Hamdo Ouga was yesterday killed in a fight with the Adoimara just up the river. I was distressed to hear of his death. He had spent a lot of time in our camp and been popular with everyone. They say he was the only Asaimara killed, and that nine Adoimara were killed. They were recovering some cattle which had been raided. It made me realize how precarious were the lives of these Danakil. Yet they were a cheerful, happy people despite the incessant killing, and certainly not affected by the boredom which weighs so heavily today on our own young urban civilization.

Numerous wart-hog along the river, but no sign of any game. Have seen none since we entered Asaimara territory, except on Mount Ayelu. Two ostrich eggs brought into camp, found close by in the hills. Innumerable tota monkeys along the river. They make a good deal of noise.

The Danakil appear never to use any form of trap for catching wild animals. They say that when they hunt they either shoot the animal or try and ride it down on horses with dogs. They kill hippo by spearing them when they land at night, using their ordinary spears. They say a hippo hide is easily pierced while it is still alive. They never fish.

February 26th
A *zabania* went out of camp after dark, was seen moving about among the trees, was surrounded and very nearly shot. Warned everyone yesterday that they must shout out when they leave camp after dark. Have told the men to shoot at anyone round camp after dark. The Danakil will probably try again to steal the camels.

February 27th
Went out in the morning along the river, but was not very successful collecting birds. Saw numerous blue kingfishers and also the miniature kingfishers.

February 28th

Left camp at 7 a.m. and marched till 9.45. For the first two hours at
the foot of the hills. A narrow belt of thick forest along the river, but
considerable open mimosa wood. Good grazing for camels and mules.
Passed several Danakil tombs. Where there are stones these tombs are
built of them, but where there are no stones they are made of tree
trunks, placed together in a pyramid. The stone one was circular, with
an entrance guarded by two piles of stone four feet high. Three solitary
stones in a line from this indicated the number of men killed, and
another stone beside these an elephant. The circle was about six feet
across. In front of the entrance were two rings of stones, with other
stones heaped in them. When this commemoration tomb is erected
there is a feast. The stones in the centre of the circles are heated by
having large fires built over them, and the fire in them removed, and
the meat cooked on the hot stones. The man is not buried here but
where he fell. These monuments along the roads are built to keep his
name alive. Passed several similar monuments in the Arussi country.
There is a great resemblance between the Danakil and the Galla. Both
castrate those they have killed. The Somalis do not, I believe, do this,
except for the Issa, who have probably learnt the habit from the
Danakil.

Dug a well in the dry riverbed to get clean water. Got a plentiful
supply of excellent water at four feet, a great relief after the muddy
Awash water. The Danakil thought us mad, and I gather from Ali that
this place will go down to posterity as the Ferengi well.

Saw no Danakil all day, except for a few who came to camp and a
small party from Daoe. The women came first, the men some way
behind. Nesbitt says this shows that they come in peace. I hear that
the Adoimara have moved their herds into the hills on hearing of my
approach.

We are still driving along a herd of twenty sheep. The men ate so
much meat in the Asaimara country that they want a rest from it. The
baby ostriches flourish. They are indefatigable, and run round gobbling
up everything. Feed them on meat, but they have also swallowed two
bird carcases which had not yet been sexed. They will soon be rather
a problem.

March 1st

Marched from 6.30 to 9.30. The men are very good at getting the camels loaded while it is still dark, so that we can start just after sunrise. Marched through country which was thinly covered with mimosa. There is only a very narrow belt of thick forest here. Low hills from four to five miles from the river. Saw eight aoul, one buck, the rest does, which Umar tried vainly to shoot.

Collected five good specimens of woodpecker. These were among the open mimosa woods. Two of them were males of the small red-crested woodpecker which seems much the least common. Also got a nightjar.

Soon after we got into camp two camels got bogged in the mud at the edge of the river while drinking. It took our combined efforts to get them out.

The ground here is very cracked, which makes camping difficult, and it is not easy to find a place for the camels to sleep. Enough grass for the mules here. Carried water from my well for myself. Saw no Danakil nor any herds all day.

March 2nd

Very hot and a bad glare from the sandy plain. At 8 o'clock I left the camels and followed the course of the river. Very thick forest, and few birds. Saw no game in it, though it is similar to the country at Sade Malka, where there are numerous waterbuck. Caught a glimpse of something which I think was an otter on the edge of the river.

Camp at Dahurtu on a steep bank above the river, which is fordable here. Dug a well on the edge of the river in clay to try and get clean water. The water was clean but salt. The Danakil swim their sheep and goats across the river here to get better pasturage the far side. An extraordinary sight of which I took several photos. The men all had a long bathe.

Had some trouble with the *zabanias* over building a *zariba*. They are inconceivably idle and their headman is pathetically devoid of any control over them. The only thing they do is quarrel among themselves morning, noon and night.

Very little grass here. There has been a drought here and the country is very burnt up, and the Danakil are having difficulties grazing their herds.

It is strange that where the river is overgrown and there are few people about the crocodiles are very wary, even the very small ones of one foot long. They are also few and far between.

March 3rd

Stayed at Dahurtu to give the camels a feed. The *balabat* gave me nine sheep and goats. My herd increases faster than we can eat them.

A long discussion with the local Danakil about the road to Aussa. From here it is four days without water across the desert, impossible for us with so many men, camels and mules, though small parties of Danakil do it. There may be a road with a well half-way from the next camp. None of these Danakil can tell you anything certain about the road, more than one day's march from their homes. I shall not attempt the desert road unless I am quite sure there is water. It will be all right if a Danakil will risk it with us; if not, I shall go by the river, however difficult the road. It is getting hotter every day, and the nights are warm. At Bilen one was glad of a pullover in the early mornings. Now we drip continuously from 10 o'clock in the morning onwards.

Doctored numerous Danakil. Eye medicine is much in demand as quite a number of them have bad eyes, but far the most common disease is a fungus-like growth, suppurating underneath and often very extensive. This disease eats away the flesh, and if the place heals leaves terrible scars. It seems, however, usually to break out again somewhere else. A hand attacked by it was completely deformed. Have seen it in the back, where there are usually deep holes from which the poison oozes, a woman's breast, the arms, hands, legs and feet. Have seen boys of about sixteen attacked by it. Many more people than usual suffering from this disease here. I am giving all my men ten grains of quinine every evening. If they should go down with fever as they did at Afdam, I don't know what we should do. But I think the Asaimara country was the worst place for fever, there were a continuous succession of villages all along the river.

March 4th

Camped by the river. The sheer escarpment of the highlands visible across the river, and seemingly quite close. The summit looks white, probably due to dried grass.

A nice shady camp, but thick bushes all round. However, we made an impenetrable *zariba* all round camp, and fortified it with boxes and sacks round the tents.

Bathed in the afternoon. Delightful and I was cool for the first time. Some sand-grouse came down to drink at sunset. I don't think this is usual. A black-and-white kingfisher here. The river is more open – I have never seen them away from the water.

March 5th

Went out after birds in the morning – got several I had not got before. Shot a greater bustard with the 12-bore at about forty yards. It weighed fifteen and a half pounds. Tried to eat it, but it was incredibly tough. They are numerous here but mostly very wide-awake.

I gather that the desert road from here to Aussa takes five days to the river. Except for one day we shall get to wells each day. They spent the day trying to get hold of the *balabat* from across the river to take me on. Yesterday he refused to come to the camp, but today he said he would join us at tomorrow's wells. The *balabat*, Muhammad Ahamado, is most anxious that his son should not come with us. He is afraid he would be killed on the way back. His other son was killed by the Asaimara and he lives in fear of anything happening to this one. A nice-looking young man with a great reputation as a warrior. They all agree that it is impossible to follow the river. The only alternative road climbs up into the mountains across the river for two days.

I was down by the river after dark and great numbers of sand-grouse came down to drink. They came some time after sunset, when it was too dark to identify them except by their cries. They remained for a considerable time, unlike in the morning when they stop only for a fraction of a second. How long they would have stayed had they not been disturbed, I don't know. Several nightjars flying round over the river.

Collected birds 254–63.

March 6th

Camped by some wells in the Masalo riverbed. This river joins the Awash two hundred yards upstream of our last camp. Very good water. The wells here were fourteen feet deep. In some wells a little lower down the riverbed, however, the water was within three feet of the surface. A plentiful supply which did not dry up, though we used a great deal.

Passed one or two lonely encampments among the sandhills, consisting of a hovel made of camel mats with a small *zariba* for the animals.

The Danakil say there are wild ass here, which come to drink from the troughs after dark. I described zebra, but they said no, they were coloured like tame donkeys, but as large as my pony. Sat over the water hoping to see one, but only saw three aoul and heard numerous sand-grouse come down to drink. They flew off again after staying some time. Two Egyptian vultures also came down to drink.

The *balabat*, Ali Muhammad, from across the river came to camp at sunset. He is dressed in a torn and dirty *shamma* and wears a bad-quality knife. He has a wild look in his eyes, and is said to be slightly mad. He is a very big *balabat* and the Adoimara as far as the Aussa frontier are under him.

A precocious young Danakil of about eight years old came to camp. Delighted Umar by reciting endless passages from the Koran. These Adoimara are far better Muhammadans than the Asaimara. In the latter country Miriam Muhammad was the only Danakil I ever saw pray. Here it is quite a common sight. Very few of these Danakil have ever seen a white person before, yet they never show the least sign of curiosity. It is true that I am burnt so dark a brown that I am not conspicuously white.

March 7th

Left camp at 2.45. The men have become very quick at loading even in the dark. Reached a dry riverbed at 8.30 and camped under some mimosas.

March 8th

Left camp at 5.30 and camped by the wells at Adiala at 8 a.m. Wells about six feet deep where we first struck the riverbed, but at camp there was water running for about twenty-six yards on the surface, under the face of a cliff. Camped among some mimosa bushes. The riverbed is in a wide valley and bordered by gravel cliffs about four feet high. These cliffs are, however, intermittent.

Found an Egyptian vulture's nest in one of the cliffs. The bird was sitting on one egg which was almost ready to hatch. The egg resembled a large buzzard's, but was more heavily marked, especially round the blunt end.

Came across numerous conical stone dwellings. These are about seven feet high, but the floor is hollowed out. Built of stones piled one on top of the other. The entrance is blocked by stones when the owners are away.

The water here was quite clear. The first time we have had clean water since we left the Awash station.

March 9th

Ali told me that it was only two hours to the next water and so we need not start till sunrise. Knowing that he dislikes these early starts I did not believe him, and we started at 3.15. We camped at 8.45 at Adaitu in a rocky riverbed where there were some stinking waters. From 5.30 till 7 a.m. we marched across very rocky ground. At sunrise I got a wonderful view out towards Aussa. Numerous mountains shown up by the sun, which was just lifting above the horizon. The vast distances reminded me of a sunrise at sea. A caravan of about thirty camels carrying salt from Aussa passed us here. Most of the camels seemed absurdly young. They carry the salt in cylinders of matting about two feet long and four inches across, sealed at both ends with salt earth.

A large number of tombs at the foot of this escarpment. One marking the graves of two men who had killed thirty-two and twenty-eight men.

Collected a large number of birds, several not yet collected. The

Danakil say there are a few oryx and an occasional leopard round here, but no wild ass or zebra. Impressed a local Danakil to show us the way to the Awash. His mother, thinking we should murder him, fetched his brother, who worked himself into a frenzy. Luckily my men got hold of his knife before he could do any harm. Everything ended all right. While struggling he blew out, vibrating his lips loudly. This is the noise the Danakil make while fighting.

A great number of baboons here. One of the *zabanias* tried to shoot one. I gave him permission as I was quite sure he would miss.

March 10th
Passed the site of a very extensive village about 6 o'clock. The Danakil build a foundation for their huts, consisting of a single ring of stones. At a distance these look like tombs. Piles of stones, three feet high, with a hole about two feet across in the middle for putting young goats or sheep in.

Also stone shelters for the animals, probably because there are no thorn bushes here. Ali tells me that when a man is married he must stay in the village of his wife's father for one year. A house is built for them at a little distance from the other houses, always in the direction of the rising sun.

An Asaimara man wishing to marry will come with about eight friends to ask the girl's father for his daughter in marriage. They all go out from the father's house. The bride's girlfriends stand about two hundred or three hundred yards off. The bridegroom's friends stand halfway between them and the house. A man specially chosen by the bridegroom then races the bride. She tries to get to her girl friends without being caught by the man racing her, or without being intercepted by the men halfway. The bridegroom takes no part in catching her.

If she gets through to her friends the man must wait a year; if she is caught she is carried to her father's home and thrown roughly on the ground before it.

The husband must live in her father's village for one year. A house is built for them at some little distance from the others towards the rising sun. He may spend odd nights with his other wives. At the end of a year the husband takes her to his village.

A man must marry his father's sister's daughter. If his father has no sister he must marry his father's brother's daughter. Otherwise the nearest relative. If a man is too young to marry his cousin, someone else chosen by the old men of the tribe and probably a member of the family or tribe takes her as a temporary wife. When the future husband is old enough he takes his destined wife and any children by her temporary husband.

The temporary husband, if not of the same tribe, has to pay ten cows for each son and twelve cows for each daughter. But if he is of the same tribe he only pays one cow whether there are children or not.

Ali Wali has a destined wife and grown-up children at Daoe. She is Miriam Muhammad's sister's daughter.

An Asaimara can have ten wives. Not all these need be related to him. If he does not wish to marry his cousins he can give them away to someone else, nor can their parents object. The husband, if not of the same tribe, must pay in cows for them.

If a man is unsuccessful in his efforts to beget a child he may order his wife to cohabit with someone else in order to try and get a child by this means.

If he himself is ugly and he desires to have a good-looking child, he may mate his wife with a good-looking man, even if he is of another tribe.

In theory at least they will not marry women belonging to another tribe and captured in a raid. These are often killed. Women who have come into the district for trade and then settled down are sometimes married by the Asaimara. This, however, is not popular and is usually kept secret.

A man can get rid of his wife if she is a nuisance. She is then probably married by another of the family.

An Adoimara man wishing to marry pays three dollars to the girl's father. The father then tells the man that his daughter is grazing goats in such and such a place, and gives him leave to go and take her. The girl, realizing what is happening, begs her girl friends to come and help her. They collect sticks and stones, and keep a good look out climbing to the top of some hill or ridge. When the future husband comes with a few friends to take his bride, she and her friends defend themselves throwing stones and fighting with sticks. The husband frequently gets seriously hurt, and has even occasionally been killed, they say. He often uses a shield to defend himself.

Having captured his bride he takes her to his house for seven days, after which time he takes her back to her father. The husband is then told by the father to bring a he-camel. This camel must be on heat and bubbling, otherwise the children of the marriage will be weak and useless. Many people assemble saying, 'So and so's daughter has received a camel.' The girl is now brought dressed in her finest clothes. The camel is made to lie down and is tied up. The girl is then tied on the camel's back, and the ropes round the camel's legs are undone. The camel, jumping about in every direction since it is very wild, is led three times round the father's house. The girl, who has been badly shaken, is now taken off the camel, and laid upon one of the best sleeping mats.

Four women take the four corners of the mat and swing it while they sing. She is next taken to a house at a considerable distance from the village always in the direction of the rising sun. She walks there but is supported by two women, and so covered up that no man can see her. Her family bring ten camel loads of water, ten camel loads of ghee and ten of rice. If they are poor they bring less. Then for seven days and seven nights the newly married couple are not allowed out of the house. The young men play outside, smear themselves all over with ghee and finish the camel loads of water, ghee and rice.

After these seven days the husband goes to his own village and the wife takes the house, water carriers, etc to her father's village. After two or three days the husband returns to his wife and may now take her to his own village if he wishes to.

As with the Asaimara, the Adoimara have to marry their father's sister's daughter. If the father has no sister or she has no daughter they marry their father's brother's daughter. If they have no cousins they marry an Issa, an Asaimara or an Adoimara girl in a like state.

An Adoimara (this applies to the Adoimara in French Somaliland and very probably does not apply elsewhere) may only have four wives. Only one of these need be a cousin.

The Adoimara do not temporarily marry the girl to someone else if the boy is too young to marry her himself. The father of the boy in such a case may give permission for the girl to marry another man. He alone can give this permission. Should anyone, even another Adoimara, take her without his permission they fight. If prevented by any reason fighting at the time, they will not forget but will fight as soon as an opportunity arises. The man who took her may, however, pay four camels and keep her, provided she has had a baby. If the girl seduces the man he still has to pay twelve sheep and give her back.

The Adaaimra never mate their wives with someone else to procure a baby if impotent themselves, or to get a beautiful child if they themselves are ugly.

Divorce is extremely simple. All that the husband has to do is to give his wife the camel which she always uses for carrying the household effects, or twelve dollars. This is called mari. *Having got rid of her by this means he is at liberty to marry again.*

Passed a great number of monuments along the road. At 7 o'clock we came on a patch of aromatic grass, growing on a rocky hillside. Picked a good deal. Struck the Awash just before it entered a narrow valley between black hills. These hills covered with grasses, monuments, and large pyramid-like heaps of rock about twelve or fourteen feet high. Ali says that these are very old monuments to famous men. There are a considerable number of them. All these monuments had one or sometimes several heaps of stones in front on which to cook the meat (220 cows killed on death of Miriam Muhammad's predecessor). The Adoimara, but not the Asaimara, erect monuments to the wives of famous men. Built smaller and lower than a man's, in proportion to the number of stones available. A heap of stones also made where a man draws his last breath: *aki*. The grave called *dico*. The monument *das*.

The large cairns of stones are called *waidella*. A double wall of stones, the space between often filled with pebbles, is built up round the corpse which is lain on the ground so as to form a cone. This form of burial is still much used. The same waidella often houses a succession of corpses.

Camped in a delightful spot, where the valley had opened out into a plain. The river has shrunk considerably in size. Trees along the river, and a yellow rush-like grass; but the hills all around black and desolate.

On the hill opposite camp are some stone wells and fortifications. These were built by a very notorious brigand, Fitaurari Miriam, a Wagerat Galla, four years ago according to the Danakil. He then inflicted a severe defeat on the Sultan of Aussa's men, who attacked him here, and afterwards systematically looted the country round. I believe he has since been captured by the Government.

I had a row with the *zabanias* in the evening. On leaving the last three camps they have set fire to all the trees, under pretext of building a large fire to see to load by. They did this again today. I made it an excuse to give them a proper ticking off. Unless I am very careful they will give the Sultan an excuse for being difficult. His country is quite independent of Chercher, and I don't want him asking why Chercher soldiers have been sent into his country to order his people about. I told the *zabanias* I should send them back if they gave me any reason to. They would hate this as they would have a long trek through dangerous country. I then had a long talk with Umar and Ali, and decided to send Ali to the Sultan tomorrow with a letter and my pass to announce my arrival. I shall stay here, just outside the Aussa frontier, until he returns.

They all say the Sultan, like his father before him, is extremely hostile to Europeans. Nesbitt's expedition seems to be the only one he has ever received. They also say that after it he begged the Emperor never to allow any Europeans again to visit his country. I should have liked to have sent Ahamado and kept Ali in camp where he is very useful, but Ahamado's family have a blood feud with the Aussa people.

Left camp 4.15 and marched till 6 a.m. on 50 degrees until we reached the top of the escarpment. Numerous tombs along the road from 7 a.m. till camp. Country rocky and desolate.

BURIAL RITES, MONUMENTS AND TOMBS

When a man dies, his mother, wives and sisters can weep while the corpse is being buried, but the other women may only weep after they have returned home, and the animals have had their throats cut. The number of animals killed depends upon the wealth of the dead man. All the cooking pots used for cooking the meat are put in a line outside the houses.

If the body is interred, the grave is known by the Asaimara as a dico and by the Adoimara as a kabaré. The burial is according to the Muhammadan law, and the grave often, but by no means always, has two upright stones at the head and feet. The graves in Bahdu, Aussa and the intervening Adoimara territory are usually assembled in cemeteries. These cemeteries are almost always close to a large village, though in very scarcely populated country they are close to the road.

The traditional Danakil method of disposing of the dead is to lay the corpse on a low platform of stones, and build a double wall of boulders up round it, gradually closing in to form a large hollow mound. This encircling wall is very often filled in with pebbles and small pieces of rock. At Abakaboro there were a very great number of these waidellas, all of the simple mound type. Some of them were extremely large. They were situated along the roadside and on every hilltop and ridge. Waidellas are placed in as prominent a position as possible. Where the road runs along the foot of a chain of hills, the skyline is broken by these endless cairns, this was particularly the case in the desolate country between Danababor-iso and Tendaho. They will also frequently erect waidellas in the middle of their villages, as I noticed on the mountain slopes above Gallefage Beda.

If a Danakil is killed by another man, his brother will often undertake to avenge him. After having killed a man belonging to the same tribe as his brother's slayer, he goes to the waidella and sets up two upright stones on top of it to show that the man has been avenged.

The Madima of Bahdu have a special burying ground not far from their chief village of Gawani. Here all the men of the tribe are buried in waidellas, except for those who have been killed in battle. Even if the

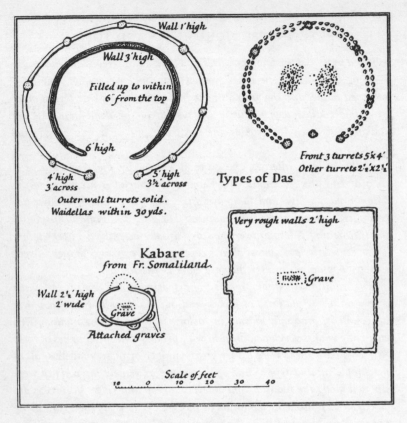

Wall 1' high

Wall 3' high

Filled up to within 6" from the top

6' high

4' high 3' across

5' high 3½ across

Outer wall turrets solid. Waidellas within 30 yds.

Front 3 turrets 5'x 4' Other turrets 2'½ x 2'½

Types of Das

Kabare from Fr. Somaliland.

Wall 2½' high 2' wide

Grave

Attached graves

Very rough walls 2' high

Grave

Scale of feet
10 0 10 20 30 40

body of a man killed in a fight is recovered, it may not be buried here but is placed in a waidella elsewhere. No women or children are buried here, but elsewhere they can be and are buried in waidellas. To be buried in a waidella at Bahdu does not entail any special recognition. It is indeed the normal form of burial.

The same waidella is frequently used again and again. The bones of the last inmate are collected and placed at one side. A whole family may thus be buried in one waidella.

The das is a monument erected by the tribe or family of a dead man to keep his name alive. It is almost invariably situated by the side of an important caravan road, since it is intended that as many people as possible should see it. It is never built till at least one month has elapsed

My camp at the Awash Station where David Haig-Thomas left me on November 28th, 1933.

Members of my expedition; Umar is in the centre with Kassimi on his right.

Leaving the Awash Station for the interior of the Danakil country on December 1st, 1933.

Watering camels at a well on the way to Bilen.

LEFT: Crossing the Awash at Bilen.

ABOVE: The Mataka Pass into Bahdu.

Asaimara warriors at Bahdu wearing killing decorations. Hamdo Ouga is on the left. The thongs hanging from their daggers indicate how many men each of them had killed. Hamdo Ouga himself was killed a few days later.

One of the *janilis* at Bahdu.

My fortified camp in Bahdu.

Asaimara whom I encountered for the first time in Bahdu.

Waidellas in Aussa.

Das with upright stones indicating the number of victims.

Wooden *das* on the Kareyu plain.

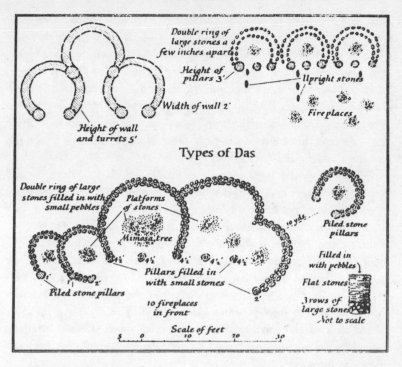

Double ring of large stones a few inches apart

Height of pillars 3'

Upright stones

Width of wall 2'

Fireplaces

Height of wall and turrets 5'

Types of Das

Double ring of large stones filled in with small pebbles

Platforms of stones

Mimosa tree

10 yds.

Piled stone pillars

1'   2'

Piled stone pillars

4½'   4½'   4½'   4½'   4½'

Pillars filled in with small stones

Filled in with pebbles

Flat stones

2'

3 rows of large stones

Not to scale

10 fireplaces in front

Scale of feet

5   0   10   20   30

since the man's death, and more frequently a year. The situation chosen for the das has no relation to where the man died and was buried. If, however, the waidella or dico should happen to be in a suitable place the das is placed nearby. But it is essential, in order that the das should fulfil its object, that it should be in a conspicuous position. A favourite situation is at the opening of a pass through which an important road goes, and in such a place there are often great numbers of das.

The das is almost invariably circular, indeed I never saw a das which was rectangular. There are innumerable different forms and combinations possible, and they vary from a simple ring of stones to an elaborate and carefully constructed stone circle five feet high and fifty feet across, decorated with numerous turrets. The simple form is usually ten to fifteen feet across. The entrance is between two turrets about three feet high, and the circle is most often a double ring of stones filled in with small pebbles and sometimes built up to form a low wall. The crudest form is a ring of large stones with two rough piles to mark the entrance. This is not, however, typical since the Danakil take an infinitude of trouble over their monuments. The walls, which may be as much as three feet wide and four feet high, are built of carefully fitted blocks of stone in order to present a smooth and level surface.

In front of the das there are two or three fire-blackened piles of small stones, circular and level. This is where the animals, killed at the erection of the das, were cooked. It is their invariable habit to kill at least a few animals when they build the monument. A great part of this meat is abandoned to the hyenas. The method of cooking is peculiar. The small stones are piled on top of a heap of wood which is lighted. When the wood is consumed the red hot stones remain and the meat is cooked on them. The Danakil say that meat cooked in this manner is delicious, having no taste of smoke. Before being cooked the meat is cut up and placed on a roughly circular platform of small stones, usually situated inside the das but not invariably. I think Nesbitt mistook this heap of stones for the grave.

Outside the entrance there should be at least one upright stone. This represents the man in whose honour the das has been erected. If there is more than one stone they represent the number of men he has killed. If a stone is flat instead of being upright it denotes an elephant or lion, the only two animals which are commemorated among his kills. These stones denoting kills are almost always placed in a single straight line.

They often build the das round a thorn bush, and will even sometimes plant thorn trees inside the das. If there are two or more trees they frequently connect them by placing a stick across from the branches of one to the other. On this stick and in the trees themselves they often hang pieces of cloth or a sheepskin. They deny that they ever decorate these trees with the trophies taken from the dead, and it is almost inconceivable that the trophy would remain so long intact. Nesbitt believes that they do this, but I think it is mere hearsay.

Very commonly two or more people are commemorated by one das.

*In this case each entrance commemorates a man and has its own line of
stones representing kills. Two brothers or two famous warriors killed in
the same fight are frequently celebrated by one das. But besides this,
numerous das are often joined one onto the other. Then there is a large
centre das with many others constructed more recently attached onto its
outer wall. There are family das. Or there may be two, three, or even
more similar das adjoining in line, frequently with the two outside das
thrown forward.*

*The Danakil do not erect different types of memorials to the dead
according as to whether the dead man was a chief, a hero, or an ordinary
man. The building of the das is in the hands of the family and they can
celebrate even the most insignificant of their members if they so wish.
Naturally, however, chiefs and heroes are usually given an extra-splendid
das.*

*Ali Wali told me that the Asaimara never build a das to commemorate
a woman, but declared that the Adoimara do so in which case the das
is correspondingly smaller and lower.*

*The most striking thing about these das is the enormous trouble which
the Danakil, usually so lazy, will take over building them. They live in
the rudest shelters, but will carry tree trunks and large stones over very
considerable distances to build the monuments to the dead. These monuments too are built with surprising skill, many of the walls being as solidly
and neatly constructed as is possible without the use of any form of
mortar.*

*Where a man draws his last breath a pile of stones is erected with an
upright stone on the top of the pile. This aki would frequently be surrounded by the circle of stones used for supporting the framework of the
house. This I think is the explanation of Nesbitt's third class of memorial
erected to an ordinary man.*

March 11th

Mosquitoes very bad last night. This is a nuisance as we shall probably
be here a week. If I move camp away from the river the men will get
knocked up by the heat, as there is no other shade.

A jackal tried to catch a tota monkey, but it got up a tree just in time chattering wildly.

Ali, Ali Muhammad, and Alamou went off to the Sultan at midday.

Saw a Danakil reed pipe. It is about two feet long and has two holes.

Tomb at foot of pass half a mile from camp. Two *waidellas*, one each side of it about 150 yards away. Ten cooking places in front of tomb about 7 yards away. Four animals recently killed and cooked here, contents of stomach still visible.

The pillars of all these tombs are very neatly built, the stones being fitted so as to present a smooth outer surface.

March 12th

Saw three gazelles which I could not identify among the black rocks on a hillside. At first I thought they were oryx, but the colouring, and the shape of the ears were wrong. Shot the two full-grown ones which I thought were buck and doe, but spared the kid which appeared to be old enough to look after itself. Found that both the ones I shot were does, but with a great difference in their horn length. The larger was in milk. They were climbing up the hill as if they were returning from drinking. A low hill of black volcanic rock with a little grass and an occasional leafless thorn bush. They can evidently inflate their noses, which makes me wonder if they are Speke's, but they seem to vary from the description given in Lydekker's *Game Animals of Africa* and Rowland Ward's [*Records of Big Game*]. If they are Speke's, it is a very considerable extension of their known range, if they are not, they are unknown.

Bought a rather ornate waterskin from a Danakil. They chop up the bark from a mimosa tree and soak it in these skins for a day or two. Afterwards water carried in this skin is said to have a good taste and to be cool. They also use this bark for dyeing the cloth for the women.

Marked these two gazelles: the smaller one 1, the larger 2, on the skull between the horns, and on the skin below the tail. Description of gazelle's skin (doe):

Chestnut-fawn colouring, with a rather darker flank and rump band. Tail black and hairy. Belly and rump white. Legs chestnut-fawn outside, white inside. Ears long but narrow 6 inches, greyish in colour. Horns nearly straight, ridged for about the first 2½ inches, measured 6⅝ inches and 4¾ inches. The larger turned in slightly at the tips, the smaller turned slightly forward and inward. A chestnut band from the horns to the nose, narrowing between the eyes. The eyes bordered by white and this band extends upwards to the base of the horns, and downwards to near the nose. Under this white is a dark chestnut streak from the corner of the eye to the mouth. Below this the colouring is light from almost white under the jaw.

The nose can evidently be inflated. Glands under the eyes. Horns small, in size not much larger than an oribi's.

March 13th

Went out shooting at 6.30. Climbed up into the black hills opposite camp. Black volcanic rock, in places large blocks of several tons piled one on top of the other, a few thorn bushes and dried-up grass in the hollows.

On the way back we descended into the plain, powdered earth with plenty of grass and numerous evergreen bushes and small mimosa. Here we at once saw five gazelles, two bucks, two does and a fawn. I shot one of the bucks. It is very similar to a Speke's, but has, I think, certain marked differences. Skinned it and started for camp. A little further on, however, I saw a solitary buck with a good head. Had a rather long shot at it and hit it too far back. Followed it for three hours but eventually lost it. It went across the plain to some low hills covered with small pebbles. Saw about thirty more of these gazelle; except for two among these hills, they were among the bush on the plain. They were in small herds of five to seven, and there were often as many bucks as does in the herd. Several of the does were accompanied by half-grown fawns. They were not wild and allowed me to pass within a hundred yards and sometimes less, only raising their heads and looking at me.

The swelling on the nose, though considerably more pronounced in the male than in the female, is not as conspicuous as the description of Speke's gazelle led me to expect. The flank and rump band too is scarcely noticeable. Lydekker gives one the impression that it is pronounced. He does not mention the black knee pads. The coat certainly is not thick.

March 14th

The Adoimara here have tried twice to lure Ahamado out of camp. Once they said they had prepared a feast for him in their village, and they next said they had some Asaimara women for him in their village. Nothing will, however, induce him to leave the door of Umar's tent.

They do not seem to have a great number of rifles here. Most of the men you meet carry spears. Several of them wear small Abyssinian swords instead of their *djambias*.

March 15th

The horse-flies are dreadful here, and the mules are literally covered with them. This makes them very restless. Today three of them wandered off a long way and we thought they had been stolen. These flies are brown and flat in appearance. They are almost impossible to kill by squashing. When out walking they cover your legs and arms. They don't bite severely, spending most of their time just glued to you, but they are intensely trying. Set the men to catching them on the mules in the evening and then drowning them in hot water. Afterwards smeared the mules over with tobacco dissolved in ghee.

March 16th

Went out for two hours in the morning into the plain at the back of camp. Saw several small lots of aoul, and three ostriches, a single cock and then two hens. Found the tracks of a single Beisa oryx. The plain is covered with bushes, mostly the ever-green, up to two miles from the river. It then merges into small stony dunes, with grass in the hollows between them. There are several rocky, flat-topped hills rising sheer from the plain. Many of these have village sites on their summits.

Abdi shot another dik-dik, a male. Kept its skull and skin. I was told at lunch time that there was a hot water spring quite close where the wild ass come down to drink in the evenings. But when I got ready to go there the Danakil began to make excuses and to say it was too far. Eventually, after insisting that we should carry water, he agreed to show it to me. Left camp at 1.30. At 2.30 we reached the entrance to a very long valley about two miles wide and bordered by black rocky hills. We saw two wild ass here resting under a small thorn tree on the hillside, and we later saw four more, in pairs. The ground was covered with their tracks. They are evidently common here.

Wild ass (seen through the glasses at two hundred yards): white nose, black upright mane and no forelock. Body uniform grey without any bars. Below the knee, however, the legs are ringed with black on a background of grey. I got the impression that the legs round the fetlocks were tinted with brown, but I was too far off to verify this. Belly and inside of legs white. White rims round eyes. Black tips to ears, and a black, rather bushy tail. The general impression is that of a very sturdy animal.

We also found a great number of oryx tracks, but only saw one, a solitary bull. We reached the hot springs at 4.30. They are called Teho. They are in the valley about half a mile from the hills on the left. There are two small patches of tall rushes but no trees. The water, which is boiling hot, bubbles up from the ground in numerous places within an area of about 250 square yards. Two of the largest of these places, about 12 yards across, are surrounded by a crater of dried mud, 2 feet high. In other places the water is under a coating of bubbling mud; such places, however, are not usually more than a foot across. The water in most of the springs is beautifully clear and often deep. There is a small area of bog which the Danakil said was dangerous. The water from the springs runs away in small channels, but all loses itself almost at once in the ground.

There were about forty aoul at the springs, who showed no fear of us, and allowed us within a few yards. The tracks of wild ass all round, but I did not actually see any at the water. When we arrived some Danakil were driving off their cattle which they had been watering.

While we were out, three Danakil arrived in camp. They were clearly out to collect information. They wandered round and looked at everything and asked Ahamado if we had a machine-gun. They then left camp again though it was close on sunset. They said Ali had taken the wrong road, and would take three days to get to Aussa. They were obviously sent by Muhammad Yaio to look us over. I am glad I have stopped outside the Aussa frontier and sent Ali on to announce our arrival. Had we been in Aussa these men might have had orders to stop us, and this would have been a bad start. I am afraid the Sultan will, however, find a pretext for detaining Ali until these men arrive with their report.

March 18th

Ali, Ali Muhammad and Alamou arrived back today about 3 o'clock. Ali saw the Sultan and seems to have spent the best part of a day with him. He is very suspicious of my reasons for coming to his country, and particularly of my desire to follow the river. He wanted to know why I had not come the direct way from Ayelu. He then told Ali I might come into his country, and he would give me men to show me direct to the French frontier. Ali said I should never agree to go this way and that I was determined to follow the river. He says that the Sultan at last agreed to this, but I expect to hear a lot more about it when we get to Aussa. The Sultan sent me a curt letter of greeting.

On the way back Ali met a party of Danakil, who thought he was from Aussa. They told him that an accursed Ferengi had arrived in their country and was encamped on the river. They said that there were three parties of Danakil hidden and watching his camp from a distance, so that he could not move night or day without their knowing. They had not heard of his hurting anyone yet, but thought he was probably waiting for a favourable moment to raid their lands. He had a machine-gun and many rifles. Ali also told me that he had heard that a large raiding party of Wagerat were one day's march up the river. They had defeated the Danakil, who were escaping with their herds to this side of the river. Got the sick camel into camp. He looks

very seedy and one of his legs is badly swollen. The camelmen think
he will die.

March 19th

We marched across a flat plain of bare sand and powdered earth. In
spite of the day being overcast, the glare was tiring to the eye. This
plain stretches south to a distant chain of mountains, eastwards to
Majenta and Galatu, and westwards to the hills we had left at our last
camp. It then appears to be completely surrounded on three sides by
an unbroken chain of mountains. We marched parallel with the Awash
and about a mile and a half away from it. The fringe of bushes along
its course is the only thing which breaks the monotony of this
plain.

I saw an extremely realistic mirage. A small lake with a few small
trees at its edge, which appeared to be reflected in the water. So realistic
was it that most of the men thought it really was water and looked
forward eagerly to reaching it.

Just before turning north we passed a large empty village. The huts
were built of tree trunks, stacked together to form a cave about eight
feet high. They were cramped inside, and there were large gaps between
the logs. Though these people take much trouble over their monuments and tombs their houses are always very rude. At a little distance
this village looked like a large number of conical wooden *das*. Among
the bushes along the river I saw several shelters of this type.

Soon after leaving camp we passed an elaborate *aki*. It was a carefully
built pillar of stones four feet high and with a diameter of three feet.
Its base consisted of a double tier of large stones. Above this the stones
were smaller and carefully fitted. It was filled up with pebbles, and in
its centre an upright stone of nine inches was embedded.

In the sandy plain we came across three wooden *das* by the road.
They were circular in shape, with a doorway. They were built of large
logs and their height was some three feet. Here, again, considerable
trouble had been taken to make the logs fit as neatly as possible (these
logs must have been brought from a considerable distance). Their
diameter was about thirty-six feet.

We also passed a grave which had fallen in. The depth was five feet and it had been covered over with logs.

We are now in Asaimara country. The district is called Adamba-roweitu.

March 20th

A nice camp by the river with good shade. Marched across a bare earthen plain. Some small rapids by the camp. The first I have seen on the Awash so far.

An important *balabat*, Kenyazmatch Wolissa, came to camp. The Government is intriguing to get him away from the Sultan of Aussa, to whom he has so far paid tribute, and place him under the Elgurash at Dessie. He has just returned from a visit to Dessie. He has no love for the Sultan and is anxious to be placed directly under the Elgurash. He says he is a Kenyazmatch and the Sultan is a Dedjazmatch, and so he is nearly as big a man as the Sultan and does not wish any longer to be under him. I suspect the Government made him a Kenyazmatch with this object in view. The Sultan is naturally far from pleased, as Wolissa controls a large section of these Asaimara. The question is as yet unsettled, but I think that there is little doubt that he will slowly come under the Dessie government. He is a slightly built man, with an intelligent and good-looking face. He gave me an ox in the evening which was useful for feeding the *zabanias*. I had also just shot them an aoul, which came down to drink.

Two *askaris* also arrived from the Sultan, bearing with them the famous silver baton [which gave the bearer the authority of the Sultan]. They told me that if I went to the end of the Awash I could not get from there to Dikil as there was no water for five days. Since I had not mentioned the subject, it is almost certain that they had been instructed to say this. I told them I would talk all this over when I got to Aussa. The best road from Aussa here is through the Galatu Pass. This would mean carrying water for one day. They say the road along the river is difficult and far longer. Ali, however, told the Sultan that I was determined to follow the river. If I now take the short road away from the river, the Sultan will think that I shall be prepared to do the same from Aussa to Dikil if I am pressed a bit. As I am determined to get to the end of the Awash, I don't wish to give him any excuse for being even more difficult than he is sure to be.

Very hot today, and a strong easterly wind. This coming off the plain smothered everything all day in dust. In the evening the wind blew a gale.

The Wagerat raiding party have withdrawn. They seem to have looted what they could lay hands on and then cleared off at once.

March 21st

Left camp at 6.15. Just as we were leaving Kenyazmatch Wolissa said that the road down the river was impassable and that we should have to come back, and that we had better go the Galatu road, etc. They are fond of waiting till the last moment and then contradicting what they have previously said. Last night he said the river road, though longer and more difficult, was practicable. Before we left, Bedi went down to the edge of the river to pray. The river came down and he was all but drowned, being soaked to the skin. I was very nearly caught by the Mullu river in 1930 and know how these rivers come down in a solid wall of water.

Marched all day through country covered extensively with the evergreen bush (Somali name *madid*), and the other evergreen (Somali name *adai*, Arabic *arak*) which is used for cleaning teeth. The arak has a purgative effect on camels. These bushes were just high enough to shut out the view. A strong wind, now from the west, blowing clouds of dust and sand. Crossed the Awash river at 9 o'clock. It was a difficult place, and Ato Shona, who tried it first on his mule, slipped and went right under. I was nervous of wetting the flour, but though we got two loads wet, they were only tents and bedding. The men prayed to Allah for help before trying it. I invoked Sheikh Husain, who saw us through so many difficulties in the Arussi. I thought Ambassa [a camel] would refuse to cross, but the bank was too slippery for him and he slid into the river against his will. From now on, we had continuous trouble with our Danakil guides, who were hot and thirsty and wished to camp. It is strange that the Danakil who live in this country are so very bad at going without water. The Abyssinians are good, better than the Somalis.

After crossing the Sade riverbed we marched parallel to a continuous chain of black and precipitous hills on the opposite bank of the river. In most places they drop sheer into the river. Cut out a clearing among some *doour* trees (Somali name) on the river bank, as this was the only available shade. These trees, which are only found close to the water, are by far the most common vegetation along the river bank. Their colouring is a light bluish-green. The river is hidden here by an almost impenetrable screen of bush. The bank was too sheer to water the camels.

Black and cloudy in the evening. The ill camel gave out in the morning, so I shot him. Two of them have had holes in their backs, and one of them has a bad cold in the head and is running freely from the nose. We are taking every care of them as we shall be done if they give out. I generally use permanganate of potash for their backs, but today I tried carbolic acid. They are rather an anxiety.

Marched from 6.15 to 12.30 on 350 degrees. At 7.45 we crossed a riverbed running west. From 9–9.30 we were crossing the Awash river. At 10.30 crossed the Sade riverbed, just where it joined the Awash. Lost half an hour here. From this point there is a continuous range of black rocky hills dropping sheer down to the Awash on the opposite bank. Marched along the edge of the river all day.

March 22nd

Left camp at 6.45. Cloudy and raining in the distance. Took a photo of Kenyazmatch Wolissa. Marched all day through country of the most imposing desolation. The river, flowing between steep banks and marked only by a fringe of doour trees, is here shut in on both sides by grim hills of tumbled black rock. The summits of these hills are covered with numerous cairnlike *waidellas*. We also passed two cemeteries of *dicos*. Both were close to the road. The first one consisting of about thirty graves had fourteen *das* about twenty-five yards off on the same mound. The second cemetery consisted of some eighty graves. There was a freshly prepared and open grave among them. These *dicos* varied considerably, some were mere mounds of earth surrounded by a ring of stones, while in others the mound of earth was overlain with a coating of small stones built up from the ring of large stones encircling their bases. Only two out of all these graves were topped with the two upright stones. Practically without exception they had one or two small and withered branches placed on them, put there by those who had prayed at them. The open grave was round, about five and a half feet across and four feet deep. Not a grave, I think, but a *mosquidi*.

The mosquidi is a round hole some three feet deep and three feet across, often ringed in with a circle of stones. It is situated close to the grave and at least once a year the family assemble round this mosquidi *to pray for the dead. They then kill some sheep or goats.*

I only saw two mosquidis *during all the time I was in the Danakil country.*

Camped at a place called Gerateaditu among some mimosa and doour trees which gave us some welcome shade. This place was like an oasis in a desert. The only patch of green in the surrounding desolation. There were even some arak bushes for the camels and a little grass. The camels will eat the doour when hungry, but don't care for it. The river bank was everywhere a thirty-foot drop, but a dry water-course gave us an approach of sorts, and we watered the camels and mules in the bath. A chain of men passed up the buckets while they sang the song of the camel. The Somalis always sing this when watering the camels, chanting the refrain in turns.

March 23rd
Left camp at 6 o'clock and camped again on the Awash at quarter past twelve.

All the hills round here are strongly fortified on their summits with well-built stone walls in some cases double. These fortifications are extremely ably constructed. They are not restricted to the north side of the river, though they are more numerous here. Ras Imru, who was related to Ras Mikael of Wollo, smashed the power of the Wagerat and of all the surrounding Danakil chiefs, except for the Sultan of Aussa. He then compelled them to build these fortifications. He lived on terms of friendship with the grandfather of the present Sultan. When this Sultan died his ten sons fought among themselves for the succession. Yaio at last obtained it. Soon afterwards he fought Ras Imru, inflicting heavy casualties on him. One of his brothers, however, betrayed him, and he was lured up to Dessie. Ras Mikael seized him and imprisoned him at Jimma for twelve years, without consulting the central Government with which he was on bad terms. The central government at last released him and reinstated him in Aussa, which it gave in perpetuity to him and his sons.

While in the rocky country we passed endless *waidellas*. These are most often placed on the skyline.

We then entered a vast plain of sand and powdered earth, with occasional patches of grass and a few thorn bushes. It is almost dead level and extends out of sight to the north. The Majenta range stands up across the river to the south, and there are the vague outline of some mountains to the eastward. Blowing sand and heat haze make it impossible to see far across this plain. Continuous mirages. Luckily the sky was overcast or the heat would have been intense.

The river here runs between high banks. It is fringed by a thick belt of doour trees. An attractive camp among these trees.

Passed the two *das* by the road. These are the first I have seen of this type. There was a *waidella* within thirty yards.

Country rocky and desolate, all surrounding hills strongly fortified. The name of this place is Tendaho. From here the river bends eastward.

We entered a vast plain extending as far as the eye could see to the north. At 11.00 we passed the end of a ridge of black rock, extending indefinitely on 280 degrees. It was covered with innumerable *waidellas*. Camped on the river.

March 24th

Left camp at 5.45 and camped at Kahurta at 8.15. I had intended to do a long march today so as to arrive at Furzi tomorrow. The *balabat* here, however, had received orders from the Sultan for us to camp here, and then to take us to Gallefage tomorrow, where we are to remain till we hear further from him. They say Gallefage is about two hours march from here. They also said that the Sultan intends to visit me there, no doubt in order to try and keep me away from Furzi, and that he will come to Gallefage tomorrow, which I am sure he won't do. They say he is a very hard man and the two men he sent me are very much afraid of him. They told Ali today that if they failed to make me camp at Kahurta they would be flogged unmercifully. Ali, too, won't be seen alone with me for an instant and won't now give me any information about the country.

This delay is a nuisance as the *zabanias* are out of food and have been for five days. I wanted to push on to Furzi and buy them some durra. I am afraid we may be detained at Gallefage for several days with one excuse and another. Today I gave each *zabania* a cup of flour, but I don't want to have to do this again. They have been working like beavers for me the last few days.

To the north there is a vast sandy desert. There is some forest along the river, and the bushes became increasingly thicker as we moved down-stream.

Camped among some tall mimosas on the river's bank. A nice camp with a good pool for bathing. Excellent feeding for the camels. Three wart-hog came down to drink on the opposite bank while we were pitching camp.

I told the bearer of the silver baton that I required some meat for the *zabanias* and my men. In the evening he produced an ox and three goats. No Danakil in Aussa may refuse anything which the man who carries this stick demands. To do so would result in his being punished with a ruinous fine.

March 25th

Left camp at 6 o'clock and arrived at Gallefage at eleven. It was considerably further than they had led me to expect. There was a thick forest of mimosa along the river. We mostly skirted the edge of this, marching along the edge of the sandy desert, which, in places, was more or less covered with thorn and *madid* bushes. There was no undergrowth in the mimosa forest, the trees of which were often of a considerable size. Under these trees the grass was high and yellow contrasting with the green of the mimosa. Mount Kulzikuma dominated the landscape. The smoke of a large grass fire hid the range behind it as with a curtain of white cloud.

This is I think the pleasantest camp we have had so far. Its only snag is that both ticks and fleas swarm in the grass. We are camped among doour trees on the river's bank. I have cut a clearing through them so as to give me a window overlooking the river from my tent. Through it I can watch the totas romping by the water. They are very intrigued by my tent and come and peer into it whenever I am still. The grass here is delightfully green and fresh. Today seemed to be the hottest day we have had to face. I stopped the men bathing as the crocodiles are said to be bad here, taking many animals and occasional people. I shot three in the evening.

There is another kingfisher here, light blue and black with an orange and white breast, which is common. It is very noisy, keeping up a fairly continuous chattering. I have seen it quite a long way from the river among the mimosa trees.

Sent one of the Sultan's men, Ali, to Furzi to announce our arrival here. Belito, the other one, I do not trust and am sure he will make difficulties for us if he can. I therefore found an excuse for keeping him with us and sending Ali. Everything will probably depend upon the report which this man gives of us – I told Ali Wali to have a long talk with him before he left.

After much talk two stringy goats were produced in the evening.

Behind Kulzikuma, which is a large mountain, there was a long range of mountains. This however was almost entirely hidden by the smoke from a large fire somewhere behind Kulzikuma.

March 26th
The Muhammadans' *Eid*. The Danakil from round about and some *negadis* who are camped here, asked Umar to conduct the prayer meeting. This pleased him enormously. All my Somalis turned out in their best clothes.

A considerable number of shots were fired off. The Danakil here don't seem to mind wasting their cartridges.

Afterwards the Danakil played '*gaso*'. They use a ball made of rolled cloth about the size of a tennis ball. This is bounced in the crowd and every man then tries to get hold of it, and to escape sufficiently far from the others to bounce it and catch it on the back of his hand. While chasing a man they make a loud trilling sound. The collaring is rough, but everyone takes it in good part. They played in two games. The boys' game played on the outside of the clearing and took care never to get in the way of the men's game. When a man has successfully bounced the ball he jumps in the air and slaps his thighs loudly.

The women danced. They formed up in two rows facing each other and about two yards apart. The dancing was monotonous, and consisted of jumping up and down together while they clapped their hands and chanted. Periodically they stopped dancing and clapping, just chanting back the words of the leader of the song. A certain number of these women wore coloured cloths. They wear the *shash* before they are married.

The black shash *which the women wear round their hair is a sign that they are married. In Aussa, however, I noticed many small children wearing it.*

A man who returns home to find another man with his wife binds him round the neck with the black shash *belonging to his wife and leads him before the* balabat *and old men. The offender is then fined from three to fifty cows or camels according to the position which the husband occupies in the tribe.*

If, however, the man refuses to go before the balabat *they fight with knives, and the death of either party starts a blood feud between the two families or tribes. If the man belongs to an enemy tribe he is killed at once.*

An Adoimara husband will ask the man whom he has caught with his wife: 'Do you know me?' If the man answers 'No' he knifes him, but if he says 'Yes' he ties him round the neck with his wife's shash *(only worn by married women among the Adoimara) and leads him before the old men of the tribe. The man is then fined twelve sheep and three dollars, and the husband keeps the child, and no one says anything. If the guilty man is an Asaimara he pays the same, twelve sheep and three dollars, but if the man is an Issa he only pays one goat. This is in conformity with the Issa custom. It was arranged between the Adoimara and Issa chiefs that in this case the Issa custom should prevail.*

Some grumbling from the *zabanias* as they got no rations today, having quantities of meat. I did this regularly at Bahdu. They say the ox was very bad meat, which is untrue. None of them can see further than today.

Ali returned from the Sultan. The Sultan sent him straight back and did not even allow him to go to his home though it is *Eid*. He is sending a Kenyazmatch and a Balambaras to me tomorrow with presents. The importance of these men looks as if he does not intend to see me himself and is sending them instead. But he must see me if I go to Furzi, so he evidently does not intend me to do this. They will probably have orders to give me every assistance to go direct to Dikil, but to stop me going any further down the river; or to take me straight to the end of the river across the desert if I insist on going there. If I follow the Awash I shall pass through the very heart of Aussa, which is what he has never yet allowed any European to do.

Whatever happens, the fact that the Government are not responsible for my safety must not leak out, since this would strengthen his hand enormously. Martin, with incredible stupidity, mentioned this fact in Miriam Muhammad's and Ahamado's letters, thus greatly increasing our danger. I had begged him to conceal this fact from the Danakil. Luckily they took the letters to Umar to read, and he suppressed this and persuaded them to entrust the letters to his keeping. They won't get them back. Some of the soldiers and a few of my men know that I am here on my own responsibility. They mentioned it to Umar, but he has, I think, frightened them into silence by telling them that the Danakil will murder us at once if they get to know this.

March 27th

A famous player came to camp in the morning. The display was extremely dull if you could not understand Danakil. They squatted in a semi-circle in front of me and he recited my praises. The other Danakil then clapped their hands and he danced for a short while, stamping to and fro and singing.

Went out after crocodiles in the evening accompanied by a party of boys. I shot five. One of them a very large one. He was in a deep pool, and had eaten many people and animals when they came down to water. There was absolutely no sign of him when we tied a kid up to the bank, but after the kid had bleated for a short while, the head of the crocodile appeared swimming towards it. I then shot it. The kid was so tied that it was not easily visible, but the crocodile can scarcely have heard it bleating while under water, and I saw it as soon as it broke surface. The death of this crocodile delighted the Danakil. I got back to camp just as the sun set. Very shortly afterwards Kenyazmatch Yaio and some thirty Danakil arrived. The Kenyazmatch was on a mule, and three bulls and some six sheep were driven before him by some of his men. The others marched behind him spread out in two lines. Their *shammas* and loin-cloths were spotlessly white and they all carried rifles. They formed an extremely striking and unexpected sight.

The *zabanias* did well and turned out at once to form a guard of honour. I gave the Kenyazmatch some tea and we then inspected the bulls and sheep, which were a present from the Sultan. He and his men went off to the village for the night. He said he would take me down towards Furzi tomorrow, but that it would be best to start in the afternoon, so that the men could see about their food in the morning.

I gave all my men and the *zabanias* some soap so that they may smarten themselves up.

Large numbers of hyenas howled and chuckled round camp during the night.

It is quite a common practice among both the Asaimara and Adoimara to file their front teeth into points.

The Danakil frequently stand resting the sole of one foot inside the knee of the other. They wear the loin-cloth extremely short.

The Danakil always try to call up a crocodile, but I have never seen an instance where I could be sure that the crocodile had come in answer to them. The call is a single rapidly repeated note from the back of the throat. They use their cupped hands to make it.

March 28th

The men washed their clothes, and cooked the meat in the morning. Had a long talk with the Kenyazmatch and was favourably impressed. They know of everything I have done since I first entered the Danakil country, but I seem to have got a good name, and I think the Sultan is going to be friendly. The fact that we are being taken down towards Furzi is in itself a good sign. I am told that Kenyazmatch Yaio is the next man in Aussa after the Sultan. He says that the Issa are making trouble near the French frontier. They killed a German engineer [Beitz] sent down there by the Government, some ten days ago, as far as I can make it out. Though the Danakil sense of time is very vague.

Left camp at 1 o'clock. While we were loading the smoke from a grass fire near by shrouded everything in a yellow pall. This and the thunder of a storm over Kulzikuma created a very eerie effect.

March 29th

Camped at 8.30 at Gurumudli in a bend of the river under some tall mimosa. Thick jungle all round, and the clearings covered with a bean-like clover with a heavy smell. Wonderful feeding for the camels and mules. The country across the river is open grassland, with numerous houses and large herds of cattle.

A shooting match with the Kenyazmatch after lunch. Used my rifle. Shot at the lid of a one-pound tin of tea at two hundred yards. He hit it once, but I failed to do so. Abdi, however, in a contest with one of his men, retrieved our reputation and hit it.

We were told in the afternoon that the Sultan was on his way to visit me. Prepared the camp to receive him, and formed up the *zabanias*

and my men as a guard of honour. Just before sunset we were informed
that he had too many men with him and that he had stopped close
by and was waiting to receive me. Took all my men, except for two
left to guard camp, dressed in their best clothes and carrying every
rifle and started off, preceded at some little distance by the *zabanias*.
There were large numbers of Danakil in the bush on both sides of the
track, and a constant stream of runners arriving and departing.

After some little time we arrived at a large clearing. Here some four
hundred picked Danakil were formed up in two long lines on both
sides of the Sultan. They wore clean white loin-cloths and *shammas*,
and all carried rifles with full belts of cartridges. They also wore as a
matter of course the curved Danakil knife strapped across the front
of their stomachs. The Sultan was dressed entirely in white, wearing
Abyssinian trousers and shirt, with a finely woven *shamma* over all.
He wore an old silver-mounted Danakil knife, probably his father's,
and carried a black silver-topped stick. He was bare-headed. He was
seated on a chair, and directly behind him was grouped a band of
slaves carrying rifles in red silk covers.

The whole formed a most impressive sight in the rapidly fading
light, surrounded on all sides as they were by the thick and silent
jungle.

The Sultan rose to greet me, but as I had brought a chair with me
we were able to sit. He then dismissed all his men except for his
interpreter, and I did the same, keeping Umar with me. The Sultan
looked round him repeatedly to see that no one approached, two or
three times waving away groups of Danakil already at some distance.
The Kenyazmatch alone was allowed near us. It was moonlight by this
time, but as the moon was full the light was good, showing up the
ranks of squatting Danakil and the solitary little group formed by my
men. I gave the Sultan an account of my travels so far, explained to
him where I wished to go, and gave him my reasons. I said that we
had all in England heard of his kindness to Nesbitt. He then told me
that he had received him at this very spot, and wished to know how
they had fared. I asked his permission to send a man to the market
to buy some durra for the soldiers, whereupon he insisted on giving
it to me.

The Sultan is known by the Danakil title of *Amoita*.

He became increasingly easier to talk to, and we arranged to meet here again tomorrow morning. He intends to spend the night here. He is extraordinarily like the Emperor in appearance. He is small in stature, but well proportioned, with small and delicately shaped hands and feet. His face, which is bearded, is oval and rather dark. His mobile features are sensitive and proud, and give a striking impression of breeding and of power.

As I looked round the clearing at the ranks of squatting warriors and the small isolated group of my own men, I knew that this moonlight meeting in unknown Africa with a savage potentate who hated Europeans was the realization of my boyhood dreams. I had come here in search of adventure: the mapping, the collecting of animals and birds were all incidental. The knowledge that somewhere in this neighbourhood three previous expeditions had been exterminated, that we were far beyond any hope of assistance, that even our whereabouts were unknown, I found wholly satisfying.

On my way back to camp I was shown his present to me. Twelve large skins of milk and two of ghee. I was escorted back by the Kenyazmatch and a large body of Danakil.

The Kenyazmatch told Umar that three Bahdu Asaimara came to Aussa less than a week ago. They made friends with an old Danakil and lived for three days in his house. He was a poor man but feasted them to the best of his ability. They then said one evening that they must return and bade their host an affectionate goodbye. That night they returned and knowing well where he slept murdered him, his baby daughter, and his companion. They were followed up and caught during the next day. They are at this moment in the Sultan's prison awaiting punishment.

I heard of this prison at Afdam and at Bahdu. If what one hears is true, it must be one of the most ghastly places on earth. The Kenyazmatch said that these Danakil will not be executed but will be kept in prison till they die.

March 30th

Sent Umar in the morning to make arrangements for my meeting
with the Sultan. He took the lunch tent, chairs and a carpet up there.
I went there myself at 9 o'clock. The Sultan was sitting in the shade
of some trees awaiting me. I escorted him over to the lunch tent,
which was pitched in the centre of the clearing, and there we had
coffee, tea and biscuits. The Kenyazmatch refused to sit and he and
the interpreter screened us on the open side of the tent with the
Kenyazmatch's *shamma*. The Sultan's retainers were formed up on
three sides of a square and some fifty yards off. As yesterday, no one
was allowed to approach us. The Sultan wished to know almost at
once if I was here to work on the Ethiopian-French boundary. This
seems to have been what the German engineer was doing when the
Issa killed him. I said that I was here to collect birds, and that this
frontier had no interest for the English. He then asked to know in
detail where I wished to go. I said that I had arranged with the French
Government to enter their colony to the north of Lake Abhe in the
area of Afamhu Mergada, and that I hoped he could tell me how was
the best way to get there from the end of the river. He said that the
French frontier was a long way off. He had heard of Afamhu, but did
not know Lake Abhe or Mergada. The Kenyazmatch went off to try
and collect some information, but failed to find out anything about
these places.

The Sultan then said he would enquire properly about the road
and make the necessary arrangements.

I then asked his advice about the *zabanias*. I said that I was anxious
not to take Abyssinian soldiers into French territory. I was afraid that
they would have difficulty in getting back to Aussa from the French
frontier, and I suggested leaving them here if he would give me fifteen
men to take their place as far as the frontier. He said that he would
think it over. I suspect he does not wish to assume the responsibility,
especially since we shall be entering the Issa country. He next asked
me to leave Ali Wali and Ahamado at Aussa since they could be of
no further use to me. As Ali is most useful for collecting information
I gave no definite answer to this. I said that the Chercher government
had ordered them to accompany me as far as the French frontier,

and I was afraid they would be punished if they left me before.

I then produced the sack of coffee I had brought from Afdam and four pots of sweet jelly. I said that I was ashamed to give him so small a present after all his kindness to me, but that it was difficult when one was on trek and so far from one's country. The coffee, I was glad to see, was too heavy for one man to carry. I tasted each of the pots of jelly and one got upset in the process. The Sultan said that this was a sign of good luck. Up till then he had contented himself with just sipping the coffee, but he now drank two cups and almost finished the biscuits. When we had finished the Kenyazmatch and interpreter and Umar drank up the tea.

The Sultan then said good-bye and moved off a little distance surrounded by his men. I returned to camp, where I found four bulls which the Sultan had said he was going to give me, and which had previously been driven past for me to see. I doctored a Shanqalla slave whom the Sultan had asked me to cure. He had been bitten some time ago in the finger by a snake and his hand was swollen and suppurating. This slave had previously belonged to Lij Yasu and accompanied him in his wanderings in the Danakil country after Ras Mikael's defeat at Ankobar.

I have two other regular patients suffering from the usual complaint which is eating away the flesh of their feet. I also had a man brought to me in the last stages of consumption, a living skeleton with his large burning eyes. There is little enough one can do for most of these people. Usually I have to give them something useless but harmless. I hate doing this, however, since they have such faith in you.

They say that a little lower down the river and especially where it disappears, the country is alive with snakes. Poor Umar is terrified of them and says that he will never dare go to sleep. Strangely enough, they don't give me the creeps as a large spider will do.

The river rose considerably today, and was even dirtier than usual. I cannot tell from the colour which kettle has tea and which has water in it.

In the afternoon the Kenyazmatch asked Umar, Ato Shona, and Basha Falega to come and see him. The Sultan was with him. He and all his men were sitting by the road in the bushes. They don't mean any of us to see his house nor even to know in which direction it is. Actually I believe it to be some little way down stream. The river divides somewhere here and I think it is between the two branches. They tried to get confirmation of what I had said last night and this morning, particularly as to whether I was interested in the frontier.

The Sultan also wished to see Ali Wali and Ahamado. I was told they would come back to camp tomorrow morning. Poor Ahamado is far from happy, as the Danakil have a blood feud here, with his family.

The Kenyazmatch is to come to camp tomorrow. For tonight we have a Balambaras with us. There is a large body of Danakil camped a hundred yards away from us on the river.

Collected birds 490–99.

March 31st

A camel with a bad head is very sick. He refuses to eat and is getting weaker and weaker. Poured some flour and water down his throat.

Two large sacks of maize arrived from the Sultan. I gave one to the *zabanias*. I must try and buy another three sacks.

Said Boy caught a catfish of thirteen pounds, and he pulled out another of twelve pounds, bitten nearly in half by a crocodile.

April 1st

The jungle here is impenetrably thick, between the river and a ridge of black rock half a mile from the river and parallel with it. Found the fresh tracks of a leopard. The Danakil say they abound here, which seems likely. Four large skins of milk arrived on a camel from the Sultan. My Somalis and then all the Abyssinians danced after dinner. The Abyssinians did the wedding dance, the Somalis the *anaharron* war dance. The Danakil encored them repeatedly. They don't seem to have any good dances of their own.

April 2nd

Left camp at 7.30. Marched back upstream [from Gurumudli] to get behind the ridge running parallel with the river. Some standing water here. This ground is evidently under water in the rains. We then marched across a sandy and rock strewn waste to the foot of the mountain mass adjoining Kulzikuma and bordering the lake. We reached here at 9.30, but now wasted one and a half hours getting the camels over a shoulder of these mountains. Huge tumbled slabs of black rock with a very ill-defined track winding in and out of them. One camel gave in and we had to unload it and carry its sacks.

The lake is some two miles long and one and a half miles across. The skeletons of dead trees standing in the water along its edge, while further out there are numerous small islands of bushes rising out apparently from the very water. Numbers of darters, herons and egrets sitting on these bushes. Saw and heard a few hippo in this lake. The southern edge of the lake is marshy. It is shut in on the west and south by dense forest through which the Awash flows. The river does not enter the lake. There is another and considerably smaller lake, one and a half miles to the east of this lake. The two lakes are separated by a spur of the mountains which runs down to the Awash. The Awash skirts these two lakes here at a distance of not more than a quarter of a mile.

The space between the lakes is very thickly covered with *waidellas*, nearly all of the chimney type. There are literally hundreds. There is also a small cemetery of *dicos* here. Passed several cemeteries of *dicos* before this along the edge of the lake and by the standing water at our last camp. Probably near water because the ground is softer. Many of the *waidellas* had one or sometimes two upright stones on the top of the chimney. The stones used in the construction of these *waidellas* were often extremely large.

Strolled round the edge of the larger lake in the evening. There are too many herds of cattle and goats here for there to be any game, except for leopards, which the Danakil say are extremely common. There are impenetrable thickets along the river which would afford them secure retreats. Saw some crocodiles, two wart-hog and numerous totas.

Took a goat and sat up for a leopard. The moon was full on the 31st. The first goat would not make a sound when left to itself, so we returned and got another one from camp. This one bleated intermittently. We sat under some rocks close to some thick bush, and on the edge of a cattle track, where we tied up the goat. Only saw a hyena. This suddenly came with a rush down the track and went straight for the goat. I scared it away with a handful of gravel. It returned almost at once and stood for about five minutes looking at the goat from ten yards off. It looked very white in the moonlight as it stood there turning its head from side to side. It then took fright and melted away. I hoped it was a leopard that had scared it. The mosquitoes were very bad and made it intensely difficult to keep still.

April 3rd

Climbed on to one of the summits behind the smaller lake in the morning. From here I could overlook the whole of Aussa, which I am afraid the Kenyazmatch, who accompanied me, did not appreciate.

We are only just camped inside Aussa proper. A comparatively narrow strip of forest extends up the river. The larger of the two lakes guards the entrance to Aussa, so to speak. North of the lake the view is enclosed on either side by two ranges of mountains, but below this the mountains fall back and the river slows into the extensive plain of Aussa. This plain is nearly square in shape and is rimmed round by barren and precipitous mountain chains. The river flows along the northern edge of Aussa, in whose north-eastern corner there are several small lakes surrounded by a lava field, it then turns south and flows into an extremely long but narrow lake at the foot of Mount Goumarri. Mount Goumarri is celebrated in the Danakil songs as the great and powerful mountain which compels the Awash river to stop. This lake extends to the south-east corner of Aussa. It then bends sharply westwards and extends at the foot of the mountains along a great part of the southern side of the plain. There is a break in the encircling mountains at this point, but the country appears to be a waste of barren desert. The greater part of the river's course is hidden in dense forest. Away from the river there are numerous and often extensive clearings, and much of the south and particularly south-east section of Aussa appears to be open plain. This is possibly where the durra is cultivated. It was too far off to see even through the glasses. Otherwise I noticed only a small area which might be growing durra, mostly round the Sultan's abode at Furzi. Furzi lies about three miles south-west of the first lake. There are no large villages. Furzi seems to consist of two or three large houses enclosed by a compound. There were innumerable herds of cattle and sheep grazing in the clearings and more open forest.

The Kenyazmatch says that during the rains Aussa is almost entirely under water. The two lakes at my feet and those on the north-east corner are left by the receding water. The Danakil then retire with their herds into the surrounding mountains. Even now large numbers of them are living on these mountain slopes. While climbing up here I passed several small inhabited villages, and the sites of innumerable others. They were situated wherever there was any clearing among these tumbled rocks. There is no shade and the heat thrown off these black rocks must be intense. There were some beehive shelters made of mats over heaped sticks, but the greater part of these dwellings were built of pieces of rock, being circular in shape.

The main road through Aussa is probably along the other bank of the Awash, through Furzi, and then across to the end of the largest lake. It would have been impossible for us to have followed the course of the Awash to here by any other road. The forest between Furzi and this larger of the two lakes is almost certainly impenetrable. Below this point, however, I think we shall have to cross the river to avoid a series of spurs running down from the mountains. From here it looks as if there is a way through the forest, which is broken by numerous clearings.

I tried hard to send one of my men to the market to buy three sacks of durra, some salt, and to try and get eggs and sugar. The Kenyazmatch, however, opposed it so strongly and said that his men would get us all that I required, that I did not insist. Ali and Belito have been recalled by the Sultan. They have taken the silver baton with them.

April 4th

Passed the Kenyazmatch village which had nothing to distinguish it from any other. It was situated on a shelf in the mountains. Large numbers of *waidellas* all round here. I wonder whether they originated this way of burying the dead on account of the impossibility of digging a grave in the greater part of this country.

After crossing the Awash we entered dense forest interspersed with large clearings of ten-foot high grass. Camped in the only clearing by the river. If we left this, they told me, we should have to march for a considerable time before we could camp again. I don't wish to tire the camels. The *balabat* brought me three goats, and ten large skins and four woven grass pots of milk. They had put *berberi* and ghee in the milk. This is a great luxury. There was so much milk that the men could not finish it. Went out for a couple of hours with the Kenyazmatch in the evening. I lent him the .450. He fired two shots with it, but it kicked him too heavily, so I gave him the .318. We each got a wart-hog. These abound here. Most of the time we were on hands and knees following the pig runs. This is the only possible way to get through the jungle. He showed me how you can get a pig to come to you by clucking your tongue in the back of your throat.

A Danakil brought back the silver baton, and it is now carried by one or other of the Kenyazmatch's attendants.

I have been collecting all the information I can about the road from here to the French frontier. The Kenyazmatch assures me that the Dikil road is extremely hard, being very mountainous with no food for the camels and almost no water. He thinks it would be impossible for my camels in their weakened state to get through. What information Ali Wali has collected confirms this. They say that the Tajura road is less mountainous with a sufficiency of water and of food for the camels.

April 5th

Left camp at 7.15 camping again at 11 a.m. Marched through more open country past several villages and large herds of cattle. These all have the same type of horns. They rise up from the skull in a sweeping half moon, bending backwards and inwards at the tips. The prevailing colour is black, but both red and white are common. Like all these cattle they are humped. I have not seen any horses in Aussa, though I have seen some mules and donkeys. In Badhu the horses were most commonly white in colour.

Crossed a shallow creek at 7.45 which seemed to run on 130 degrees. At 9.15 we crossed a lava-field, which in places was thrust up to form considerable ridges. The river flowed between two of these volcanic hills which, nearly three hundred feet high, are extremely precipitous. There were some reed beds here contrasting vividly with the black of the surrounding lava. There was a thin belt of trees along the river.

Camp was under a few mimosa on the river's bank and surrounded by a dusty expanse of beaten earth sprinkled with *kimbo* bushes. The river here flows between dense beds of tall rushes with feathery tops. From my tent I could just see the top of the Goumarri escarpment over these rushes. There is a large village here situated on the mountain side and the *balabat* is a man of considerable importance. He was a close friend of the present Sultan's father, and this Sultan has implicit trust in him. He brought me two oxen, three extremely fat sheep, three goats and nine bags of milk with *berberi* and ghee in it.

The Kenyazmatch gave Umar and the soldiers each a skin of ghee. A large grass fire down towards the lake. The sun blood red as it set.

Overlooked the bird skins. The Somalis gave the Kenyazmatch a dance after dinner, and put up a very good show. The clouds of dust which they raised rather added to the effect, making the scene shadowy and unreal.

As I was going to bed I killed two tarantulas in my tent. Beastly things. A considerable difference in size, the largest being four inches across.

I have discussed the question of our road to the coast at great length. Danakil do use the Dikil road, but they go in small parties with fresh and lightly loaded camels, and even then they say it is difficult to get there. They say that I should never get my camels there, and that if my camels fail there is no water.

My camels gave us a considerable amount of trouble on the shoulder of a hill on the second. The Danakil say that the best of the road we should meet is as bad as this, and that there is a mountain to cross between here and the French frontier where the road is practically impossible for any camel. Most of my camels have been trekking since early November and are now in a very weak condition. There is, they say, no food for a camel on the Dikil road, and the lack of water would make it impossible to rest them even for half a day. Between Dikil and Jibuti the road is passable, but bad, and there is but little feeding. This I know to be true.

The Tajura road is the one almost invariably used by the Danakil to get from Aussa to the coast. The Assab road is difficult for water. They assure me that there is sufficient water on the Tajura road, and that it is possible to rest and feed the camels on the way. The country is inhabited, while between here and Dikil is mostly uninhabited.

The Kenyazmatch says that they are responsible for me and that if I take the Dikil road I shall probably die. He cannot understand why I should hesitate between a good and a bad road. I cannot see what motive they could have in saying all this unless it is true.

Time makes it impossible for me to return to Afdam or the Awash station and in any case, it would be too far for my camels.

If there was any real object to be gained I should attempt the Dikil road, but it seems idiotic to jeopardise everything when I have obtained my aim for what I suspect is red tape on the part of the Governor. All the French in Jibuti, particularly the Government officials, believe in a terrifying Danakil bogey. If the Danakil do scupper us I shall have acted on my own responsibility in opposition to their instructions, and they cannot be held responsible. I shall think this over carefully, but it involves forty-five lives besides my own and I must follow the safest road.

A Danakil boy stole one of the bird knives. The Kenyazmatch ordered four men to take him by each arm and leg and to pull him slowly apart to make him confess where he had hidden it. He confessed almost at once. This will probably stop anyone else stealing. Though this was the first thing we have had taken in Aussa.

The Kenyazmatch has recently got a consignment of stuff through for the Elgurash at Dessie. I asked him how he got it here from Dikil if the road was impossible. He said that he had fresh camels and a great number of spare ones, and that he had arranged to be met half-way with fresh camels, and water. He said that having just been on this road, he could speak with authority about it.

If I go to Tajura I think I must take the *zabanias* with me. I don't know what the reaction of the Jibuti Government will be to this unauthorized intrusion of eighteen Abyssinian soldiers into their colony. They cannot get to Dikil if I cannot. I had intended to send them back on the railway from there. I don't think they would ever get back to Afdam by themselves. If the Danakil don't touch them they will I think certainly fight and murder each other and the Danakil would then mop up the remainder. At the moment they are split up into three parties and ready to come to blows, and Ato Shona, through fear of what they will do to him, has left them and sleeps with Umar. I can keep order while they are with me, but Basha Falega admits he cannot control a single one of them. Glad as I should be to be rid of them, I cannot abandon them now that they have served my purpose. The Abyssinian Government will think I have taken them with me to ensure my safety in French territory now that I am going by an unauthorized road. They can easily find out the truth from them when they return. For my part I should have no hesitation in going to Tajura without them.

April 6th

Left camp at 6.45, camping again at 10.45. Crossed the Awash river an hour after leaving camp by a deep ford. Two camels fell and swamped their loads, but no flour got wet.

We marched down the river along a grassy plain between the river and the Goumarri precipices. A succession of villages among the rocks at the foot of the mountain. An albino Danakil living here. I saw his brother who was perfectly normal. The albino was rather pinkish-white like an unsunburnt European. In the distance he certainly looked exactly like an old and dirty European gone native. My men were convinced for a long time that he was a white man, probably a Greek, living with the Danakil. They none of them seemed to have heard of an albino. He was bald, but his eyebrows and eyelashes were white.

He kept his eyes so screwed up that I could not see their colour. He later came into camp. He seemed to be on perfectly normal terms with the other Danakil.

The *balabat* here gave me fifteen skins of milk and sixty pieces of durra bread. Danakil hospitality is lavish.

The Goumarri escarpment is a series of terrific precipices. The whole of this face appears to be absolutely sheer, an unbroken wall of rock from top to bottom. In the evening with the light on it, it is extraordinarily impressive. The Awash river, after thrusting its way through endless descent to here, gives up the unequal contest at its foot.

Doctored a great number of Danakil, several children with abscesses in their ears. I am also treating the Kenyazmatch for a cough, which is a proof of confidence on his part.

I have decided to take the Tajura road after getting down to the end of the river. I shall write to Barton giving him my reasons. The Sultan is sending letters to the Government of Jibuti, the French headman at Dikil, and the Abyssinian consul at Jibuti.

April 7th

Left camp at 7.15, carrying some wood, intending to march down the lake. At 8.15 we arrived at the place where the Awash river runs into the lake. Marched through tall reeds. The lake here is bordered by an expanse of soft mud. Numerous waders, herons, and ibis, also a few Egyptian geese. The Danakil insisted that it was impossible to take the camels any further so I marched them back to close to yesterday's camp, but found a rather better place for feeding them. I am sorry I loaded them, but I hoped to be able to get some distance down the lake. Tomorrow I shall take three men, the mules, and some food and push as far as possible down the other shore of the lake. Overlooked the birds.

Marched 7.15–8.15, returning 8.30–9.15. Three sacks of durra for me and one for the Danakil who are to accompany me, arrived from the Sultan. He returned the twenty dollars I sent to buy them with. This durra is about half chaff. Given six skins of milk.

April 8th

Took Kassimi, Said Boy, and Abdullahi with me with Desita. Fitaurari, Tinnish and the cook's mule. Abdullahi made a useful pair of saddle-bags last night out of sacks. Carried my bed and mosquito netting, some dried fruit, raisins, rice, sugar, coffee and tea. The Kenyazmatch, Yusuf and another Danakil came with me and brought the silver baton. The Kenyazmatch and Yusuf rode mules. At 6.40 we reached the foot of the Goumarri escarpment and turned down the lake. The going was too bad to ride. We followed the water's edge except when forced up onto the mountainside. Except for a few bushes and a little green growing in places at its feet, the mountainside is devoid of any vegetation. Buttresses of black and reddish rock seamed by water-courses, where the lighter coloured sub-soil shows through the crust of volcanic rock.

We killed a seven-foot python which we found asleep under a bush. There were the remains of a great number of catfish, partly eaten, along the edge of the lake and often at some distance up the mountainside. I wonder what killed them. There are also quantities of small white snail-like shells all along the shore.

The rocks between the low and high watermark are thickly encrusted with a white coral-like growth. The highest watermark is eighteen inches above the present level of the lake. This would, I think, be sufficient to flood the greater part of Aussa.

There are hippo tracks everywhere and I heard them grunting far out in the lake but saw none. In every direction there were crocodiles lying on the top of the water. Several of them must have been ten feet long.

The northern and western sides of the lake are low and thickly fringed with reeds, and there are patches of aquatic grass at some distance from the shore. I could see several flocks of large white birds, probably pelicans, on the water near the western shore. Herons, some very large, egrets, ibis, the chocolate and white rail and sandpipers common. Several pairs of Egyptian geese, but nowhere did I see any duck. There were one or two pairs of fish-eagles yelping over the lake. The southern side of the lake is indented by several bays, separated by spurs running down from the mountain mass. Camped in the first of these. Here the mountains stand back a little from the lake and there are a number of mimosa and some tall grass. There is a village here, and several herds of goats and cattle were grazing on the green grass near the water. Found a tree which gave some good shade.

This lake is called Adobada (the White Water).

April 9th

Explored the southern shore of the lake in the morning. Left camp at 6.30, reached the summit of the range in the south-west corner at 10 a.m. Started back at 11.15 and arrived in camp at 1.30.

The Kenyazmatch and Yusuf made every effort to stop me climbing the last hill, assuring me that there was nothing beyond it. When I offered to climb it alone with Abdullahi they said that the Danakil here are dangerous and that they must come. The Awash, after flowing into Lakes V and VI, disappears in an extensive swamp. A second branch of the Awash, probably leaving the main stream north of Furzi, since I had heard that Furzi was situated on an island, loses itself in this swamp without entering any of the lakes. There is a break in the mountain chain south of Lake VI, but through the glasses the country appeared to be arid desert. From the hill behind Lake II, I took this swamp to be cultivated land. There was a large village in the flat below our feet. The pass over the hills here is surrounded by a great number of *waidellas*.

The Kenyazmatch shouted down to a man in the village below us to bring us up some water. This was most welcome. We then had several very long shots at the crocodiles in the lake. They would all submerge at each shot. Those close to the edge stirring up the mud and leaving a dark stain on the water. On the way here we shot and landed two which measured nine feet long with a girth of forty-two inches, and eight feet six inches with a girth of thirty-eight inches. They did not appear to be exceptionally large. Some of those I have seen in this lake must be ten feet long. Both were males. The Kenyazmatch cut off their sexual organs, which are retracted. He assured me that with the Arabs on the coast it has a commercial value. It is probably attributed with aphrodisiacal properties like shark skin.

We had another drink on the way back. The Danakil here dig shallow wells close to the water and then build a roofed shelter of stones round them. The water is clean and cold. The woven grass jars give it a smoky taste. I also had a very good bathe while Abdullahi bombarded the surrounding water with rocks to keep the crocodiles off. The Danakil assure me that they will seize a man if given a chance. Certainly the way they sneak close up to watch you when you stand near the water's edge looks as if they were contemplating an assault.

A small naked herd boy in camp, probably seven years old, who was circumcised. This is very exceptional. Usually performed at the initiation ceremony when the boy is fifteen years old. They are then careful to keep themselves covered. The strict observance of these customs is no doubt relaxed in these outlying villages. Women never remove their clothes, even when wading across the deepest stream.

Among the Asaimara boys are circumcised when fifteen years old. Before circumcision they may not wear a dagger, except in play, or go raiding.

There is a special day for the ceremony, usually at the end of the rains, but sometimes at the beginning, and the operation is performed on all boys of a suitable age. They are allowed no food in the morning. All the ponies are saddled, and the warriors and old men collect at a given spot on a main road. The operator is any famous warrior, and he circumcises the boys at some little distance from the crowd. After the operation each boy endeavours to call out the names of cows, camels, sheep or goats. Some succeed in naming as many as twenty or thirty, while others overcome by the pain fail to call out any names. The boy is later given the number he has named. He is then given a root to eat to give him clearness of brain. No medicine is put on the wound, though it is wrapped round with a piece of cotton. As soon as they have all been done they mount their ponies, wearing their knives and carrying shields, and go hunting. They must kill something, even if it is only a rat or a young bird, though they naturally try to kill a gazelle or a pig or something large. They do not blood their knife, killing the animal indiscriminately with rifle, spear, knife, or stick.

They eat no food till the evening, when everyone brings cows, sheep and ghee and there is an enormous feast. The janilis give a dance and the girls sing the praises of the young men and recite what they have killed during the day.

The boys wear a bead necklace until the wound has healed.

The Adoimara observe a strange form of segregation where circumcision is concerned; this is neither a tribal nor even a family matter, but purely the concern of the parents of the child. This is the division of the Adoimara into those who will and those who will not marry an Issa woman. Those who will never marry an Issa woman are circumcised at birth (common at Dikil). Those who will marry an Issa woman are circumcised between seven and ten years old. In both cases the family assemble and dance and play.

There is no special day for the circumcision of the ten-year-olds. Until the wound is healed he is fed on the very best food. He wears a bead necklace for seven days. After this he may go on a raid, and they say there are several instances of boys of nine having killed a man. This second group is common at Tajura.

Girls are circumcised either before marriage or more generally on reaching the age of puberty. The wound is sewn up with long mimosa thorns bound round both ends with cotton. She has her knees bound together and remains like this for a month or more. After having a baby she is sewn up again, and has her knees bound together until she has had three children. She is sewn up again each time.

April 10th

I put a scorpion, luckily a small one, on with my trousers after a dip before starting, and got rather severely stung.

There is a plague of bluebottles in camp. I have given up lunch since the sight of them on my food makes me sick and it is impossible to keep them off.

Umar has stitched the rubber soles back on to my shoes. They have worn wonderfully. In the Arussi I got them wringing wet most days. Except that the uskhide soles have come loose, they are still as good as new. Crêpe rubber is very good.

I told the Kenyazmatch that I intended to push down the other side of the lake to explore the marsh and verify that the river really ended there. Until I do this I shall not be satisfied, especially since Umar has gathered that the river continues down to the edge of the Issa country, and ends in some salt lakes. The swamp could easily be formed by the smaller branch of the Awash.

It was impossible to continue from yesterday's camp, since I was short of food, and it is a long way. I think the best road is on the other side of the swamp. It would be difficult to get the mules further along this side of the lake and Lake V is shut in on this side by a precipitous escarpment.

The Kenyazmatch was very angry and upset and declared that I had seen everything. He said he had some stuff to take up to the Elgurash, for which he was sending repeated requests. He sent off a man to the Sultan for instructions. He says that the Danakil round here are getting out of hand because of my prolonged stay, and grumble that he is mad to show their country to the Ferengi. They expected me to leave tomorrow and they might make trouble if I went off again in yet another direction. I told him I had run risks to get here, that I was now within reach of the end of the river, which was my objective, and that I intended to get there. Ali Wali is most anxious for me to leave tomorrow. The Danakil from whom he got this information was very reluctant to speak, saying that if they found out they would shave his head with a blunt knife.

April 11th

Collected birds with Abdi round the edge of the lake. The Kenyazmatch insisted on accompanying me, and carried the silver baton with him.

Spent the remainder of the morning doctoring Danakil. One of them severely cut about in a fight. They had stitched up the worst cut in his hand and put an effective bamboo splint on it, a long upright with two cross-pieces. They also brought me a man who seems to have gone suddenly mad. He won't speak and allows himself to be led anywhere by the hand, remaining where he is left. He can hear and will do anything he is told, but seems to have lost the power of initiative. He stares unwinkingly at you. I gave him some castor oil.

Another man, a mere skeleton, was brought in a stretcher. He was yellow in colour and seemed absolutely devoid of any flesh, merely dried skin and bone. His testicles were enormously swollen, being the size of a football. They said they had been like this for years and wanted me to operate. I refused to as I said it would almost certainly kill him. I suspect there is something else wrong with him. In Addis Ababa a man whose testicles are twice the size of his head sits by the Makonnen bridge. Otherwise he seems quite healthy. The Shanqalla picked a quarrel with one of the Kenyazmatch's men and was nearly knifed. It was entirely the Shanqalla's fault, and I was going to tie him up by the hands for the night, only the Kenyazmatch asked me to pardon him. The Kenyazmatch has recovered his equanimity. I have the very greatest respect and liking for him, and am sorry to put him in this position. The Sultan is sending his interpreter.

They tell me that some years when it is unusually dry, Lakes I, II, III, V and I think VI, dry up completely, and Lake IV is divided into two – the Awash river disappearing in Gallefage near Gurumudli. The Danakil then come from all round to water their herds in Lake IV. This has never been known to dry up. They also dig wells in the dry riverbed.

April 12th

Collected birds round the lake in the morning. Shot two pythons which were lying together in some thick rushes close to the water. The only one I brought ashore measured nine feet three inches. They have two small horns close to the vent, probably rudimentary legs.

Gerazmatch Talahun, the Sultan's adviser and interpreter, and Balambaras Ahamado arrived in camp about midday. Talahun was the old Sultan's trusted adviser. He strikes me as being plausible but I don't think I trust him. They brought me a letter from the Sultan. This said that he was replacing the Kenyazmatch, who had to go to Dessie, with Talahun and Ahamado. It was a very busy time of the year for him, and I must either take the Tajura road as arranged, leaving at once, or follow the river with my camels and then go on to Dikil. It was impossible for him to allow me to remain here encamped while I explored down the river in order afterwards to take the Tajura road.

I then said that I intended to go to the very end of the river, whatever the risk, since this was what I had come to do. They said I could only do so if I took my camels and then left by the Dikil road, and asked for a letter when I left Aussa, saying I had done so in safety. Very well, I would go by the Dikil road and give them a letter saying that I had been most hospitably received and had left the Sultan's territory in safety; but I should be obliged to add that they had compelled me to leave by a road which they had previously said would prove fatal to me. If the Sultan would allow me to remain encamped here I would follow any road however bad, to get to the end of the river with a couple of mules. It was not my object to explore Aussa in different directions, but simply to get to the very end of the river. After having done so I would leave their country at once.

They then said that I had agreed to take the Tajura road if I saw the end of the Awash, and that they had made all the necessary arrangements for me to go by this road. The Awash ended when it flowed into this lake, but they had even shown me the end of the lake. The other lakes I had seen were standing waters left over from the rains. Thus having seen the end of the Awash I should do as I had said and go off at once to Tajura.

I replied that I had seen the Awash flow out from the big lake again. I had always said, even when I sent Ali Wali to the Sultan, that I must go to the end of the river. If it ended near by I must verify this, while if it flowed down to the Issa country I must follow it there. I had said in the first place that I believed that the river ended on the Issa border (Lij Farada told me that the river ended in the Chercher section of Danakil). It was they who had assured me that it ended at the foot of Goumarri, and believing myself to be at the end of the Awash, and my object accomplished, I had agreed to take the safer Tajura road.

Then having drunk four pots of tea and eaten my last box of biscuits they adjourned to talk it over. They came back at 7 o'clock, and told me that since I was in great need to see the end of the river they would show it to me. It was, however, a very long way off, much too far to get there and back with mules, so that I must take my camels. The Awash ended within one long day's march of Dikil, so that it was useless to come back here to go to Tajura. The road from the end of the river to Dikil was passable. It was the first part down the Awash which had made them say the road was impossible. The water at the end of the Awash being salt made it difficult about water. There was no road down the Awash, since no Danakil ever went there, and the country was intensely mountainous. The river ended in a no man's land of the Issa Asaimara and Adoimara, and was consequently dangerous.

I thanked them for saying they would show me the end of the river. I offered again to take sufficient men with me for safety, and to go there on foot, despite the distance. If I took my camels and they gave out we should be stranded. They then said it was too far. They would be with me, and consequently in the same boat, and they would arrange with the local *balabat* for camels to carry water and help mine over the more difficult places. The road is the same I followed on the 8th and 9th.

I said I would start tomorrow morning. The Kenyazmatch then said goodbye. He assured me, however, that he will meet me again at the end of the lake. I think he is going to make some arrangements about camels.

I called the men and told them that we start tomorrow for Dikil and have got a difficult time in front of us.

The Danakil have lit all the reeds opposite camp on the far side of the river. A most impressive sight, as the fire is not a hundred yards off. I hope the sparks won't start a fire on this side.

April 13th

Left camp at 7 o'clock and camped at 10 at the promontory. This is really an island uncovered by the low water. Collected three herons and a larger darter. Tried hard to get a specimen of the herons which live in the trees and bushes on this promontory, but they were too wild. A nice camp on a stretch of green grass between the precipice and the rocky end of the promontory. A few *waidellas* among these rocks. A small village on the mountainside here and they brought me three skins of milk. There was a small spring of wonderful water here. It bubbles up absolutely clear in a small basin of ground. This water leaves a lingering sweet taste in the mouth. We have not had clean water like this since we were in the Arussi, and it is an enormous treat. I would sacrifice any other comfort for good water. The water of this lake is unexpectedly dirty. The Danakil dig wells at the edge of the lake to clean and cool it. It blew a gale towards sunset, and the camp was very exposed and my tent facing the wrong way. Piled boxes in front to try and keep the wind out.

April 14th

Blew hard till the early morning when the wind dropped. Left camp at 6.45 and camped at 11.15 in the same place as on the 8th. We had some difficulty getting the camels along this road. Nagadras Haile Miriam was the first camel in camp. He is everyone's favourite.

April 15th

Left camp at 6.30 and camped again in 'Crocodile Bay', opposite the island. Took a circuitous road inland as it was quite impossible to get the camels along the lakeside. The Kenyazmatch was waiting for us. The Sultan is sending twelve of his *askaris* with us to Dikil.

We had a long discussion about the road. I told them that I wish to see Lake VI close and must spend a few days at Abhebad. The Dikil road, they say, does not go near either of these lakes. They went off to discuss it, and talked without a break till sunset. The Kenyazmatch showed himself extremely quick at grasping a map I drew on the table filling in Abhebad. The Awash after leaving Lake VI seems to cross back round the far side of Gera Mountain to Abhebad, which appears to be south of Lake V. They finally suggested that we should leave here tomorrow afternoon, march halfway to Lake V, getting there early next day. That the camels should then go direct across to Abhebad, and that I should follow the river round with the mules. There are some springs of fresh water round Abhebad. Tomorrow we shall overlook it all from camp and settle it then.

There was a storm with lightning and thunder over Kulzikuma at 4 o'clock. We got a few big drops. Went across into the next bay and shot a few crocodiles with the Kenyazmatch just before sunset. Tarantulas as usual.

Darling Mother

I am now within reach of the end of the river and hope to get down there shortly. I thought it ended in a big lake by which I am now encamped. The Danakil assured me that it did not flow out again. I explored this lake however and found the exit, and they now admit that it goes down into the Issa country through three more lakes, two of which I have overlooked from a mountain here. It will probably take me some little time to get there. I don't want to spoil everything now that I have come so far by skimping the end. I cannot, I think, expect to get to Jibuti till towards the end of May. I will then catch the first boat home and be in England in early June. I will wire you at once from Jibuti.

I have written to Sir Sidney and asked him to wire you now.

I have had a completely wonderful time and no trouble of any sort. The Danakil have received me most hospitably, and since I left Afdam I have been given two hundred sheep and thirty oxen besides hundreds of skins of milk. My men in consequence have had more than enough to eat. They have been splendid and will go anywhere and do anything. We have been lucky and had almost no fever, and I have kept very fit.

It is exciting to think that I have penetrated into a country where no white man has been allowed before. Nesbitt never got down into Aussa and all other expeditions have been turned back at its frontier. It is an extraordinary oasis shut in all round by sheer precipices of black rock. The Awash flows round it on three sides seeking an exit and at last finds a crack in this wall of rock, and flows down into the Issa desert where it ends in a vast lake.

Coming here we passed through a veritable land of death. Black volcanic rock tumbled and piled in every direction and not a sign of life or vegetation except on the very river's edge. If my photos come out I shall have some good ones. Then suddenly the mountains open out and you find yourself on the edge of Aussa. This is roughly square in shape and the whole plain is wonderfully luxuriant. Half of it is dense forest with clearings where they graze their flocks and cultivate some durra; the other half is extensive swamp. There are five lakes varying from five to eighteen miles in length.

I met the Sultan twice, in itself rather a feat, after nearly three weeks wasted in preliminary negotiations. We had a moonlight meeting in a big clearing surrounded by the silent forest. He had some forty of his picked troops lined up round him, and I and my small band felt rather overwhelmed as we advanced towards him. He was very friendly when once he had got over his preliminary suspicion and we met here again the next morning and had a long talk.

They want one to see as little of Aussa as possible and ever since it has been a constant battle of wits. I have however succeeded in following the river's course as far as this and they have now agreed to show me the real end. He has given me the silver baton, without which it is impossible to move a step, and thirteen *askaris* to add to our forces in the Issa country. From the end of the river to the French post of Dikil is only two days march.

I cannot hope to describe anything in a letter and am reluctant to spoil what I have to tell you by a bad description. I have kept an extremely full diary. I long to see you again and to tell you all about it. It has been wonderful, in very truth a dream come true.

There is one horror here and that is the tarantulas, large, hairy and four inches across. They scuttle round camp as soon as the sun sets. Last night we killed twelve in camp. In my dreams they assume the most nightmarish proportions.

There are also great numbers of pythons round the lake and we usually kill two or three when out after birds. The largest was thirteen feet long. Crocodiles abound.

I have collected some six hundred birds, and have I think got a new species of Speke's gazelle. Previously it was only believed to exist in the Haud in Somaliland. It stretches all across this country at a much lower altitude. I have also mapped Aussa.

The Sultan has agreed to get this letter down to Dikil for me.

Darling Mother, I think of you endlessly and would give anything to get a letter from you. I do pray you are all well and

happy. What fun we will have when I get back and it is not long
now. I shall wire the boat from Jibuti so that you will know
when I shall arrive. Do bring my brown suit up to London with
you as I have no tidy suit with me. I long desperately to see you
and the others again and shall be filled with impatience all the
way back on the boat. God bless you and keep you safe and
happy.

Your loving son,
Wilfred

April 16th

There was another storm round us during the night. Both my ther-
mometers are broken, but the following were the aneroid readings at
11.45 a.m.: A41 = 2100; Ax = 1130.

Collected some good birds. Started to load at 12.15, left camp at 2.15
and camped again on the summit of the mountain behind us at 5 p.m.

Climbed incessantly and had a wonderful view from camp. There
is no vegetation on these hills, except for an occasional leafless thorn
which merely increases the sense of barren desolation. The ground is
everywhere covered with a layer of volcanic boulders, black with a
reddish tinge, and generally of a size which you can just lift. In some
places, particularly along the ridges, however, rocks of a considerable
size are tumbled together. The going was bad for the camels. We
camped on a rock-strewn plateau and had hard work clearing a space
for the camels to lie. A storm over Abhebad so I put up my tent.

Below us, far nearer than I had expected, set in a limitless waste of
volcanic rock, lay a great expanse of water, sombre under threatening
storm clouds. That was where the Awash ended. I had come far and
risked much to see this desolate scene, a striking contrast to the
marshes, pastures and forests of Aussa.

April 17th

Left at 6 a.m. and camped at 9.45 on Lake V. Very bad going, rocky
and several steep descents. Had some difficulty getting the camels

down the escarpment to lake, which is very sheer and runs on 320 degrees. Then crossed over to the other bay and camped. This is much the most attractive of the lakes I have seen so far. The water is clean, and the lake, unlike the others, looks blue. The rocks run out into the lake, and are white from constant submersions during the rains. Numbers of darters and herons sitting on them. The white of these rocks contrasts with the black of the surrounding lava: there are several small reed-beds of a vivid green, the largest by camp where a spring runs into the lake. A good place for birds.

The Kenyazmatch and Talahun suggested carrying water and marching again in the evening. I then told them that I was going to stay here four days to rest the camels and to give me time to go and look at Lake VI.

It also seemed most convenient to stay here a few days in order to explore Lake VI. I had told them that I intended to see this Lake from close. They went off grumbling. I think they have sent a man off to the Sultan.

In the evening I strolled a short way round the lake. The Kenyazmatch came with me. He never bears malice when we disagree. He shot at and stunned a small crocodile, about two and a half feet long. I took it into camp and put it in the bath for the night. None of the men will touch it. They stand round at a respectful distance and scatter when it moves its head.

These clean blue depths were not to be resisted and we both had a bathe after bombarding the surrounding water with stones. It was well out of our depths. But as far as I was concerned, the thought of crocodiles rather spoilt it.

April 18th

Three *balabats* have arrived from the Sultan, and thirteen *askaris* and a headman. The Kenyazmatch and Talahun are to return, and these *balabats* will take me down to Dikil. These *balabats* are: Essa, who controls the country between Abhebad and the French frontier at Gobad and claims control over Dikil. (This Dikil dispute is of long standing and I think the French are too firmly entrenched ever to be ousted. These Danakil hate the French very bitterly.) Sheikh Husain, who is *balabat* of the country round Abhebad, and Badhoul Ahamado, who controls the country round Lake VI and behind Giaru Mountain. The Kenyazmatch ordered them to accompany me to the French frontier and to show me what I wish to see. I have agreed not to cross to the far side of Abhebad, which is Issa country and not under the Sultan. The Kenyazmatch has asked me to be careful here, as the Aussa Asaimara, the Badhu Asaimara, the Adoimara and Issa all border on Abhebad. They say there is a big Issa chief called Adi Fara Matal across the lake who pays tribute to neither the Abyssinians nor French. He also admitted that the Aussa Asaimara here are savage and difficult to control. He said that they hate white people and asked me to be tolerant of them. But I shall be safe with the silver baton.

I arranged to go down to Lake VI early tomorrow morning, with Kassimi, Said Boy and Abdullahi, and Badhoul Ahamado, with as many Danakil *askaris* as he thinks necessary. I shall take food for three days and go at least as far as the exit of the Awash from the lake, probably camping and exploring round from there.

April 19th

The Kenyazmatch, Talahun, and Yusuf went back to Furzi as soon as it began to get light. I was intensely sorry to say goodbye to the Kenyazmatch as I like him enormously. Despite our frequent clashes we parted friends. I think I have won his confidence and that he knows I wish his country no harm. I gave him the Lebel rifle and twenty-one cartridges, a spare mosquito net, which I knew he wanted, and several pots of jam. I gave Talahun twenty dollars and several pounds of coffee, and Yusuf five dollars and some coffee.

We marched for two hours down the lake and then for three-quarters of an hour down the Awash. There was no road, and we had to pick our way as well as possible across an extensive lava field, which has flowed down from a succession of craters along the face of Giaru. This lava was seamed and cracked in every direction, and we several times had difficulty in getting the mules round long fissures thirty feet deep. We passed one village built of rocks and endless *waidellas*. As

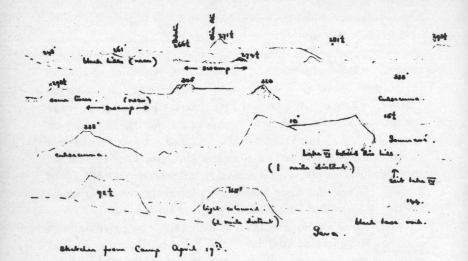

we passed a large herd of baboons ran across in front of us into the
village and stopped among the houses. They appeared so much at
home that it was difficult to believe that they were not the inhabitants
of some weird city built by apes. Lake VI is entirely enclosed on this
side by impenetrable reed beds, and we were unable to get anywhere
near it to camp. These reed-beds extend to the very foot of the lava
wall. Further on, however, there is a strip of grass-land sprinkled with
mimosa bushes between the lava and the reed-beds which enclose the
Awash river. With some difficulty we got the mules down the descent
to this plain, and continued down the Awash until we found an opening in the reeds where it was possible to get to the river. We made
the best of some scanty shade and camped after a reviving bathe. It
was intensely hot here, the ridge shutting off any breeze, and the
surrounding lava radiating the heat. There is a table-topped hill just
across the river with a village on its lower slope. The Awash river here
is both wide and deep. There were several herds of cattle and goats
being grazed here. During the rains this plain is under water and the
grass is now good. A large number of Danakil collected to look at me.
None of these people have ever seen a white man before. They looked

The entrance into Aussa: Kulzikuma foothills and dense forest.

Soldiers of the Sultan of Aussa arriving in camp.

The Awash river in Aussa.

Fording the Awash in Aussa.

Goumarri precipes and Lake Adobada.

My caravan on the way to
Lake Abhebad.

The swamps of southern Aussa.

Lake Abhebad where the Awash ended. I had come far and risked much to see this desolate scene.

LEFT: Sinter formations in the south-east corner of Lake Abhebad.

ABOVE: My camp on the way to Lake Assal.

BELOW: Two mimosa bushes near Lake Assal which we cut down to feed our starving camels.

Camels carrying the salt which the Danakil collect from Lake Assal.

Some Adoimara we encountered near the coast. They were hostile to the French.

We camped in the boulder-strewn
Marha riverbed.

This photograph of me was taken by Umar when we reached the coast.

I crossed from Tajura to Jibuti on a dhow like this one.

me over with a dispassionate curiosity, very much as we should inspect a previously unknown animal in the zoo. They are as wild looking as the Badhu Danakil, and most of them had either cut their ears or wore other killing decorations. In Aussa proper no one ever cuts his ears, and the silver bracelet worn on the right wrist and elbow is now largely decorative.

In the evening I strolled down the river. The Danakil use a raft of sodden rushes, rather like a huge dabchick's nest, to get across the river with. They pile their clothes on it and anyone who cannot swim sits on it and the rest push it across.

I returned as the sun set and we then moved to the very foot of the lava in order to try and avoid the mosquitoes. They soon followed us up and were very bad during the night. There was also a small midge which penetrated my mosquito netting and bit severely. The Danakil would not camp us in the only level place as there were some *dicos* there. The local people brought us some milk and durra bread, so that my three men had plenty to eat. The Danakil, who squatted round my bed with their spears stuck in the ground beside them, talked endlessly. This, the midges, and the stamping of the mules attacked by the mosquitoes, made sleep difficult.

I sent a Danakil to Umar with a note telling him to cross over to Abhebad where I would meet him, after following the Awash round to the lake. I have sufficient food.

April 20th
Halted by the Awash at 9.20 having passed the crater, which is on the far bank of the river. There were some trees and bushes which gave us shade. The river is swift and shallow, and is fringed with bulrushes and choked with aquatic vegetation. The water, which is beautifully clear, flows in channels through this vegetation. Several Danakil appeared from nowhere and brought us a little milk, and later some herds of goats were brought down to water. Each goat was ducked in turn. Six Speke's, two bucks and four does, came down to drink at midday and I shot the best, which seemed to have a rather good head. I then shot three crocodiles, all small. After a few minutes the sun

makes your rifle barrel too hot to hold with comfort, and the wind blowing off the lava feels like the draught from a furnace. It seemed hotter even than yesterday.

I insisted on marching again in the afternoon, though the Danakil assured me that we were very close to the camp. They wanted to stop and drink some more milk, which was being brought, and they don't mind if we don't get to camp tomorrow.

April 21st

Left camp at 5.45, marched on 50 degrees, and reached the main camp at 10.30. At 6.30 we passed a small village and a clump of doum palms. There was a large herd of she-camels grazing on the grass by the lake side. I saw two Speke here. We followed the lake side from here on, usually at some little distance, until we reached camp.

The country is incredibly desolate. There is no vegetation of any sort. The lake from here on was bordered by a stretch of black mud intersected by white reefs. The black volcanic rock is encrusted and whitened by the action of the water, sometimes as much as a mile inland. I think there is probably a difference of as much as sixty feet between the present level of the lake and the highest watermark. In the rains it must rise very considerably, but the Danakil deny that it ever comes half as high as this. Certainly these higher rocks do not look as if they had been submerged for a considerable period. I took several photos to illustrate this.

Along the present level of the lake, however, there are the remains of a considerable number of trees, in one place quite a big grove. All these tree-trunks are thickly encrusted. It is an interesting problem when these could have grown.

We came along fast today as the going was good and we drove the mules along quickly. We probably managed as much as three and a half up to four m.p.h. The glare off the sand and white rocks was tiring to the eyes. At 9.30 we reached a small spring issuing out from under a shelf of rock on the lake's edge. The water was clear and fresh. Half an hour later we reached another spring, which flows a short way and then loses itself in a clump of rushes. There is a narrow border of green grass along its course. Shortly after this we reached camp. It is some little way from the lake by a spring of excellent water in a dry riverbed. Between camp and the lake there is a small reed-bed formed by two or three small springs. There are numerous dead tree-trunks here which the men have used for building shelters. These are all below the highest level of the water and a few are still growing. A cool breeze off the lake. Everyone is well, though Demise has been bitten by one of our tame baby crocodiles. It has since died, possibly assisted.

Abhebad means 'the Smelling Water', and this lake deserves its name. The water is intensely salt, and soapy to the touch. It is a dirty dark green in colour with some large red patches near the shore. In the distance, however, it looks an attractive blue.

Umar's party with the camels marched for three hours to get here.

April 22nd

Out early after birds. We got a flamingo, but had the devil of a job getting to it as it was on waist-deep mud. This water burns like *berberi*. We put up a large sandy-coloured jackal, a wolf-like brute and very mangy, from a cleft in the rocks. Here were the remains of innumerable and full-sized goats, a half-eaten flamingo, and a freshly killed baby crocodile, two feet long. I don't know if this was the jackal's lair, or whether he was invading a hyena's in its absence. I saw the tracks of several hyena round the lake.

April 24th

A discussion with the Danakil first thing. They are anxious to get us down to Gobad and to return to the flesh-pots at Aussa.

A bad sandstorm as the sun set. It must have lasted twenty minutes and was extremely unpleasant. It came across the lake, a huge yellow cloud blotting out each headland in turn. Had all the men holding the tent by the ropes to save it. Afterwards it was cool and fresh, having been very hot all day and last night.

The Danakil, instead of building themselves a comfortable rush thatched shelter, as all the men have done, climb the ridge, which is extremely steep, behind camp and spend the day squatting like a lot of baboons, in the scanty shade of a small thorn bush. They chose two stones and as soon as they get stiff from sitting on one they move across onto the other. As the sun sets they come clambering down into camp.

April 25th

There are a succession of hot springs under the hill on the far side of the valley. The water is too hot to put your hand in. There are three fair-sized basins, but beyond these the whole hillside oozes out hot water, always, however, within a few yards of the lake's edge. The whole shore is a quicksand of thick black mud in consequence. We got a camel and an ox bogged on arrival, but got them out. I don't think these quicksands are deep enough to be dangerous. They are unpleasant, however, as the mud is extremely hot.

The Danakil have heard that the French are squabbling with the Adoimara at Gobad. There is also a small party of Issa raiding here. They have killed two Asaimara coming from Dikil, and I believe wiped out a small encampment of Danakil, mostly women and children. This has given my Danakil something else besides the heat of the valley to talk about.

April 26th

Took a camp photograph in the afternoon which I very much hope will come out. Gave the camels a feed of durra, as there is no food for them here. There was a thunderstorm and dense black clouds to the south and east of us in the evening, evidently very heavy rain. We got a strong wind and some big drops. Lashed everything down and dug trenches round the tents.

Tomorrow I intend to go and have a look at some strange jagged rock projections, probably marking an extensive hot spring, on the south-east edge of the lake. If there is any exit from the lake it must, I think, be in this corner. The south-west is entirely shut in by a continuous mountain range. I have inspected the other two sides. The Danakil swear I cannot get there and back in a day. If this is true, the coast must be very indented, since it does not look more than three and a half hours' walking. I shall take Abdullahi, Birru and Goutama, and as many Danakil as they think necessary. I shall take a teapot and some raisins and hope to get back.

April 27th

Left camp at 5.30 and reached the pinnacles at 11.30. We reached another extremely enclosed valley, with two large pools of stored rain water in the basalt rock, overhung by a precipice. A path winds down the hillside to these pools. The water looked very green in the pool, but proved cold and fresh tasting. The Danakil started out without water, most unusual for them. They vowed there was no water ahead. They probably thought this and the distance would make me turn back. When they saw I was going on, they quickly found this water and filled up their skins. They next started to grumble that they had no food with them. They all got very hot and cross. We started on again and reached a riverbed with a little running water in it from last night's rain. There are four riverbeds all draining into this corner of the lake and close together. The going was very bad and there were numerous inlets of the lake to circumvent. There was a continuous quicksand along the lake from camp till about 7 o'clock, caused by a seepage of hot water. In one place on the hillside clouds of steam were being puffed into the air. I should have liked to have climbed up to look at it, but did not wish to waste time.

The pinnacles consist of sinter formations, the highest perhaps thirty feet high. They are extremely numerous and extend for about three miles. Several rise out of the lake at a considerable distance from the shore. I took a great number of photographs. There were several hot springs here. I believe this hot water to be necessary for their creation. About one hour after leaving camp we passed several small ones on the water's edge. These had hot water trickling out round them. In the big group at the end of the lake, a large number were stranded on dry land by the receding water. These have, I think, stopped growing. Some of them were extremely beautiful, appearing to be covered with the most delicate tracery.

I had thought that the lake extended considerably beyond this point, whereas this is its southern limit. There is no question of any outlet here. It was satisfactory to have established conclusively that the Awash did end in Abhebad.

We started back at 12.30 and reached the riverbed with the trickle of water at 1.45. Made some tea and stayed here, despite the absolute lack of any shade till 4 p.m. The Danakil then raced along to get back before dark. Despite the going, which was largely over stones about the size of melons, too small to give a proper foothold, we must have kept up a steady four m.p.h. We climbed onto the plateau, thus avoiding the inlets and valleys, and marched on 310 degrees. We struck the valley where the camp is situated about two miles away from the lake. We reached camp at 6.45. The moon is almost full.

The camelmen have found some trees for the camels and a small spring up the valley. Except for a few trees in this valley I saw none all day. The sides of our well are falling in and the water is becoming increasingly brackish. I shall leave here tomorrow afternoon, and carry water for one night.

Abdi got several birds, including a small nightjar, among the trees up the valley.

April 28th

Loaded the camels at midday as the Danakil said that if we marched for three hours this evening we should arrive at Gobad tomorrow morning. The Danakil carried water for us on the four camels the Sultan sent with them for this purpose. Left camp at 2 p.m. and marched on 90 degrees till 3.15, climbing steadily the whole time. A good view from camp which I sketched. From 3.15 till 4.15 we marched along the southern wall and roughly parallel with a sandy plain some one and a half miles across, and extending a considerable distance. It was half a mile north of us. The going was extremely bad, even for a man on foot. A camel, Elmi, gave out suddenly and had to be left behind about a mile from camp. Camped on a level sandy stretch, the first place we had encountered where it was possible to unload the camels. Put up no tents, but built a rough wall round my bed to keep the tearing wind off.

The Danakil tried to give my men six skins of water, keeping six for themselves. After a bit of a row I made them give up another four. They now say that we cannot possibly get to Gobad tomorrow, but must camp by some rain-water half way. The existence of this water seems dubious depending, as it does, on the recent rain. I have insisted that they should send a man there tonight to verify that there is sufficient water, and I have told them that unless I am absolutely convinced of this I shall march my men back to the lake tomorrow. Why did they not send off a man to do this during the last few days? They talk and talk, re-opening the whole argument for some new and trifling point. It is now 10 o'clock before I can get any food and go to bed.

April 29th

The Danakil who went off last night arrived back with a skinful of water. At 6.15 we passed a few small pools under a rock. Camped by quite a large stretch of water with some mimosas for the camels. This water is running, but is only on the surface here. It is due to the recent rain and will, I think, dry up very shortly. The camels are ravenous. The going was as bad as ever over piles of these beastly stones. A strong wind blowing clouds of sand which penetrates into your eyes, ears, and mouth, and covers everything inside the tent. When closed down the tent was too hot to be bearable. Sent two camel men and some Danakil back in the afternoon for a last try to bring in Elmi. They returned at 7 p.m. with his tail.

Sheikh Husain now says that we cannot get to Gobad tomorrow and must camp again on another rain water. I intend, however, to march tonight about midnight, and push hard, carrying water. I won't trust to another of these rain waters. The Danakil are making every effort to induce me to start tomorrow morning, but we have a full moon and had better profit by it. To march during the heat of the day and short of water would be very hard on the camels and men. We can only carry enough water for one day, so that we must march hard in order to make sure of arriving at Gobad at latest the day after tomorrow. These Danakil can see no further than their immediate comfort.

April 30th

The moon was obscured practically all night by thick clouds. After we had been marching for an hour a camel suddenly collapsed and was unable to go any further, even when unloaded. I shot him. This was disturbing, since I was afraid that others might also suddenly give in. He was carrying a very light load.

We reached the summit of this range from where we overlooked Abhebad and now had a very nasty descent in the bad light, which took us till 4 o'clock. The Danakil lost the track and got my camels tangled up among the rocks on a steep mountainside. The greater part of the Sultan's *askaris* refused to go any further and lay down and went to sleep. They joined us again later in camp. We then crossed a sandy plain, shut in by volcanic hills. This was where Sheikh Husain said we should find water to camp by, but though the ground was soft, there was no water. At 5.15 we reached the hills on the far side of the plain, and the going became very rough again. Except for this one stretch of sand we marched unceasingly across rocks and boulders until we entered the Gobad plain. My feet became very bruised and several of the men became lame. Most of the Muhammadans remained behind here for a short while for the morning prayer. We descended this hill by way of a riverbed with a few pools of rain water in it. This valley smelt delicious, there being much aromatic grass and a heavily scented shrub here. We entered the Gobad plain camping on the Dagadli riverbed. There are some trees and *arak* bushes here for the camels, and water within a few inches of the surface. I sent a Danakil to Aseila, notifying the French officers there that I had arrived on the French frontier. In the evening two *askaris* arrived. The lieutenant has just left for Jibuti, but the sergeant expects me tomorrow.

Intensely hot all day.

Collected birds 765–73.

May 1st

The wind got up at 1 o'clock and blew a gale. This was followed by a downpour of rain but the tents were out of its reach. Camped opposite the Aseila post, but on the other side of the riverbed. The sergeant arrived shortly afterwards and invited me to live at the post during my stay here. This post was established in 1928, following a big raid by these Adoimara on the Badhu Asaimara. A *peloton méhariste* of sixty men patrol this corner of the frontier. During the dry season lack of pasturage compels them to remain here and they have in consequence built a permanent post. When they are absent on patrol the post is handed over to the Adoimara to be used by them in the event of a raid. There is a square dug-out roofed with bushes and grass surrounded by a single trench with three machine-gun emplacements: the whole protected by a barbed-wire entanglement. The post is on a small rise and has an extensive field of fire. Except for a few Issa, the men are all British Somalis. They impressed me as being alert and well disciplined. They possess one machine-gun, rather obsolete, and two repeating rifles, also hand-grenades. They are armed with short carbines taking three cartridges. They are dressed in khaki with red capes.

This corner possesses the best grazing in the colony. It is an ancient point of friction – the Adoimara–Asaimara and Issa territory converging on it. The establishment of this post appears to have quieted things. They inflicted heavy casualties on a Badhu raiding party last year. Last year the patrol visited Henle, claimed to be, and I think it undoubtedly is, French territory, but never before visited by them. The Sultan arrived with his whole army and gave them two hours to leave. They were entrenched and invited him to turn them out. After a lot of talk the Sultan withdrew and the French gave up their intention of visiting Lake Ali. This was made an excuse for stationing a company of Senegalese at Jibuti. It received some mention in the English papers last April. The Abyssinian Government seems to have admitted afterwards that the French were inside their frontier. The Sultan was called up to Addis Ababa.

One of the *askaris* told them, however, that the machine-gun jammed and that it might easily have been a defeat for them if the Asaimara had kept up their attack for a few more minutes.

The Adoimara here are Debinet.

The rain is two months later this year and the Adoimara here were getting restive about grazing. The condition of the Adoimara at Borharamela must be desperate, since they were already suffering at the end of February. I heard the other day that they have recently had heavy rain at Bahdu. The sergeant says that the heat becomes intense as soon as the first rain falls. The river came down in flood in the afternoon.

May 2nd

The baby ostrich was found dead. I think he must have poisoned himself with the preservative I used for the bird and animal skins. This is a tragedy.

I got rid of the Danakil *askaris*, and Ali Wali and Ahamado went back with them. Actually they have gone down to Dikil to sell some oxen they have brought along with them. I gave Ali a *gras* rifle and twenty cartridges, and Ahamado chose Fitaurari and five dollars. I gave the *askaris* twenty dollars to divide amongst themselves. They all went off very happy. I gave Ali and Ahamado each a letter for Martin. Ali has been intensely useful, and Ahamado, though useless by nature, has followed me without grumbling. I liked them both.

They have a garden here and it is a great treat to get fresh vegetables and a change of cooking.

Sergeant Antoniali, a Corsican, is most hospitable. He says that he prefers being stationed here to Algiers, Morocco or Senegal. As he expresses it, digging trenches and posting sentries have some point here. The soldiers had a Thanksgiving dance in the evening to celebrate the coming of the rain. They marched round carrying torches behind the bugler and the small boys beating empty petrol tins. They then let off three rockets, fired off several shots, and danced.

I cannot see the value of a Camel Corps among these broken mountains. Sergeant Antoniali says they never use the camels, always marching on foot. For such employment they seem a mobile and effective force. The useless upkeep of the camels wastes a lot of money.

May 3rd

Inspected the gardens in the morning. A great achievement. They have induced the local Adoimara to take up cultivation, and to irrigate and plant quite a large area. They have planted durra, maize, wheat, vegetables, grass and palms. There is a most varied assortment of vegetables, lettuce, leeks, tomatoes, radishes, carrots, and melons. It all seems to be growing well except for the melons, which won't ripen properly. They have built several small wells, and one large one with a reservoir and a machine worked by a mule or camel for drawing water. When they leave here, on the 15th, they will hand it all over to the Adoimara chiefs. They have promised to build further wells if the Adoimara make a success of this garden. They have trained six Issa and six Adoimara as masons under an Arab foreman. This work is entirely due in conception and execution to the initiative of the lieutenant and sergeant. The Governor declared that they were attempting the impossible.

I think it will go ahead now that they have successfully made a start and interested the Adoimara. The Adoimara must see the advantage to themselves: if it succeeds, it will have more effect than a dozen posts in quieting this area.

Heavy rain over Aussa in the evening. Arranged for my caravan to leave soon after midnight. I hope this will enable them to get to the second water close to Dikil, where the grazing is better. Here there is nothing but *arak* which, owing to its purgative effect, weakens the camels. I sleep again at the post and leave at dawn. I shall keep Abdullahi and my mule, Desita.

May 4th

The camels left at 1.30 a.m. I left at 4.45, arriving at Abeyufus riverbed at 8 a.m. The camels had not yet arrived. They straggled in very done at 8.30. The *askari*, who was guiding them, lost his way in the dark and took them in a wide half-circle over bad going. I marched straight on 80 degrees over a sandy plain, almost parallel with the escarpment behind Aseila, which runs on 90 degrees. Saw no game. The camels are very done, and there is almost no food for them here. This stream joins the Aseila riverbed. Dense clouds all round in the evening.

The ground is crawling with thousands of ticks – beastly.

May 5th

Marched east from 5.15 to 6.45, camping on the Sheikh Ketu riverbed by the well. A heavy downpour at 3 o'clock and the river came down. A good camp with enough feeding for the camels which will improve every day. Took Said Boy and Abdullahi and went up to Dikil as soon as the storm was over. It is an hour and a half away, going fairly fast. The *Commandant du Cercle*, Captain Bernard, his wife and child, and the wireless operator here. I liked Bernard and found him very welcoming.

The French have recently built a most impregnable fort here. It covers a large area. The walls are twenty feet high, loop-holed, and topped with broken glass and a barbed-wire entanglement. There are two large observation towers. They have bored a very deep well through the solid rock to get water. The whole thing must have cost a fortune. There is a motor road from here to Alisabiet, and continued on, though rather rough, to Aseila. They are now joining Alisabiet and Jibuti with a road. They say, proudly, that they are going to take the road as far as Abhebad. What value it will have, beyond facilitating a bathe there, I cannot see. The Sultan will never allow them to bring it across the frontier in order to tap the Aussa market. No *negadi* will bring his stuff to Dikil, the mountains are too bad, and when it is there, there is either the freight on the railway to pay, or a waterless trek from Alisabiet to Jibuti to face. They have always gone to Tajura and I think always will. I do not believe Dikil can ever offer them any advantage over this traditional road. Dikil has been created by the French. Had the site had any real value it would have been used before this by the natives.

I tried to sell or get rid of three camel saddles, but the Arabs in Dikil said they had no use for them as there was no trade. The only work they had was for the garrison here. This, I think, is probably true.

May 6th

Talked over the road to the coast. The Jibuti road is difficult for water. There appears to be sufficient water on the Tajura road, and it is far more interesting. Wired the Governor, Chapon Baisac, for permission to cross to Tajura. Received a reply at mid-day granting me permission to go there. This rather surprised me since they had previously refused it. I think the reason is that they are nervous of the Issa on the Jibuti road since the murder of Beitz. The adjutant arrived at 1 o'clock on the motor from Alisabiet and brought me my mail. I had so many letters that it took me the rest of the day to read them. A downpour at 5 o'clock preceded by a violent gale.

May 7th

Went down to camp in the afternoon and found everything all right. I wish I could stay there instead of living at Dikil, but this is impossible. I cannot sleep and feel imprisoned in a house after so long in a tent, and I am obliged to drink endless different wines, which I dislike.

Offered the *zabanias* fifty dollars for their two camels, which they accepted, as no one will buy them here. I gave them all *bakhshish* and Ato Shona and Basha Falega each a letter for Martin. They will go up to Dikil tomorrow and can catch the train to Asba Tafari from Alisabiet.

Rain in the distance and the river suddenly came down. A wall of water.

May 8th

Visited the garden among the palms in the afternoon. The floods do a lot of damage. Said good-bye to the *zabanias*. Bernard is sending his subordinate, Dongradi, and twelve men with a machine-gun with me. We shall be safe! His excuse for this army is that no one has ever crossed from Dikil to Lake Assal. I think he is scared of the Danakil at Guda.

When I said goodbye to Bernard, I never expected that nine months later he would be killed with all but one of his men, in a battle with the Asaimara on the Gobad plain.

I have taken the following translated extracts from a published diary, written by Dr Henri Huchon, which includes part of the official medical report presented to a Commission of Inquiry at Jibuti, in January 1935. This report was based on the testimony of the only soldier who survived the massacre and the French doctor who later visited the scene and examined Bernard's remains.

Reading later about Bernard's death in this report, I realized how easily this could have happened to us. We had been fortunate indeed to escape massacre when we first arrived in Bahdu. The Asaimara had recently been fighting with the French and had suffered heavy losses. All whites to them were the same. When I returned to Bahdu I was welcomed because I brought back their Hangadaala. None the less whenever I went out shooting I was at risk of being killed by a trophy-hunting Danakil – Nesbitt had had three of his followers murdered like this.

DEATH IN BATTLE OF A COLONIAL ADMINISTRATOR

Dikil, 17 January 1935

It was 5 p.m. The compound was quiet and peaceful. The women were coming back from the well, below the outpost. The men sat, silently sipping their tea. The Commandant du Cercle, *Bernard, clad in pyjamas, was busy among the clutter of his verandah, typing the last chapter of his annual report. This half-finished paper, headed 'Political Situation' was later discovered in his typewriter.*

Outside, a sound, faint at first, increasing as it came closer, rose to a loud cry. A local Issa appeared, covered in blood and dirt, breathless and exhausted, waving his arms: on the Gobad plain, Asaimara raiders had attacked a douar *in Issa territory. Men, women and children had been slaughtered, goats and camels driven off. This wounded survivor, worn out by his long run, pleaded for assistance . . .*

The garrison at Dikil normally consisted of sixty-five militiamen. On the day in question, there were only twenty-five. The other forty, commanded by Dongradi, the adjutant, were patrolling fifty kilometres away. The chef de poste *was an elderly sergeant, a veteran of the 1914–18 war.*

Bernard could not afford to delay. The raiders had devastated the plains ... Time was of the essence. He assembled eighteen of the remaining twenty-five soldiers, except for the oldest, put the sergeant in charge of a machine-gun, took two cases of ammunition, requisitioned the van belonging to the Syrian storekeeper – the only motor transport in Dikil – loaded it with his men and hurried off to the battleground ... After a while, the sandy going became too soft [for the van] and they were obliged to continue on foot. Bernard hid the van in a gully, guarded by two soldiers. He would also have liked to leave behind a corporal, who was too old for the rigorous march. But the corporal refused, saying, 'Why do you treat me like a woman?' The following day, this man would be the first one killed ... On the way they encountered Issa survivors whom they enlisted ... Eighty kilometres west of Dikil, four kilometres from Maraheito, a brackish spring among the rocks ... Bernard and his men reached ... a small hill which overlooked the pass ...

Daybreak revealed the enemy, nearly a thousand warriors. They had with them their trained war-horses and four thousand head of livestock, including eight hundred camels ... It seemed foolhardy to engage them, but how could Bernard now retreat?

Bernard opened fire, 'from too far away', as his sergeant pointed out. The raiders, however, taken unawares, panicked and scattered. But after firing for five minutes, the machine-gun jammed and the shooting suddenly petered out. The tribesmen regrouped and launched an attack.

The Asaimara were armed with daggers, spears and small, round hippopotamus-hide shields capable of deflecting a bullet. The Issa, who were poorly armed, fled. Left by themselves, the soldiers retreated to the high, rocky ground. Half-way up the slope they attempted a stand. It was there the first of them, the corporal, fell ... Two of the soldiers tried to rescue Bernard. They led him across the hillside .. through the encircling warriors ... A wounded soldier, the sole survivor, recalled:

'The administrator ... called out to the others, believing they would follow him. But they were already dead; one of them a few steps away from him. On the hilltop only the veteran sergeant remained, fighting, lashing out furiously with his [empty] rifle. Then I saw [Bernard] scrambling up [the hill]. He cried out ...'

THE REPORT

Three days later, the investigating commission from Jibuti retraced Bernard's last footsteps. His corpse, what remained of it, lay behind a heap of stones. The medical examination showed the relentless beating by the Asaimara.

I WOUNDS

On the head: multiple bruises on the forehead, the cheeks and nose, the scalp, with subcutaneous bleeding over the face and a heavy flow of blood from the nostrils.

On the neck: the throat had been slit across from ear to ear, in a series of strokes down to his spinal column. The edges of this gaping wound were clean cut, but at the two extremities below his ear lobes, many jagged serrations to skin and muscle were observed consistent with the sawing movements of a dagger.

The right forearm, underneath, had a 50 mm cut above the elbow, an oblique clean-edged wound, 30 mm long from a dagger blow or a spear.

On the left arm, in the deltoid muscles, a clean-edged vertical wound 50 mm long from a dagger or a spear; one at the nape of the neck, three superimposed on the right shoulder blade, one level with the last vertebra, two in the lumbar region.

II MUTILATIONS

From the collarbones to the crotch the whole front of the trunk was missing. The throat and abdominal cavities were wide open. The windpipe had been slit. The right lung and the heart were missing. Only the left lung remained. The diaphragm, the stomach, the liver, the spleen and most of the intestines were missing from the abdominal cavity ... The penis had been cut by a dagger and both the testicles removed in the scrotum ...

May 9th
Left Dikil about 8 o'clock. Arranged to meet Dongradi at 2 o'clock. Five camels missing when I sent for them, and it took two hours to find them. Left at 2.45, arriving at the rendezvous with Dongradi at

4 p.m. Camped in a riverbed with a few palms and good permanent water at 5.30. Marched on. One of my camels, Karayu, gave out and had to be left behind. Two others, Farur and Hawiya, are on their last legs and I don't think they will get much further. The country is broken and extremely stony.

May 10th

Crossed the valley of Galamo, then started to climb. Several *dicos* here. One of the camels, Hawiya, collapsed and I had to shoot him. Descended and camped by a pool of water in the Marha riverbed. The country was incredibly desolate, and very broken. The going was rough, especially on the hillsides. A fine view from the summit at 8.15 which I sketched. The Danakil guides, previously so certain of the waterholes, caused considerable anxiety during the last hour by saying we should only find water if it had rained. Actually I am convinced that this water is permanent. It is in a basin of rock and is more than six feet deep. The high-water mark is two feet above this level. The pool is some twenty-five feet across. There was another small pool close by. The water was fresh and good. There is almost no food for the camels here, and they don't seem to have the energy to look for the little there is. Camped among the rocks on the hillside, and had some heavy work clearing a space for the camels to sleep. Dongradi and several of the men have had headaches. Kassimi has a very poisoned hand. A bad camp, hot, rocky and almost without shade.

Dongradi, as always, camped slightly apart, after positioning his men to defend our camp. I had been apprehensive that he might expect to take charge, but he accepted without question that this was my expedition and though he was helpful when I asked his advice he left decisions to me. I saw little of him, since he preferred to feed on his own and spent most of his time with his soldiers, who obviously had great respect for him. A dark, tough, undemonstrative Corsican, he confessed he was fed up with the colony and hoped shortly for a transfer to Algeria. He had been maddened by the constant interference to which they were subjected at Dikil, from officials in Jibuti who never ventured outside the town.

Collected birds 821–25.

May 11th

Left camp at 5.45, crossing the hill till 6.15 on 340 degrees when we rejoined the Marha river at the point where the Danbaulu river joined it to form the Kuri river. Palms and water here and good feeding for the camels. I wish we had pushed on to here yesterday. From here till we camped we marched in the Kuri riverbed. The river is enclosed by black rocky hills devoid of any vegetation. There are doum palms growing in clusters throughout this length of the riverbed. Most of them were either being or had been tapped for wine. The sap is run into conical cups about nine inches deep, extremely neatly made from the palm fronds. We passed one family encamped busily collecting the sap. We passed numerous pools of rain water, but the only permanent water was where we camped at Dalibuyi. They dig a well here later in the year. The water was cold and clean, protected from the sun by a large rock. An attractive camp in a palm grove. Some feeding for the camels.

Killed a black snake two feet long which was beginning to eat a lizard. The snake disgorged the lizard which was none the worse. The Danakil guide collected a large number of different coloured stones on the hill above yesterday's camp. Extraordinarily light and often hollow. Oval or round in shape.

Climbed the hill above camp and drew a sketch in the evening. The overwhelming desolation of this country is most impressive. Except for the palms in the riverbed, there is not a sign of vegetation anywhere. You look out over range upon range of hot black rock vibrating in the heat.

The Danakil guides seem unable to give us any indication as to how many days it will take to get to Tajura. At one moment they say four, which is obviously impossible, and the next they say eight or ten. I have only got nine more days food for the men and a little durra. The French *askaris* brought ten day's food since Bernard assured us that we could get to Tajura in six days. I think it will take us another ten days. Bernard claims to have a most extensive knowledge of the colony. In actual fact, I think his knowledge is confined to the posts in which he has been stationed. He told me that we could get to Lake Assal in two days, marching six hours a day.

May 12th

Started to load at 3.15 and left camp at 5.00 marching on 300 degrees down the Kuri riverbed. At 5.30 we came to a large grove of palms and a fair-sized spring of warm water, which flows down the valley. At 5.50 we left the valley climbing over the hill on 55 degrees. At 7.15 we rejoined the Kuri again by some pools of rain water and further palms. The Kuri here runs on 290 degrees. We marched down the valley of the Kuri till 9 o'clock. From 7.30 till we camped in the plain of Gagada under the Lacfonta escarpment at 10.15 we marched on due north. There were a succession of palms all down the Kuri. At 8 o'clock we came to some fairly good pasturage and a small herd of camels feeding there. The plain of Gagada is largely sandy and almost devoid of any feeding for the animals. This was disappointing since the Danakil guides had assured us that the camels would get a good feed here. The Danakil have moved from here to Heute and the Aussa frontier where the feeding is better at the moment. There were only an odd camel and a few goats here, all very scraggy. There are almost no mimosa bushes here so the Danakil camels must live on the grass. The plain here is covered with a small bush but the camels practically refused to eat it. This plain is ringed in by mountains. Dembin, Golodaba and Gagalu are large mountains. Another camel, Neali, gave in after half an hour's marching and I shot him rather than leave him behind to die of thirst and starvation.

I saw a few Speke's gazelle, two lots of four, and a single buck close to camp which I shot for food.

The Kuri is an attractive valley and I took a lot of photos.

The camels stood this march well. The going on the whole was good. The wells which the guides expected to find were filled in and I had some anxious moments since the last water was a very long way off. We found some standing water left by some recent rain. A considerable part of the plain here has been under water within the last few days. The plain is flooded at the moment at the foot of Golodaba.

The guides now say that for the next three days there is no feeding for the camels, no grass, and not even any wood for fires. They seem certain of the water; if this is really true we are going to have a desperate time and are certain to lose a lot of camels. They have not had a proper feed since we left Sheikh Ketu and today they are eating almost nothing. I abandoned two loads, smashing everything to prevent its being surreptitiously put back on. As a last resort we could load the mules. They are getting oats, and have not been ridden since we left Aussa. But if the camels give out we may be done. However, yesterday the guides said it was impossible to reach Gagada today and we did it in five and a quarter hours. It may therefore not be so far as they say. They are so unreliable over distances and times.

May 13th

We passed a very considerable pile of stones. The Danakil each picked up a stone and cast it on this mound crying out 'Hess! Hess!' It appears that a very great many years ago a man committed incest with his sister here and the child was born here.

We camped in the riverbed at the foot of Awadu mountain, marching again in the afternoon to Gugumpta. The Aluli appears to change its name to Gugumpta at this spot for no very obvious reason.

This valley is magnificent. The riverbed is shut in by jagged and precipitous mountains, rising in crowded tiers one upon the other, so falling in thousand-feet precipices to the scanty pools below. The valley twists and turns and every hundred yards reveals a gorge more stupefying than the last. In many cases scarcely twelve yards separates the two walls of rock, which shut out all but a narrow strip of sky, immeasurably distant as if seen through a prison window. The colouring of the mountains endlessly changes for here the rock is of sandstone which permits of every shade: rose, orange, brick-red, purple, cinnamon, umber, olive-green, and blue-grey are streaked and splashed upon the mountain face, but the prevailing tone is red. The green tuft of an occasional doum palm serves merely to throw into stronger relief the barren desolation of this place, nor does the spoor of an odd hyena dispel the conviction that life is here extinct. The water trickles underground from one slender string of pools to the next, but though beautifully clear it has a stale flat taste, and there is not a blade of grass along its course.

We camped at 9 o'clock by two mimosa bushes and a few doum-palms which we cut down for the camels, but they seemed too tired to eat. We found some little shade under the overhanging rocks, but nothing could shelter us from the scorching wind which drove before it a perpetual cloud of sand.

In the evening the setting sun made the valley sombre and mysterious, but it became delightfully cool. I found a pool just out of my depth and long enough for half a dozen strokes. We also found a small pool of rain water which was clean and sweet-tasting.

Camp is at the entrance to a large shadow-filled gorge and the precipices tower round us on every side. A caravan attacked in this valley would not stand a chance however well armed.

May 14th

Left camp at the first light of dawn. Where the valley opened out, we came in sight of Lake Assal.

At 6 o'clock we descended onto a plain of salt. This was as white as fresh fallen snow, and as hard as a rock. I think this salt is about three inches thick. In numerous places there were small holes through the crust of salt, and water underneath. It took us three-quarters of an hour to cross this plain to the hills opposite, and the salt plain extended a considerable distance in other directions. The lake is bordered on the south, west and north-west by this expanse of salt which must be considerably more than a mile wide.

The colouring of the lake's edge is a series of vivid contrasts. First there is the mixed sandstone and lava on the mountain side, then a strip of yellowish-white encrusted rock, showing that the lake's level was once more than a hundred feet higher than today, next the spotless white expanse of salt and finally the deep blue of the lake. The lake is ringed round by black volcanic hills and dominated by the towering masses of Harod and Garba. Nowhere was there any vegetation to be seen, not even a leafless thorn bush.

At 6.45 we climbed a low hill, and crossed some very broken country. The ground here is covered more or less thickly with a layer of lava, but the sandstone is exposed in the valleys. The going was difficult for the camels and Farur gave in and had to be left behind. At 9 o'clock we turned onto 80 degrees. There was a very small pool of rain water in the rocks here.

At 9.30 we arrived at a string of pools in a riverbed and camped. There are a few mimosa bushes here and quite a lot of other grass-like pasturage. This grazing is invisible from a distance of more than a quarter of a mile and was absolutely the first thing I had seen all day. I think it will save the camels. We collected as much as possible in the evening so that they could feed during the night. We also got my camel, Farur, brought in in the afternoon and he ate greedily. He is not ill, only dying of starvation and weakness. Farah has got a bad attack of fever. I cannot think where he got it.

There were a few Danakil encamped on this water when we arrived. They left in the afternoon.

We have still got two full days marching, with little or no food for the camels, according to the guides.

May 15th

Went down to the lake in the morning with Abdullahi and Abdi. Left camp at 4.45 and arrived at the water's edge at 5.45 walking on 315 degrees. There is no salt this side except for a little in the creeks. The lake is bordered by a low sandstone cliff covered with a coating of lava. A succession of large hot springs run out from under this cliff into the lake. This water was salt. It seemed to be far too salt to have become impregnated as it came out of the ground. The country here is extremely broken and jagged, being covered with lava. This lake is, I think, below sea level. It is shut in on all sides by endless lava fields. I wonder if it is not literally the hottest spot on earth.

Left camp at 3.10. I carried no water on my camels but Adjutant Dongradi carried two of my water tanks full on his camels.

A few doums here but no water. Farur gave out and I gave him to a Danakil who was here. Poor Farur, he was a most attractive camel.

May 16th

Left camp 5 o'clock, marching due north across the valley. At half past five we turned nearly parallel with the precipice opposite, climbing it on a long slope. Even so it was desperately steep. We heaved gurgling, snorting camels from one block of lava up onto the next to a deafening accompaniment of shouts and whistles. Abdullahi's blood-curdling yells got several camels back onto their feet when they appeared insensible to further blows. At the bottom of the escarpment there was a freshly made *waidella*. The guides said that it was that of a man who died of thirst just before the rains broke. I don't think the water at Alexsitan would last for more than three months after the last rain.

The *askaris* say that the Issa who live near the Danakil bury their dead, at least sometimes, in *waidellas*. Some Debinet they killed in a fight at Gobad were all buried in *waidellas*. They think that the Adoimara always bury those killed in battle like this, but I question if this is true.

We reached the summit at 6.30 then came to a further escarpment and marched down this on 320 degrees. Luckily we were able to skirt it, marching on 110 degrees until we camped at Dafarai at 8.15.

Camp was extremely hot and the wind only got up as we left. There was no shade except in the ravine and that was stifling.

I managed to hire two camels to take us to Tajura off some Danakil who are camped near here. One of them is not half-grown but they have agreed to lose their money if their camels fail to get there.

We left camp again at 2.30 going due East. I had a very good bathe in one of the pools. The water was unexpectedly cold below the surface.

We took the larger valley on the left. The other continues roughly due East. At 4 o'clock we had a long and extremely steep climb over a shoulder of the hill. Several of the camels were trembling violently when they arrived at the top and one collapsed, but by carrying his load we managed to get him into camp.

We camped at 4.45, having been marching since 4 p.m. on 100 degrees. We camped early as there were several green mimosas for the camels here, and I want them to get some food before tomorrow's march. They had practically nothing at Dafarai and the two climbs today have been a great strain on them. I am afraid I shall lose several tomorrow. I abandoned a lot more stuff.

I was talking to one of the men when a hover-fly flew round his head. He immediately took a piece of grass and stuck it into his hair above his forehead. He said that otherwise the hover-fly would lay eggs in his nose, which would later be filled with maggots. He believes that the piece of grass effectually prevents this.

This valley, which is extremely narrow and precipitous in places, is called Asbina. It is mostly of red sandstone. There is a sprinkling of mimosas along the mountainsides, a very welcome sight since I hope it means that there may be feeding for the camels in front of us. The guides say we have passed the worst of the road.

May 17th

The Danakil camelman I engaged yesterday tried to knife Abdullahi during the night, accusing him of attempting to rape the woman they have with them.

Had to abandon Nagadras Haile Miriam and another camel here. I hated leaving the Nagadras. At 7 o'clock we left the valley marching on 90 degrees and camped at 8 at Hedeita. The road today was far better, though the country all round is broken by numerous ravines. We saw the sea first at 7 o'clock. This is the Gubat al Karib, generally believed by the natives to be the stronghold of the king of the devils. It is narrow and shut in on the far side by precipices.

We passed two cemeteries at 7.30 and 7.45. The Adoimara call these graves *kabaré* instead of *dico*. I have noticed several *kabaré* recently ornamented with white pieces of rocks, and I saw one *waidella* the top section of which was built of white rock. There was a round hole three feet across and three feet deep in the second cemetery. I thought this was the beginning of a grave, but the guides say it was a *mosquidi*. The family assemble round it to pray for the dead once every year.

In the French Danakil country burial in a waidella *is only used in three special cases (women dead in childbirth, persons dead in an area where there are but few people to bury them, and men killed in fights). The dead are normally buried in a grave or* kabaré *according to the Muhammadan law. These* kabaré *are sometimes found together forming cemeteries. This is always the case near a village or town. There is a large graveyard in the centre of Tajura. The graves are then usually simple mounds with an upright stone at the head and feet. Sometimes, however, they are surrounded by a ring of stones enclosing one, two and occasionally even three graves.*

There is quite good feeding for the camels here. The mimosas being green after the recent rain. I shall stop here until tomorrow afternoon to feed and rest the camels. It also seems doubtful if we could get to the next water in one day, and we should suffer badly if we started at dawn and failed to do so.

I have hired two more camels for one dollar a day to take us to Tajura. I hope we are through now. Even if the rest of my camels fail we could I think replace them from here on.

The well here, though deep, only has a little water in it, and that is brackish though drinkable. The whole life of this district revolves round it since there is no other water anywhere near.

The Adoimara here are Adevassul, and their territory stretches almost to Dikil which is Debinet. The women are nearly all dressed in coloured cloths and silks, and some of the men wear coloured loin-cloths. They have suffered severely from famine this year, losing a large part of their herds in the drought. They graze as far as the Aussa frontier and the greater part of the tribe is on the Heute plain at the moment. There were a few Sugha Guda at the well and they were inclined to be truculent, trying to prevent the men taking water. The Adoimara in the Guda mountains are the most troublesome in the colony. A *Commandant du Cercle* some years ago tried to get through to Lake Assal, and the Sugha Guda ordered him to turn back, which he did. They also killed three French *askaris*, and the government did not attempt to avenge them. They have in consequence no respect for the French.

I shot a Speke's gazelle with a very good head on this hill since we have no meat.

May 18th

Spent the morning questioning the guides on Adoimara customs. Collected quite a lot of information, most of which tallied with what I had already heard.

We passed an extremely large *waidella* close to the path. The two turrets are to act as scarecrows to prevent the hyenas from digging out the corpse.

At 5.15 we entered the riverbed of the Gelalipaaon, marching on 110 degrees till we camped at 6 a.m. We left the riverbed a quarter of an hour before camping. We just had time to get things a bit straight before sunset. Everyone was thirsty after four hours marching, and very few of them had any water left. There was a nice fresh breeze off the sea, which was half a mile away.

I am disappointed by Mount Guda after all I have heard. It is not as imposing as either Garba or Harod.

I told my men that I had decided not to go to Jibuti but to cross the desert to Asmara. All they said was, 'We want three days in Tajura.' I have no desire to go back to civilization, and wish I was just starting out from the Awash station with the whole Awash river still before me to explore.

CONCLUSION

May 19th

Left camp at 4.15, marching for half an hour with lamps. Camped at 6.30 at Sagalu where there is a well of good water. It is an attractive spot with a grove of date palms along the sea shore. Here we were met by the Sultan's brother. There were two dhows anchored off the oasis. They collect wood and charcoal. The Danakil pile these ready for them at various places along the coast. Dongradi took a photo of me and the men. We left at 3.45 and marched along the seashore. There were hundreds of small crabs. These live in burrows just above the high tide mark and the excavated sand forms a small pyramid before each hole.

Camped at Ambabo. There is a well of rather brackish water here. I sent two men to get water from a well about two miles further on. This water is good. Birru gave us an enormous dinner.

May 20th

Tajura is considerably smaller than I had expected. This is in part explained by the very crowded houses. There are numerous mosques and a few white houses, belonging to the Sultan and rich Arabs. Otherwise the houses are built of mats over a wooden framework. They are, however, very much more solidly constructed than any other Danakil houses I have seen, and a great contrast with the native quarters at Jibuti.

The post is situated on a hill dominating the town, and the top of the hill, which is extremely steep, is surrounded by an entanglement of barbed wire. There is a large grove of date palms round the well on the western side of the town, and a considerable number scattered among the houses. The town is extremely attractive. Behind it are the foothills of Mount Mabla, across the bay are the successive ranges of the Issa mountains, and to the westward at some distance, yet dominating the whole, is Mount Guda. On the evening of the 18th we were too close under the mountain to have a proper view of it, but from here it looks worthy of the numerous legends, both native and European, which have assembled round its summit. The oasis-like nature of the town is emphasized by the barrenness of its immediate surroundings, for between it and the hills there is nothing but a waste of stone-covered sand.

I was young, highly impressionable and incurably romantic, and Tajura was a marvellous place to end my journey. For me it belonged to that authentic Eastern world of which Conrad wrote, a world remote, beautiful, untamed. Its palm-fringed beach and sparkling green and blue sea; the sombre outline of mountains across the bay; dhows at anchor offshore, with dugouts passing to and fro; white mosques among the palms; narrow passageways between crowded mat-roofed dwellings; Somali and Arab merchants, stately in ankle-length robes, embroidered sleeveless jackets and coloured turbans; Danakil from the desert, shock-headed, half-naked, armed and unpredictable; groups of women in colourful dresses, who as I passed covered all but their eyes; harsh Somali voices; the sound of a stringed instrument, the throb of a drum; long-drawn, sonorous calls to prayer, taken up from one minaret to the next; the distant roaring of refractory camels at the wells; the sound of surf on the beach; the smells of dried shark's meat, clarified butter, wood smoke and spices.

I camped under a few mimosas at the foot of the hills to be at some little distance from the town. The sergeant here wished me to camp among the palms under the post, but I refused as the ground was too dirty. Though there is little shade where we are, I think we get more breeze.

I had lunch at the post. The *Commandant du Cercle* has his wife and children here. He has only very recently arrived here. He is a fat little gourmet, with an embarrassing lack of assurance and a self-assertive manner. He is afraid of the Danakil and is careful to confine himself and his family within their barbed-wire entanglement. He told me the town is dangerous and I am not to go there unless escorted by his troops and two *askaris* have orders to follow me everywhere. I said I might if I could find the time climb Mount Guda. He at once got very excited and said that even he was forbidden to go into the Guda zone without a special permit from the Governor.

The Sultan of Tajura had asked to meet me, so at 5 o'clock I came back to the commandant's house. The Sultan, a good-looking young man in an immaculate white robe and closely wound white turban, had a quiet-spoken dignity, unlike our host, who waved his hands about, lit one cigarette from another, and hardly stopped talking – mostly about the advantages of a refrigerator. I invited the Sultan to visit my camp, which next day he did.

He asked many questions about my journey, and seemed especially interested that I had met the Sultan of Aussa and been allowed to travel through his territory. He asked if I had had a large force of Abyssinian soldiers with me. I knew that Umar had already heard that before my arrival wild rumours had been afloat in the town: I was said to be accompanied by an Abyssinian army that intended to seize Lij Yasu's son. I had never heard of this son, but it was not improbable that among the Danakil the lecherous Lij Yasu had produced several. The Sultan was non-committal about the French administration, though he did mention that the commandant had not left his house since arrival, and that his predecessor had never ventured outside Tajura.

I gave the men four sheep, rice, flour, coffee, and a large quantity of sugar to celebrate our arrival. A great number of Arabs, Danakil and Somalis inspected our camels during the day but we reached no agreement as to price. I was getting desperate about the mules since they have been very short of food for two days, only having a little corn each evening. Here there is absolutely nothing, nor can you buy anything but a scrap of hay at a fantastic price. However, we got rid of them all in the evening. I did not think there was a chance of selling them here and I got double the price I expected. Desita fetched sixty dollars, Shaitan fifty dollars, and the other three each forty dollars. I shall take my mule, Arat bin, to Jibuti.

May 22nd

I asked the *Commandant du Cercle* for permission to have a dance and fire off cartridges after dinner. He said it would be all right if he warned the Sultan about the shots. This he did.

My Somalis gave a tremendous show, and a large number of Arabs and Danakil came and watched. I gave them the remainder of the cartridges to fire off, but after they had let off about fifty a breathless Somali sergeant arrived from the *Commandant* to tell me to stop. Once the town was warned I cannot see that it mattered how many we fired off. A pity, as it added zest to the dancing, and the echoes thrown back by the mountains were most effective.

May 23rd

I saw the *Commandant du Cercle* in the morning. He stopped the firing last night since it was more intensive than he had expected, and he was afraid of a dhow from lower down the coast carrying a report across to Jibuti that the post at Tajura had been attacked during the night, or that it might draw in the Danakil from outside. A good reason.

A message has come from the Governor asking me to cross to Jibuti as soon as possible, since the presence of all my armed men in Tajura is disturbing the Danakil. I have six rifles besides my own! A detachment of Somali *askaris* from Jibuti arrived here the day before I did and were all sent back, without relieving anyone, with Dongradi. I wonder if they were intended to protect the town from my savage hordes. On our arrival we were asked by numerous Arabs and Somalis where all the rest of my men were.

I chartered a dhow to take us to Jibuti and we left in the evening of May 23rd. A storm was threatening but luckily passed over the land, for we were on an open deck without shelter. Tajura vanished into the distance and the sun set behind Guda. As night fell, the moon lit the sea. With small waves breaking against the bows the boat rolled slightly, her long raking yard dipping and rising against the stars above the much-patched lateen sail. I was very content, travelling like this across a sea which de Monfreid had made his own.

In Jibuti I spent three days waiting for a boat to Marseilles, and I did not find a congenial soul in the town. Chapon Baisac, the Governor, summoned me for an interview. After I had been kept waiting a long time I was shown into his office, where I had hardly sat down before he asked me abruptly why I had brought Abyssinian soldiers into French territory, and why I had not handed over my weapons before leaving Dikil for Tajura. He barely listened to my explanations, which I should have thought self-evident, and during the half-hour I spent with him never spoke a gracious word. This corpulent, pompous and short-tempered little man was certainly not one I would have wished to serve under.

I had bought *Secrets de la Mer Rouge* and *Aventures de Mer* written by Henri de Monfreid while I was in Addis Ababa and I had been fascinated by de Monfreid's account of his adventurous and lawless life. He had come to Jibuti in 1910 as a clerk in a commercial firm, but he had found himself frustrated and bored by the life he was leading, having no interests in common with his fellow Frenchmen among whom he was living. The Danakil however appealed to his romantic nature and he spent all his spare time associating with them and learning their language. The French community was scandalized by his behaviour and he was sent for by the Governor and reprimanded. He resigned from his job, abandoned his association with the French, and joined the local Danakil. He became a Muslim. He bought a dhow, enlisted a Danakil crew and made a living by fishing for pearls off the Farsan isles and smuggling guns into Abyssinia through Tajura.

I had just finished reading de Monfreid's books when I reached the French outpost at Aseila, commanded by Sergeant Antoniali. He made me very welcome and I stayed with him for days before going on to Dikil. I was interested to find that his cook, Fara, had been one of de Monfreid's crew and was evidently devoted to him.

I had hoped when I got to Jibuti to meet de Monfreid. He had however gone on a visit, I think it was to France, but his dhow, the *Altair*, was anchored in the bay. I went on board her and met his crew. From his books I already knew their names. I heard he was selling the *Altair*. I thought fleetingly of buying her and leading a life resembling his, but reality took charge.

My men were anxious to return to their homes and families, and on the evening of our second day at Jibuti all but Umar and his servant left on the train. I went to the station to see them off, and the parting with them deepened my depression. Kassimi and Goutama, Birru and Said, Abdullahi, Said Munge, Abdi, Bedi and his fellow camelmen, and the rest: they were twenty-two in all, and some had been with me since I left Addis Ababa with Haig-Thomas for the Arussi mountains eight months before. All had proved utterly reliable, often under conditions of hardship and danger. None had ever questioned my decisions, however seemingly risky, and I had never doubted their loyalty. Despite their fundamental religious and racial differences as Amhara, Galla and Somali, they had never quarrelled or intrigued among themselves, but had worked side by side throughout.

I was glad to leave Jibuti next day, even third-class in a Messageries Maritimes boat returning from French Indo-China to Marseilles. Umar accompanied me on board and there we parted. As I watched him descend the gangway I was more conscious than ever how much of my success was due to him. He had ensured the loyalty of my men, accurate information, and the successful outcome of negotiations with tribal chiefs and with the Sultan himself, and his imperturbability had given me the assurance that I had sometimes needed.

I had come far, overcome many difficulties and risked much, but I had achieved what I had set out to do.

GLOSSARY

aban	protector, ensuring safe conduct of, for example, a caravan
Abuna	Archbishop of the Ethiopian Church
aoul	Soemering's gazelle
askari	soldier
bakhshish	gratuity, tip
balabat	tribal headman
Balambaras	junior military rank
bongo	large striped forest antelope
chef de poste	officer in charge of administration
choum	village headman
Commandant du Cercle	commander of fort or outpost
dagnia	Danakil elder
Dedjazmatch	rank equivalent to senior general
dik-dik	small African antelope
djambia	broad-bladed Danakil dagger
douar	encampment
durra	Indian millet
Eid	Muslim holy day, e.g. end of Ramadan
Elgurash	the Ethiopian Crown Prince (Asfa Wossen)
Etchege	prior of Debra Libanos monastery and senior monk of the Ethiopian Empire
Ferengi	European
Fitaurari	'Commander of the Spearhead', an official rank
fracilla	a measure of weight

genet	species akin to, but smaller than, the civet (civet: a large nocturnal carnivore of the cat family)
Gerazmatch	title of lesser seniority
gerenuk	long-necked African antelope
ghee	clarified butter
Gibbi	palace
gougsa	equestrian game of skill using throwing-sticks or spears
Hangadaala	spiritual head of the Bahdu Asaimara
janili	Danakil soothsayer
Kenyazmatch	'Commander of the Right', title of intermediate seniority
kopje	small hill
kudu, lesser and greater	large African antelopes. The greater kudu has long spiral horns
medaqua	duiker, a small African antelope
méhariste	soldier of the French Camel Corps
mountain nyala	a large antelope indigenous to Ethiopia with a resemblance to the greater kudu
negadi	muleteer
Negus	Ethiopian King
oribi	small African antelope
oryx	an African antelope with long straight horns that inhabits desert or semi-desert terrain
peloton	squad, a main body of French soldiers
Ras	most senior rank or title, often equated with that of Duke
shamma	Ethiopian cotton toga-like garment
Shanqalla	tribesman of Negro origin in Ethiopia
shash	black, shiny gauze
Sheikh Husain	pilgrim shrine in Ethiopia, built to commemorate a place where the saint had lived alone for years, praying and fasting

shifta	widely used Amharic term for brigands or bandits
shikari	hunter, native attendant of sportsman
shola	wild fig-tree
syce	groom
teff	small grass cultivated in Northern Ethiopia for flour
Timkat	a blessing ceremony in Ethiopia
tukul	thatched native mud hut in Ethiopia
warquah	representative
zabania	guard
zariba	thorn fence

INDEX

Wilfred Thesiger

Desert, Marsh & Mountain

In this lavishly illustrated book, Wilfred Thesiger recreates a lifetime's journeying in some of the world's least-known places.

His is a romantic but austere vision, redeemed by the companionship of peoples who accepted hardship with fierce pride. Five years with the Bedu, just before oil transformed them, placed the author in the front rank of British Arabists. Later he lived, as no Westerner had lived, in the strange world of the Marshmen of Iraq. Here, also, are memorable accounts of his travels in Iraqi Kurdistan, Iran, the Yemen in time of Civil War, and the mountain country of the Hindu Kush and the Karakorams.

Thesiger's world is tragically contracting, and societies are crumbling at the intrusion of the West. Only just in time to see and share the harsh nomadic life he so admires, he draws a poignant picture of its strength and beauty in fine prose, and unforgettable photographs.

'This book establishes Thesiger as one of the greatest travellers and travel writers of the century'   *Spectator*

'A most beautiful and memorable book, capturing the last possible moment of a way of life'   DAVID PRYCE-JONES, *The Times*

'A declaration of faith that goes a long way to explaining the "strange compulsion" that drives men to seek, and find, the consolation of the desert . . . his descriptions of raids, blood-feuds and reconciliations give his prose the character of an ancient epic or saga . . . breaking into images of great beauty'
                          BRUCE CHATWIN, *London Review of Books*

0 00 654817 2

▲ *flamingo*

Wilfred Thesiger

The Life of My Choice

Wilfred Thesiger is the last of the great British eccentric explorers, a legendary figure, renowned for his travels through some of the most inaccessible places on earth. As a child in Abyssinia he watched the victorious armies of Ras Tafari returning from hand-to-hand battle, their prisoners in chains; at the age of twenty-three he made his first expedition into the country of the Danakil, a murderous race among whom a man's status in the tribe depended on the number of men he had killed and castrated. His widely acclaimed books, *Arabian Sands* and *The Marsh Arabs*, tell of his two famous sojurns in the Empty Quarter and the Marshes of southern Iraq. But Thesiger's true character and motives have until now remained an enigma. In this, his autobiography, he highlights the people who most profoundly influenced him and the events which enabled him to lead the life of his choice.

'One of the very few people who in our time could be put on the pedestal of the great explorers of the eighteenth and nineteenth centuries' DAVID ATTENBOROUGH

'One of the most engrossing life stories I have ever read' RICHARD HOLMES, *The Times*

'He is unquestionably, one of the greatest travellers the British have ever produced, the last of our recognizable primitives. He also writes with much distinction and honesty' GEOFFREY MOORHOUSE, *Daily Telegraph*

0 00 637267 8

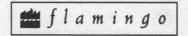

Wilfred Thesiger

My Kenya Days

Wilfred Thesiger is one of this country's greatest travellers and explorers. His books *Arabian Sands* and *The Marsh Arabs* have been hailed as classics of modern travel writing. This book, which follows on from his bestselling autobiography, *The Life of My Choice*, provides a compelling record of Thesiger's thirty years in Kenya.

My Kenya Days offers fresh insights into Thesiger's motivations and enigmatic personality. Lavishly illustrated with his extraordinary photographs, it contains superb evocations of Kenya's vanishing tribal heritage, of the dramatic landscapes of Thesiger's Kenya journeys, and intimately portrays his Samburu companions and surroundings at Maralal, where he made his home.

'A remarkable man whose love for Africa shines through this book'
The Times

'Magnificent photographs . . . almost religious in nature, displaying a reverence for their subject matter, both human and inanimate'
Sunday Telegraph

'A book worth pondering deeply' FRANK McLYNN, *Guardian*

'More than a sum of its parts: it reads as a threnody for a world we have lost and which will never be recreated'
ANTHONY DANIELS, *Sunday Telegraph*

0 00 638392 0

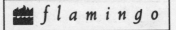
flamingo

Stanley Stewart

Old Serpent Nile
A Journey to the Source

'Like a cross between Eric Newby and Bruce Chatwin'
Daily Telegraph

Late one night in Rome, Stanley Stewart found himself by Bernini's *Fontana dei Quattro Fiumi*, beneath the figure that represents the Nile. Its head was enveloped in a veil – a reference to the fact that the sources of the Nile were then unknown. Seduced by this image of concealment and expectation, he resolved to travel the length of the Nile from mouth to source, from the moment of promise to the moment of revelation.

The journey, from the Nile Delta to the Mountains of the Moon, was arduous, colourful, funny, horrifying and often wildly dangerous. Whether on a pilgrimage to desert monasteries, aboard a felucca sailing to the splendours of ancient Egypt, crossing the Nubian desert, meeting the victims of famine in Sudan, or narrowly escaping the attentions of the Ugandan army, Stewart tells his story with wit, understanding and an eye for the telling detail.

At the heart of the book is the great river itself, constant, incredible, beguiling, source of life and of death to the millions who live along its banks. Evocative and compelling, *Old Serpent Nile* is in the finest tradition of travel writing.

'Immensely well-written . . . as intriguing and as changeable as the Nile'
Sunday Times

'Understated, elegantly written and impressive'
ROBERT CARVER, *New Statesman*

0 00 655028 2
£6.99

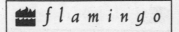

Stanley Stewart

Frontiers of Heaven
A Journey Beyond the Great Wall

'Stewart must now be considered among the small number in the very first rank of contemporary travel writers'

ROBERT CARVER, *TLS*

For the Chinese the Great Wall defined a psychological frontier. Within it lay the Celestial Kingdom, the compass of all civilization. Beyond lay a barbarian world of chaos and exile. Chinese journeys to the west, along the ancient Silk Road, were passages into the unknown, often into legend. Today, the great western province of Xinjiang is still a land of exile, the destination of soldiers, reluctant settlers, political prisoners and disgraced officials.

Following in their wake, Stanley Stewart journeys halfway across Asia, from Shanghai to the banks of the Indus, and along the way encounters the modern Chinese for whom these regions beyond the Wall still hold the same morbid fascination.

Whether describing the lost cities of Central Asia, a Buddhist monastery in the shadow of Tibet, a Kirghiz wedding on the roof of the world, ballroom dancing in the Mountains of Heaven, an escape from the secret police in Kashgar, or a love affair in Xi'an, Stewart tells his story with wit, charm and affection. In a book packed with character and incident, Stewart explores the paradoxes of travel, the lure of far horizons and the isolation of exile.

'Like a cross between Eric Newby and Bruce Chatwin'
Daily Telegraph

'Bewitching . . . subtle observation runs like a fine silk thread through the text'   *Irish Times*

0 00 655029 0
£6.99

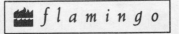 *flamingo*